Wrist Locks:
From Protecting Yourself
to Becoming an Expert

by
Keith Pascal

*An extra gift.
Enjoy!*

*Keith Pascal
2009*

Kerwin Benson Publishing
Eugene, Oregon

This book is designed to provide authoritative information with regard to wrist locking. It is sold with the understanding that neither the author, the publisher, nor anyone involved with the book is engaged in rendering legal advice, or advice and expertise for your specific situation or set of circumstances.

If expert counseling of any kind, including legal, is required, the services of competent professional people should be sought for each specific area in question. And you should do a lot of your own research too.

Original hardback edition, 1998 – This new edition (2008) is completely revised and updated. Sequences of photographs have replaced the simple line drawings. The text has been edited, yet again. Additional wrist locks have been incorporated into the instruction.

ISBN: 978-0-9666828-7-8

Pascal, Keith.

Wrist Locks: From Protecting Yourself to Becoming an Expert/ Keith Pascal.

Martial Arts

Self Defense

Printed in the United States of America

Dedication

This revised edition of *Wrist Locks* has had such an overhaul that it's like a new book, with the need for a new dedication and acknowledgments.

You'll recognize some of the names from the first edition in the Acknowledgments section on the following page, along with some new names.

With the indulgence of all who helped with this edition, I'd like to dedicate *Wrist Locks* to our close friend, who was a fine martial artist:

With the fondest of memories to:

C. Perry Burdon (1935-2008)

Acknowledgments

Of course, I'd like to acknowledge my family: Specfically, thanks to my **Grandma (Rhea) Shulman** (1908-1995) for helping to shape me.

To my parents, **Ilene Pascal** and **C. Bennett Pascal**, for helping to edit both editions of this book, and for their constant support.

To my wife, **Kate Pascal**, and our daughter, **Quinn Pascal**, who brighten my day, provide constant love, and... put up with me.

Next, there is the Golden Connection: To **Steve Golden**, for teaching me *most* of what I know about martial arts... and wrist locks. To **Nancy Golden**, for helping **Steve** on the first edit of this book.

And to anyone who has a martial connection to **Steve**, especially his students, seminar attendees, and those who appreciate his influence on the martial arts world.

Finally, let's talk about those who helped with this edition of **Wrist Locks**:

To my editors. Thanks for being so prompt. Appreciation to **Kate Pascal**, **Jay Frasier**, and **Mike Russell**.

To everyone on the photo shoots, whether posing, shooting, marking chapter and photo numbers, or controlling the dog. Many thanks to **Mike Russell**, **Jay Frasier**, **Kate Pascal**, **Ben Rayack**, and **Quinn Pascal**.

Thanks to my bonus-chapter models: **Steve Golden**, **Nick Campolongo**, and **Tom Iddison.**

And finally to **Lee Asher** for the cover design and being my business confidant. Check out LeeAsher.com.

Contents

Introduction

What you have before you is a completely revised and updated copy of **Wrist Locks: From Protecting Yourself to Becoming an Expert**.

This updated guide puts you on the path to wrist-lock expertise and is filled with over 400 photographs and specific, updated how-to instructions.

In the first edition of *Wrist Locks*, I stated that no single book could make someone a wrist locks expert. Yet, after nearly a decade in print, many claim that it did just that.

I am impressed, but I still believe that you need more than one resource, even this book.

So, if this book by itself won't make you an expert, what exactly will it do for you?

It will make you a much better martial artist. (If you get one useful thing out of this book that saves your life, or even makes you a better martial artist, then the price of the book was worth it; wouldn't you agree?)

If you were to take two identical martial artists (clones, if you will) of exactly equal ability and give one of them this book and thirty days, the clone with the book would win in a confrontation against his twin—guaranteed.

In this book, you'll find a bunch of professional locks that work.

Let me emphasize this point.

They actually work. I can make them work. My students and friends can make them work. My wife can make them work. My dog, Lucy … She does the best she can, lacking a certain prehensile advantage.

You'll learn how to make these locks work for you. Even if you can already do some of these wrist locks, this book will help you go beyond others to become a real expert.

And if you own a copy of the first edition, then you are in for a treat. Not only do the sequences of photos do a better job of demonstrating each lock and point, but new locks and variations have been added.

Like the first edition, this completely revised edition definitely *points you* in the right the direction. You'll have to provide the initiative.

In no time at all, you'll be flowing from one lock to another, deftly avoiding your opponents' attacks. You'll even learn to invent your own locks, to really confuse your opponents. (This is definitely a prestige builder.)

While this book gives you the tools to know that you'll always react with the best move possible, probably its best benefit is that it teaches you to counter all opponents who try to wrist lock you.

You will react by instantly flowing into a counter or reversal. You'll react smoothly and confidently in almost any wrist lock encounter.

Some of the specific techniques and benefits to be found in these pages:

- A great nose control to take the opponent to the ground in an instant.

- 3 steps to becoming a lock inventor.

- 7 specific recommendations for going beyond others to become a **real expert**.

- 8 tips for when NOT to use wrist locks.

- Techniques for getting better faster.

- When to strike instead of lock.

- Arm bars and their reversals.

- 6+ reversals and counters.

- 9 pattern tips to speed you on your way to expert status.

I could go on.

You'll learn to check for other attacks while locking. You'll learn some locks that are so impressive, they're suitable for demonstrations. You'll learn follow-up techniques that will leave others in awe.

There's a single move that will make you look like an Aikido expert. There's a great tip for memorizing long sequences of material, one you can apply to other areas of your life.

Rather than tell all now, let's get started.

Two last pauses, before you jump in — make sure you have read the disclaimer on the copyright page and read the safety tips on pages 12 and 13.

Let's keep everyone safe and happy.

May you learn lots of expert techniques as you progress towards protecting yourself and achieving expert status.

Sincerely,

Keith Pascal

P.S. If you'd like to contact me, try either
info@kerwinbenson.com or keith@keithpascal.com

About the Photographs

In 1999, Nancy Golden helped edit the first edition of *Wrist Locks*. Her suggestion for improvement was to use photographs instead of line drawings.

I didn't have a choice then. My only photo model was my wife, Kate, and she was pregnant with Quinn, at the time. So, I took photos of Kate, and I adjusted her size and belly in the line drawings.

In this completely revised and updated edition of *Wrist Locks*, I am proud to announce the inclusion of over 400 photographs.

In the first edition of *Wrist Locks*, all of the locks were from a right-handed practitioner's perspective. This time, I added a little more variety. All of the complicated sequences have been shot from a right-handed perspective, (even though I am a lefty).

Some of the shorter sequences have you locking with the left hand. I do this when you have to combat someone else right handed, using your left.

I encourage you to master all locks and sequences using both hands. It makes sense, if you truly want to become an expert.

Finally, some of the locks are repeated in different chapters. These have been shot from slightly different angles, and the photos show different points in the lock sequence.

I hope these photos help you learn quickly and precisely.

And yes, Mike R. really is almost seven-feet tall.

1
Practice for Fast Improvement and Great Results

Before we jump in and learn wrist locks and martial arts principles, we need to make sure we're on the right track to fast learning.

Specifically, this chapter discusses:

- safety considerations,

- the method of approaching wrist locks so you learn the most,

- and the best practice tips to improve at a fast rate and really become an expert.

You might be tempted to skip to the tips at the end. Don't do it!

To use an old cliché, *safety comes first*. In this chapter, it really does.

Don't skip it; if a quick, five-minute read prevents an accident, wasn't the time more than well spent?

After safety comes methodology. This is where you learn how to get the most out of each chapter.

Once you know how to learn better, you'll be ready to get good *fast* and fine tune your technique.

Safety Considerations:

- *If you're under eighteen years old,* **have a responsible adult present** for consultation to monitor your practice. Also, get permission from your parent or legal guardian.

- **Before you practice, stretch!** Find a good routine. Read books on stretching. Look to Hatha yoga's Salutation to the Sun. It's a wonderful full-body stretch, because it takes you to the limits of the body's range of motion. Look into ads stretching videos in the martial arts magazines and online.

- **Remember to stretch out your wrists** thoroughly. No strains or sprains, please.

- **Wear loose, comfortable clothing to practice**, but if you normally wear restrictive suits or tight dresses, you'll occasionally need to practice in those outfits, so you don't get any surprises in an actual confrontation.

  You want to know your limits of movement, and how to compensate, before a real situation occurs.

  Also, no jewelry. You don't want to snag someone's clothing, get strangled by a necklace, or scrape your partner with a watch or a ring. Remove earrings and other piercings.

  Earrings are painful when pulled.

- **Consider your practice area.** If you're going to throw each other around, or take each other down to the floor, you need an area free of sharp corners, and objects. You don't want to get thrown into a post in a garage; use your head before you start the practice session, so you don't hit it during.

- **Have a good emergency release system.** Be sure to agree how long after you tap on a partner's arm or leg, he should release the grip; this is referred to as a *tap-out* in martial arts.

  For us, two or three light taps on any part of the partner's body signifies that the pain or pressure has become unbearable. We don't tap out at the first feeling of pain; we wait until it's almost unbearable. That's why we tap out: we can't stand it any more and anymore would cause injury.

  A decision you and your partner will have to make is what exactly a tap-out means. Does it mean "freeze" all movement; in other words, stop applying *more* force? Does it mean completely release the hold, NOW? Or is it something in between, like let up a little pressure, please? You have to decide.

- **Practice for position first.** Go slowly. Apply pressure in small increments. Learn your limits. Even though you should simulate realism in a practice session, make every attempt not to cause damage to your partner. Remember, this is your partner, not a real enemy.

How You Can Get the Most When Practicing

When reading this book, you could just skip around and look at specific locks and holds that interest you.

You'd probably learn something. It might even be of some use. But I can almost guarantee that this information wouldn't be of as much use to you as it potentially could if you thoroughly studied each chapter.

By learning the sections of the book, you are learning beyond the specific techniques. You learn principles. You learn to go beyond this book and develop your own personal method of self-defense.

This is much more valuable to you than a few moves. Sure, the moves are good; that's why they are in this book. And yes, you will need to learn them. But try to get more out of this book than a few moves. Be a good learner.

I have taught long enough to be able to see the difference between good learners and poor learners.

An obvious factor in the skill that one obtains has to do with the amount of contact that the learner spends with the target material, (the thing to be learned). The more practice you get, the more fluid and competent you'll become.

Break the moves down and analyze them; put them back together and figure out how to make them smoother. Really work with the material. Take the time to learn the technique correctly.

Eventually, you'll have to go beyond technique, but that's a different lesson. For now, technique is a pretty good crutch to rely on.

Not only is the amount of time spent important, but the quality of practice counts a lot towards rapid improvement. People with a goal are more motivated. The more motivated you are, the faster you'll learn. Your learning will be smoother. And the faster you learn, the sooner you'll achieve the specific goal. So, let's talk about your goal.

Read with a Purpose

Why did you buy this book? If it's borrowed, what about this book grabbed your attention?

What interested you? What motivated you?

Now, as you read this book, what do you hope to get out of it? What is your desire? What do you want to be able to do?

Are you looking for a gentle way to defend yourself, when your opponent is out for blood, and it's much easier to hit?

Are you a martial artist looking to round out your style by adding a wrist lock component to the system? Are you looking for a quick route to becoming an expert?

Are you a senior citizen looking to protect yourself and others?

Will you primarily be defending yourself while riding a bicycle?

There is a difference in the way each person should approach this book. Maybe you're a general reader not yet committed to one discipline or another. Maybe you're comfortable with your self-defense technique, but you've just never been able to easily snap a good lock on someone.

Or maybe you've been on the receiving end of a good lock, and you wish there were something impressive you could do in response other than cry out in pain and agony at the top of your lungs.

Your perspective and previous experience should shape the way you approach this material.

Your perspective will also help define your goal. And a specific goal will help you get more out of each practice session. Consider linking your perspective with your purpose.

Why not base each practice session on a different section of this book, at least for a while? Sessions could cover generalizing, feeling where to go, reversals and counters, patterns, or inventing.

After you are fairly proficient in each area, you should definitely practice several areas in each practice session. Mix and match. You could still have an overall theme, even with several different lessons going on.

For example, your overall theme could be experimentation and invention, even though you specifically practice arm bars, the first pattern, weapon disarms, and single wrist grabs.

When practicing with a purpose, you will almost automatically start to pick out specific locks for your repertoire; you will definitely learn at a faster pace than someone going through blind, aimless practice.

Even though you'll be selective, you should still go through as many locks as possible.

Never forget. There are other people out there who know and use these principles. You may have to defend against some technique found in this book someday.

The more you know and can do, the better prepared you'll be.

Try It; You'll Like It

As martial arts videos sweep the market, I worry about the future of martial arts books.

In today's fast paced world, everyone wants instant gratification. They want to see the moves performed. They don't want to have to actually think about the technique.

Obviously, I approve of the written form of instruction; after all, you're reading this book.

When you watch someone else perform the move, whether from a video or in person, you end up trying to mimic them. After all, it *looked* good. And if they didn't happen do the move well, and it didn't impress you, then there's no chance that you'll want to do that particular lock or move.

When you learn a move from a book, you have to figure out the best angles, you play with alternate timing, and you get to adapt the move to your specific needs.

You have no preconceived notions, good or bad, about the technique.

Don't get me wrong, videos are a great learning tool. When you watch someone good, you can pick up good habits.

With a video, you do get to see exactly how it was done, even if you don't feel the technique performed. (If there is enough interest, I'll eventually produce a video series on wrist locks.)

I just think that vide make us a little mentally lazy.

Remember, there is value in the analysis of technique – you have to come up with the best angles, speed, and timing.

You will become a better martial artist.

Besides, you'll have your own creative counters while your opponents will be stuck in their "video mold." They won't be able to respond to your creativity.

Since books lack the visual glamor of a video, some of you may pass by excellent material. Keep in mind, that it's often too hard to recognize the gems just by reading about them.

I remember hearing about my teacher receiving a copy of Bruce Lee's notes shortly after the legend's death. These notes were later to become *The Tao of Jeet June Do*.

My teacher tried to impart the value of the advice contained in the book.

Even though I had my black belt, I wasn't ready for the gems of knowledge in the book. I read the book and said to myself yes, this makes sense; yes, I understand ... but I didn't really. I couldn't appreciate the depth of advice contained within that important volume.

Years later, I began to appreciate the information that had always been there. I would pick just one kernel from the book and practice it all day. Once I started actually practicing the principle, I really began to appreciate it much more than when I had only read it.

The story continues a few years later.

My wife was studying in Mexico, (before we were married). As a gift, I sent her a copy of *The Tao of Jeet Kune Do*.

On the inside cover I wrote her a note about her liking the gift but not appreciating it until she was ready.

She really did like it, but as predicted, she wasn't ready for the depth of information either.

Recently, she has been intently studying *The Tao...* again. There is a sparkle of new understanding in her eye.

These Techniques Work

Since you're going to practice some proven winners, will you do both of us a favor and really learn to do them?

If these moves don't eventually work on your practice partner, you're not doing the move correctly. These moves work. I can successfully put any number of these techniques on many people, including seasoned fighters.

I'm not saying I'm the best out there; I'm just saying that these moves work. And my students over the years have perfected these techniques in a minimal amount of time.

So, if you're not wrist locking successfully, you have some more practicing ahead of you and maybe even modification of your technique.

Don't discard these locks prematurely, especially if you are unsuccessful because you are being out-muscled by your partner, and you lack the finesse to adjust at this time. Patience and practice.

If eventually you eliminate a move from your arsenal, you'll know you didn't make a haphazard decision. Just because you discarded a particular move, doesn't mean that you wasted your time learning it.

Since now you know how to do the technique, and you know how to do it well, you are much more likely to recognize someone else pulling the move on you. You'll be prepared, and you will have ruined your opponent's element of surprise; if you're good, you can surprise your opponent.

A definite bonus.

Tips for Fast Improvement

- You've already read about **practicing with a specific goal in mind.** So, you're already practicing with a purpose. Good. That's one tip out of the way.

- **Use the principle of reverse learning.** If you have to learn a routine or any kind of sequence where you have to memorize the order of the movements, practice it backwards.

  Begin by practicing the last move. Next, practice the next-to-the-last movement; then do the last movement again. You continue with the-third-to-last, second-to-last , next-to-last , and then last movement. You get stronger as you move toward the end.

Have you ever tried to memorize a speech or report in the correct order? You know the beginning very well, but you falter near the end. The beginning is well rehearsed, the end less so. With this reverse-order method, you'll always be progressing toward more familiar ground. It's a good feeling.

• **Check your positions out in a mirror.** If your body position looks awkward, maybe there is something wrong with it. Correct the position, then perform the entire sequence over again the proper way.

• Take mirror evaluation one step further; **video tape your practice sessions.**

Evaluate your technique. Look for the bad to change it; look for the good to continue it.

If your ego can take it, have someone else evaluate your tape. Exercise care in whom you pick. Egos are fragile. Make sure this gentle soul is a competent wrist lock artist, otherwise you may not get useful feedback.

• **Work out with someone better than you.** You'd be amazed at how much faster you'll improve as you try to keep up. Just working with someone better will help you improve, but if this person is willing to coach a bit, so much the better.

Having another wrist lock expert as a teacher is probably the best thing you could do for yourself; you'll have to make do with what's available in your area. Of course if you're rich, you could bring a teacher to you.

• **Evaluate yourself and your technique frequently.** Don't get depressed as you reach plateaus; we all do. Just keep plugging away. Change the pace of your practice sessions.

Take a break and get some exercise. Then go back and work until you progress to the next level. Even an expert can improve, and should maintain one's level of skill. Never give up.

• **Visualize doing successful wrist locks.** When not physically practicing, you can practice in your mind.

It's a good mental exercise anyway, but it's a lot more. You truly will improve. All sorts of studies have been conducted where mental practice of a kinetic act is almost as effective as the actual practice.

You should do both; this way you get double the amount of practice. Go through practice sessions in your mind. You should also visualize going against real attackers.

Visualize yourself as being successful with your self defense in both the imagined practice sessions and against your imagined attacker.

- **Collect lots of books and videos that contain locks.** Try to incorporate movements gleaned from these books and videos into practice sessions.

  If you're already a video junky, I won't be able to change you into a book person; even *I* learn from videos. I just prefer books for learning.

  Always try to add something that's fresh to your practice session. Since you should spend most of your time perfecting and honing your core knowledge even further, these fresh little breaks add spice to your workouts.

  Look for a balance between old and new. You'll improve faster if you blend the two.

- **Keep notes.** I keep collecting more and more wrist locks, and I take notes on them. You could keep video notes, so you don't have to write or worse – sketch your techniques. But I prefer getting it down on paper.

- **Pascal's Personal Technique: I keep notes on myself.** I have my own personal tips.

  To improve quickly, I developed my own set of tips from analyzing my technique.

  I took notes on everything, from my body positions to my mental attitude, from practice sessions that went very well to techniques that I actually had to use. Anything that caused me to evaluate my performance was fair game for the notebook.

I was diligent in my collection of data, and I know that I benefited so much from this exercise. It was worth the effort.

• **Make a game out of it.** You'll have to get creative; it takes work to turn a dull, repetitive activity into a fun, repetitive activity.

Adding a competitive edge to your game can make the practice go faster. It can also help you to get faster, or stronger, depending on the goal of the game.

Be careful that your technique doesn't suffer. Sometimes technique can get sloppy, when we're trying to win.

Now you have the framework to learn and glean the most from the material presented in this book. Let's continue....

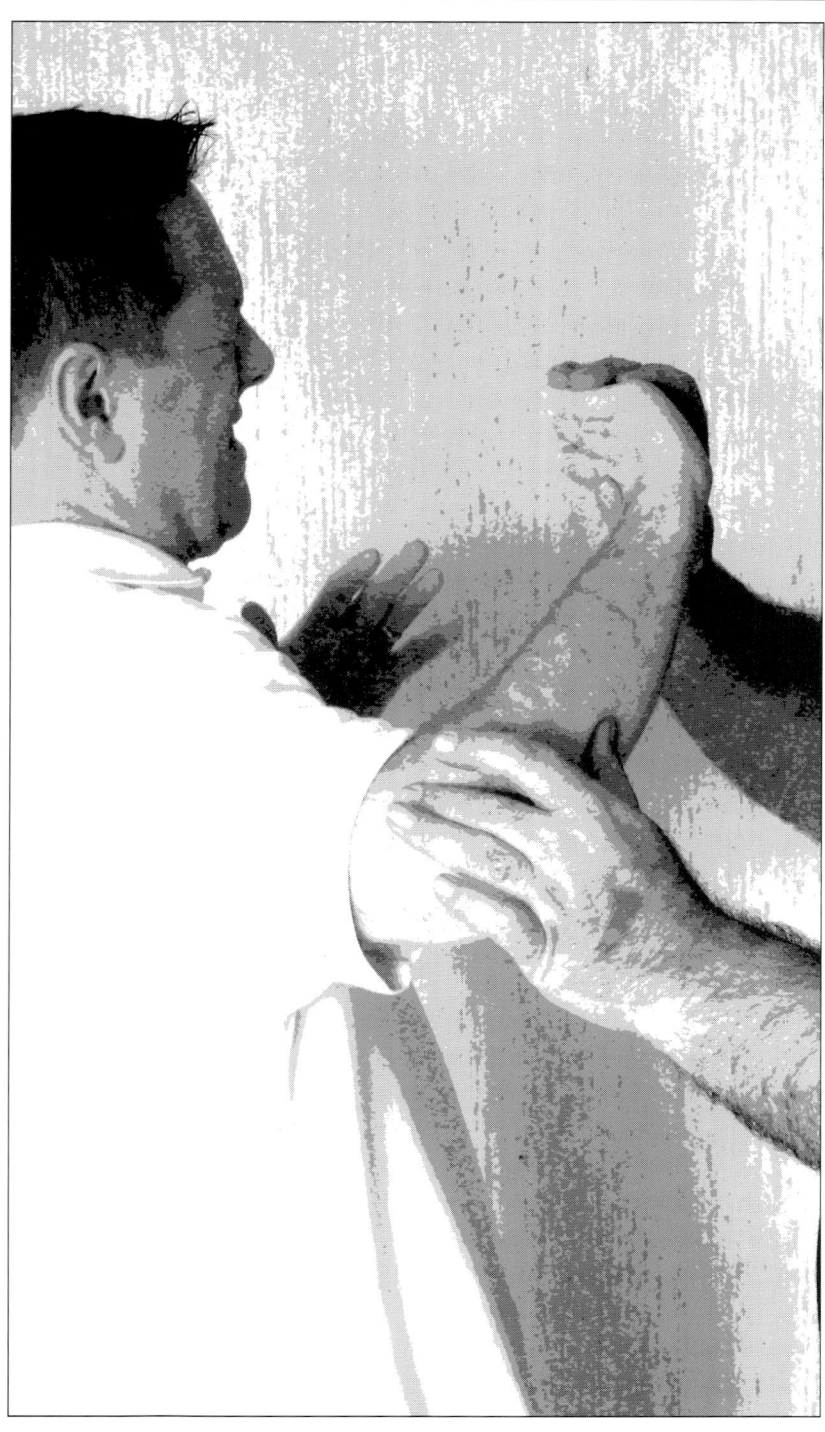

2
What's In a Name?

How do Names Fit in Your Expert Status?

Are you going to have to memorize a bunch of names of weird locks to be considered an expert?

Not necessarily.

You should learn some of the conventional names if you intend to communicate with martial artists outside of your system. It's just like a second language; you don't want to always force everyone to communicate in just your language.

It's impolite. It's not considerate or classy. It's the same with locks. Sometimes, you should help out others by using their terminology.

Other than communication, and having an established "tag" for future reference, there's no reason you shouldn't stick with names you've invented for your own convenience.

So, do you need to know a lot of names to be considered an expert?

There are several routes you could take. One answer to the above question is **no**. Ignore everyone else and become really good at what you do. Anyone who plays with you loses. You're good. But you either can't talk about your style, because you don't have any names for the moves, or you force everyone else to learn your names. Hmm – calling yours a secret style is one way to communicate that you can't communicate.

Another scenario is that you take this expert status so seriously that you go out and learn every name of every move.Not only do you learn the names of your style, but you memorize the name of every lock from every other style too. You can even cross-reference.

Somewhere in between would be to learn the names of all the locks in an established style, and then learn a few names from other styles.

Memorizing all of the names from one style can still be quite a feat. You don't have to know all names from all styles to be an expert. (Although for some it's an admirable goal.)

If you were into an eclectic style, maybe your approach would be to learn some names from one style, other names from another. You'd mix and match. Eclecticism lends itself to a refreshing unorthodox quality.

Advice for Beginners

My advice to beginners is to take life easy.

Don't spend a lot of time on names, right now. Either use my *tags* to start with, or invent your own.

At this stage, the acquisition of names should be used as memory aids, not to elevate your professional status. As you pick up new moves, learn the names that go with them.

When working with others, if someone calls a familiar move by a name that's unfamiliar to you, take the time to memorize it. You'll gain an eclectic knowledge this way.

Of course, if you practice a specific discipline, I also highly encourage you to research that discipline thoroughly. Really become an expert in your own style. Know locks better than anyone at your gym, dojo, or even garage (where I teach).

Feel free to create your own names. But be careful!

Sometimes the move defines the name, but unfortunately sometimes the name defines the move.

For example, if you were to call a Basic Wrist Lock a Circle Throw Lock (because that's how you primarily used it), you'd be limiting the definition of the use of the lock. You'd miss the downward-pressure variations, and the non-throw controls.

Make sure that your name doesn't limit. The exception to this is if you have a reason to break down a move into subcategories. Then the limiting names would help to further define the difference between one variation and another.

To get you started, I have listed a few of the names of locks found in this book, with some of their equivalents from Small Circle Ju Jitsu and Shaolin Chin Na.

If you are really going to become an expert, you could spend years on locks from those two styles alone. Then, if you were to add Aikido into the mix – wow!

Memorize names, if they are a component of your definition of a wrist lock EXPERT. To get you started:

- A **Wing** in my system is called an arm lock in Small Circle Ju Jitsu. (Wally Jay is the founder of the style.)

- A **Basic Lock** is also a Basic Lock in Small Circle, but if it's executed with the same hand (right to right), it's called a Cross Arm Wrist Lock.

- A **Double 90** is called a Bent Elbow Wrist Lock.

- **Pattern #2, Position #3** is called a Goose Neck Hold, in Wally Jay's system.

- Our regular **Arm Bar** is his Reverse Arm Bar.

- My **Kickstart with a Vertical Twist** is called Send the Devil to Heaven, in Shaolin Chin Na.

- An **Arm Bar** with a face strike at the end is called Old Man Promoted to General, in Shaolin Chin Na.

- If you dropped off the biceps rotation and bending your opponent's elbow inward, then our **Weird Lock With No Name** would become Bei Ping Kao Ya (Roast Peking Duck).

Now, let's learn some great locks and martial principles....

3
Getting Out of Unfamiliar Locks by Feeling Where to Go

To really become a master of wrist locks, not only do you have to be able to put a variety of locks on different people, but you have to be able to get out of, and even reverse, locks that other people put on you.

By practicing specific reversals and counters over and over, you'll remember what to do in a variety of situations. A true master can feel his or her way out of an unfamiliar lock, which is the focus of this chapter.

I have to get you to the level where you can *feel* your way out of almost any wrist lock or arm bar.

You gain a feeling of safety when you know you can escape from, and even reverse, almost any lock.

Releasing Pressure

Let's talk in general terms first.

In general, a lock reversal begins with a release of pressure and ends with a similar, or sometimes different, pressure being applied to the instigator.

You will need to learn various methods of releasing pressure.

In this chapter, there is an arm bar lesson with three techniques for releasing pressure. Two of the techniques are true reversals ending up with an identical arm bar placed on your opponent. One is a release where you finish in a different lock, although you can very easily flow back into an arm bar. *"Isn't it beautiful the way it all fits!"*

You'll get suggestions for reversals of specific locks in Chapter 9. After this chapter and the one on reversals, you'll find it easier to experiment and develop your own logical counters.

You'll probably come up with a great reversal or two.

If you do, write me. I'll see what I can do to make sure you get credit, if it ends up being an innovative move.

The Point of No Return

Besides a release of pressure, there is usually a critical "point of no return."

There is a certain point in a lock technique beyond which it becomes impossible to execute a reversal, or for that matter, even an escape. This point is achieved when a specific angle or leverage on the body is reached, or when a specific amount of pressure or tension is placed against the joint.

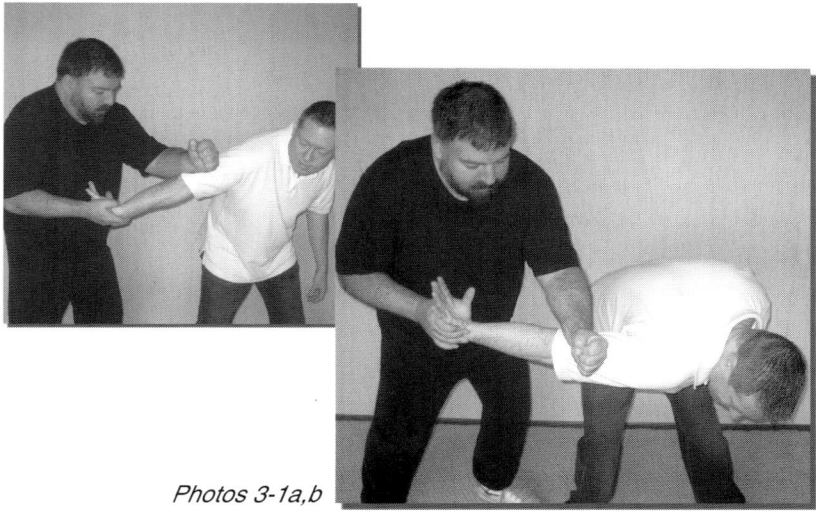

Photos 3-1a,b

Sometimes it's just pure pain that keeps you from trying an escape.

My first piece of advice is to learn where the point of no return is for as many locks and techniques as possible.

Learn to feel that specific point beyond which you really will be trapped. Once you know enough of these specific points, you'll start to recognize critical points on new moves.

Photos 3-2a,b

The technique may be new, but the pressure will remind you of a familiar lock.

Once you feel the direction the pressure is going, you'll instinctively know the limit of your body's range of motion.

To learn the point of no return, have your partner put a lock on you very, very slowly. Try to feel at what point your range of motion becomes so limited, because of pain or pressure, that you can no longer attempt to escape.

Eventually, when you really know that specific point, and you have begun to practice counters and escapes, you'll have your partner execute the lock at continually faster speeds.

When you can successfully reverse this specific lock at full speed, against a variety of opponents, (see Chapter 7 on generalizing), then it's time to move on to a different lock.

The Arm Bar and Its Reversals

Maybe you'd get a better idea of the general principles of finding the point of no return and releasing a lock's pressure, with a specific sequence.

What follows is the way that I teach the arm bar with three reversals.

To make the sequence more realistic, we begin by defending against a punch.

> Later, if the student fails to take the proper steps to generalize the arm bar to different situations, at least he (or she) can use the technique to control a punch.

Take either a right lead stance, (right foot forward,) to your opponent's left stance, or take a left stance (left foot forward) to your opponent's right stance (photo 3-3a).

Your opponent steps in with a punch with the lead hand; the punch extends toward your face (photo 3-3b).

Both of your hands are just below chin level. Now everything happens at once. Punch with your lead hand towards your opponent's face; your rear hand serves as a light check hand against your opponent's punch; step slightly forward and to the side with your lead foot, a right lead steps slightly to the right, and left to the left.

You should end up with hand positions as in Photo 3-3e.

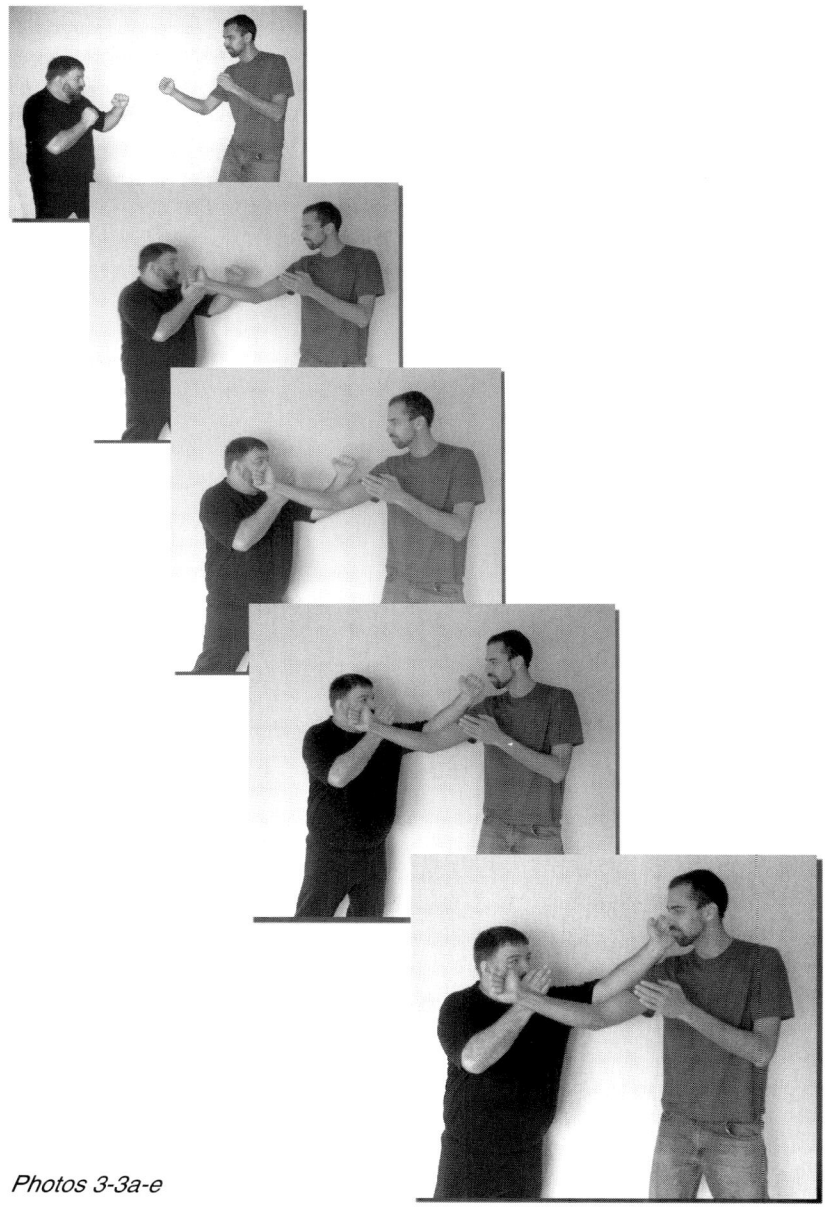

Photos 3-3a-e

All of this should happen almost simultaneously. If you feel the need to lead with something, lead with your weapon; in this case, your striking hand. Don't lead with a body movement that telegraphs everything, unless you're planning some sort of a fake.

If you are, be careful.

This would probably be an appropriate place to mention timing. OK. I'm mentioning it. It is beyond the scope of the book to teach you how to employ timing and rhythm in situations other than wrist locks.

Suffice it to say, I'm not a proponent of single-step sparring, where each movement falls on the beat. I prefer the Bruce Lee philosophy of interruption of movement.

If you find yourself countering at the end of your opponent's motion, then *get thee to a progressive martial arts school or a boxing club now.*

Choose your school carefully. In fact, there are some great articles about choosing martial-arts schools on the Internet. You need advice about contracts, fees, style or system, goals, and so on. (Write me for recommendations.)

Back to the arm bar ...

If either your check hand or punch hand slowed down your opponent's punch enough for you to grab it, proceed.

If it's retracting too fast you'll have to do some other move to slow that arm down, or give up on a grab and take the easier way out – hit.

Use your check hand, (rear hand,) to grab your opponent's wrist and rotate it palm up (photos 3-4e-j).

Retract your lead hand, (right hand,) from its punch to apply pressure with your wrist to the lower part of the opponent's triceps (photos 3-4a-d).

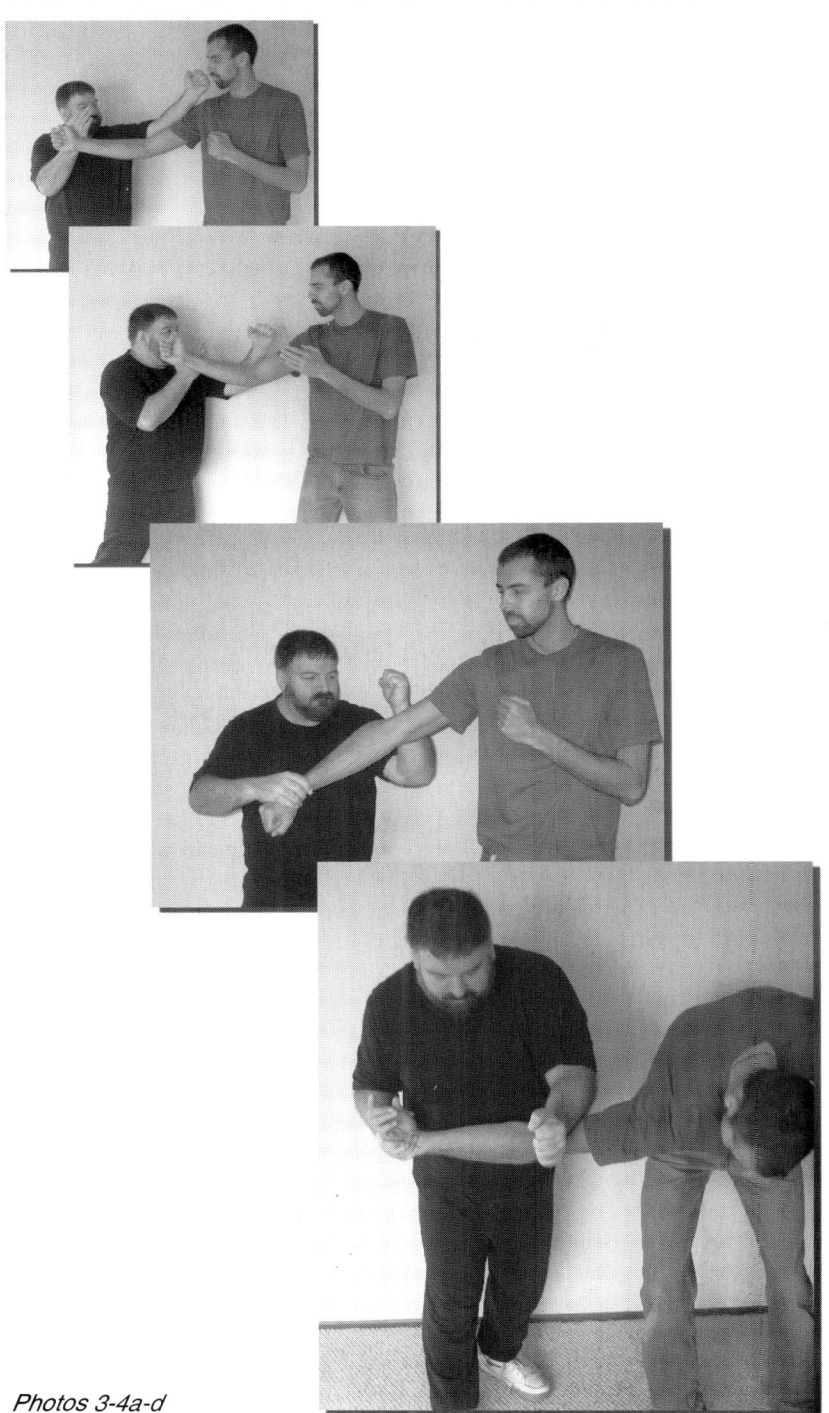

Photos 3-4a-d

Study Photos 3-4e-j to see how to rotate your opponent's wrist to the proper position. Keep constant pressure on the wrist while rotating.

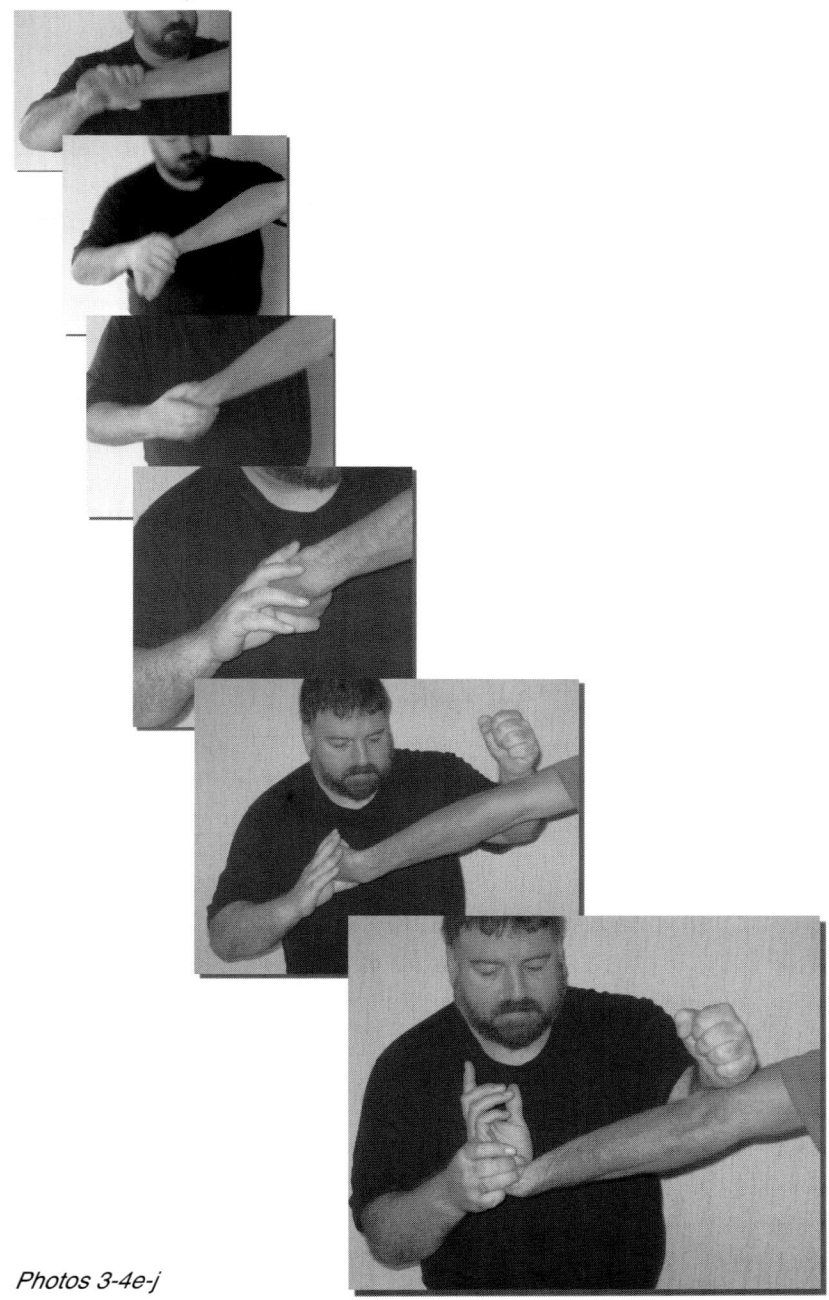

Photos 3-4e-j

That's the arm bar in a nutshell. You can take your opponent down to the ground with enough pressure, or bend the arm behind their back with an extra finger or wrist lock added to the arm twist (see pages 146-148).

Oh, what fun! You have several possibilities, but right now, we're dealing with the basic arm bar.

After mastery, teach it to someone else, so he or she can perform it on you. After all, don't you want to be the one to learn the three reversals first?

Pressure-Release Reversal

Have your partner put an arm bar on you, *lightly.* "Lightly" because you want to learn how to perform the counter correctly first (photo 3-5a).

Practice *the point of no return* later, after you can perform the move.

With your free hand, reach up to the hand that is applying pressure above your elbow, grab his (or her) wrist, and release the pressure from your arm. Release by pulling the wrist and arm forward and off your arm (photos 3-5b-f).

Rotate your other hand up, so you can apply pressure to his triceps with it (photos 3-5g-j).

> If the opponent's other hand is still holding your hand while it starts to rotate upward, that's fine. Take his hand with you; he'll let go when you start applying pressure to the back of his arm.

Position both hands so you're in an exact reversal of where you started.

By the way, this means that your partner could now reverse you. Then you could put the reversal back on your partner. And so on ...

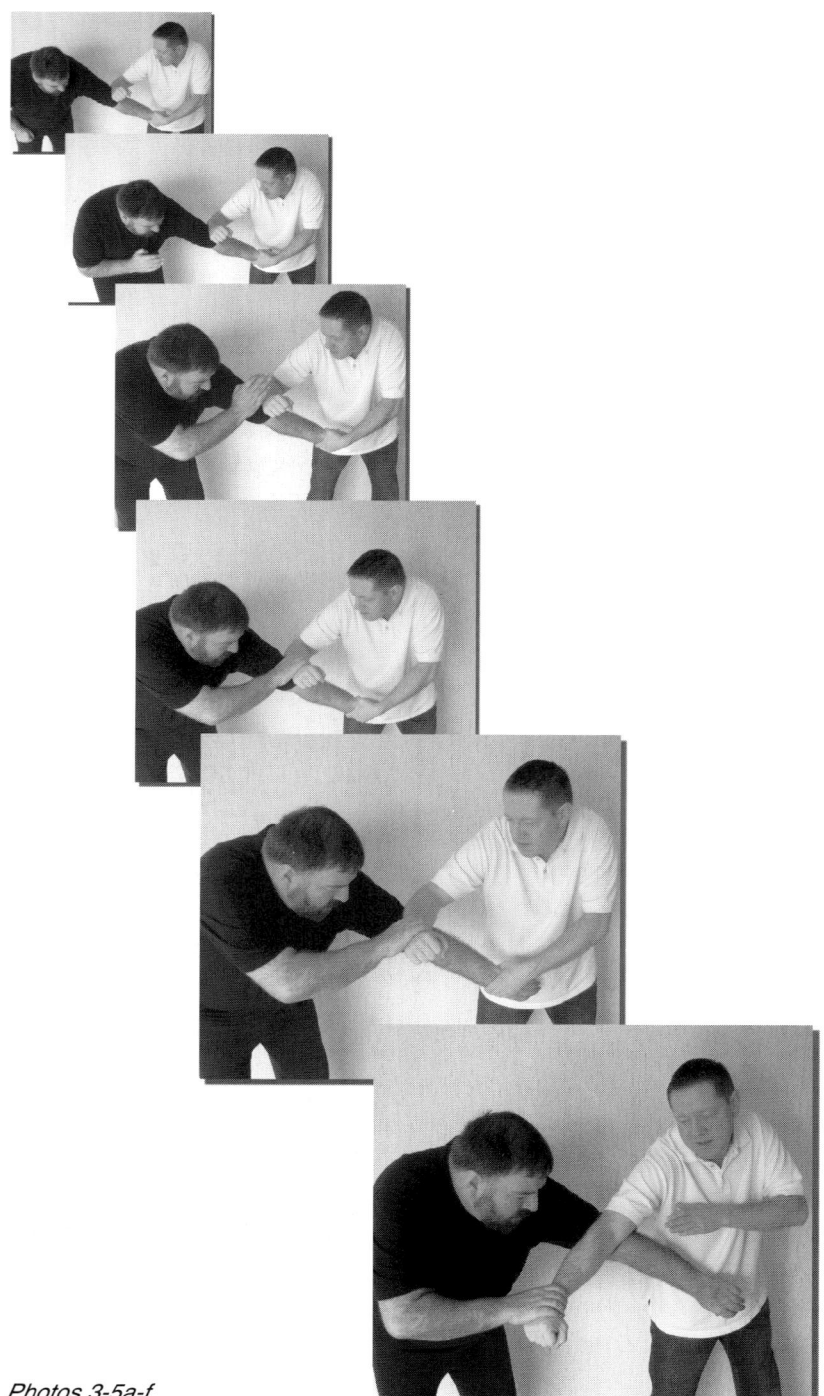

Photos 3-5a-f

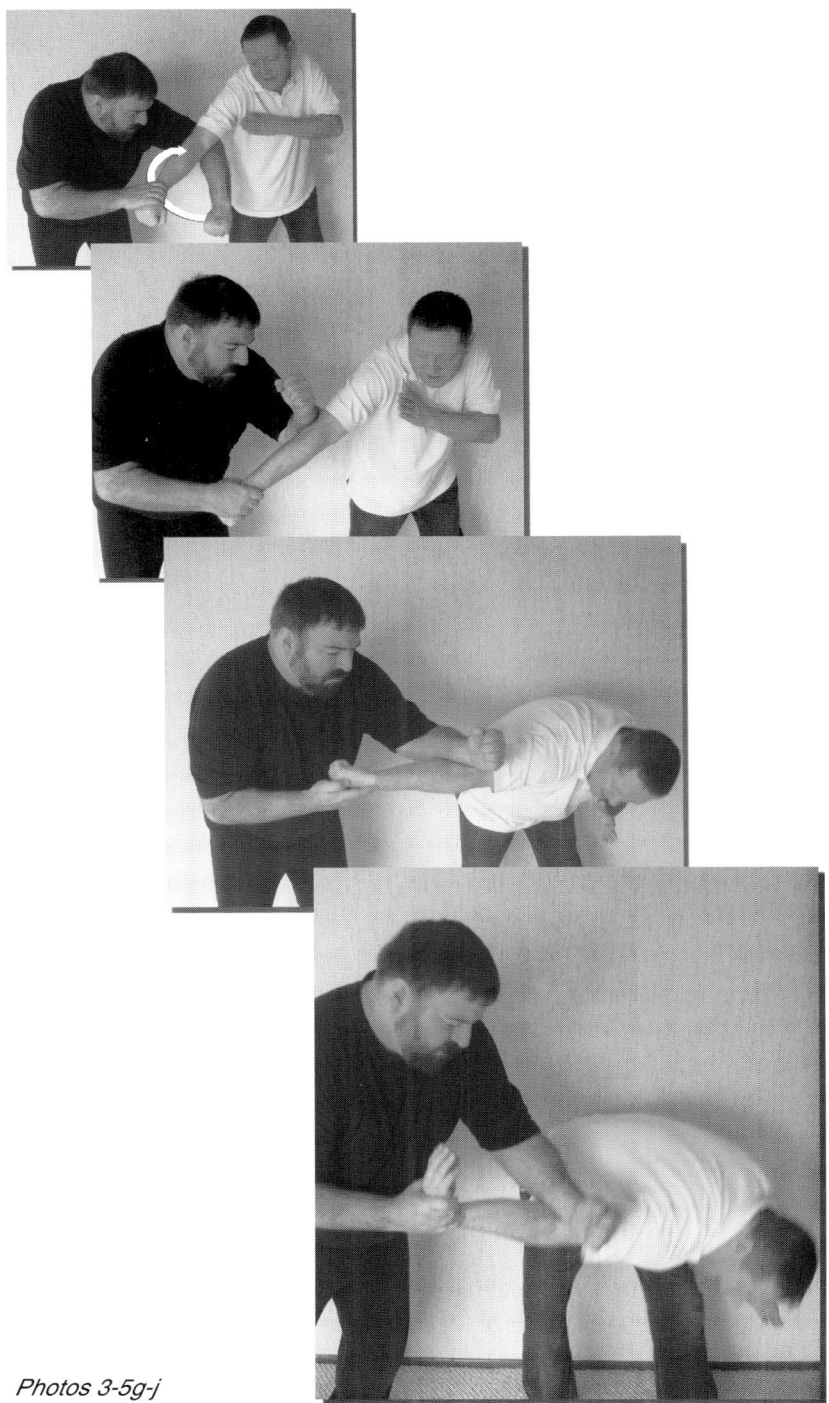

Photos 3-5g-j

Before you experiment with endless reversals, spend some time finding the range for effecting the reversal....

It's time to find that critical "point of no return."

Have your partner put an arm bar on you, applying continuously more pressure. Try your reversal with different amounts of pressure applied incrementally.

Eventually, there will be too much pressure for you to properly respond. Just before that moment is the critical point.

Your partner may have to ease up a bit to help you find the right spot. You and your partner need to pin down the point for your benefit. Learn instinctively when you're about to lose the ability to counter.

Make that point your *friend*. Learn it well. Know exactly where your "point of no return" is at all times during the move. Execute your reversals before your *friend* shows up. If your timing is right, you'll never meet your "friend" in a real confrontation.

Wrist-Grab Reversal

Now on to the second reversal:

Again, have your opponent put an arm bar on you *very lightly*. (Remember, always experiment very lightly at first, so you can *find* the move, but remember to make it realistic later.)

This time, reach using the fingers of the hand that is being held forward and up, and grab the wrist of the hand that has hold of your wrist (photos 3-6a-c).

It is a very tight circular motion with your wrist.

After you grab your partner's wrist, pull the arm until it is straight in front of you (photos 3-6d, e), turning your body inward towards your opponent, to facilitate pulling out the arm.

Continue holding your opponent's wrist, making sure to turn the wrist palm up. Use your free hand to put pressure with your wrist against the arm, above the elbow, as usual.

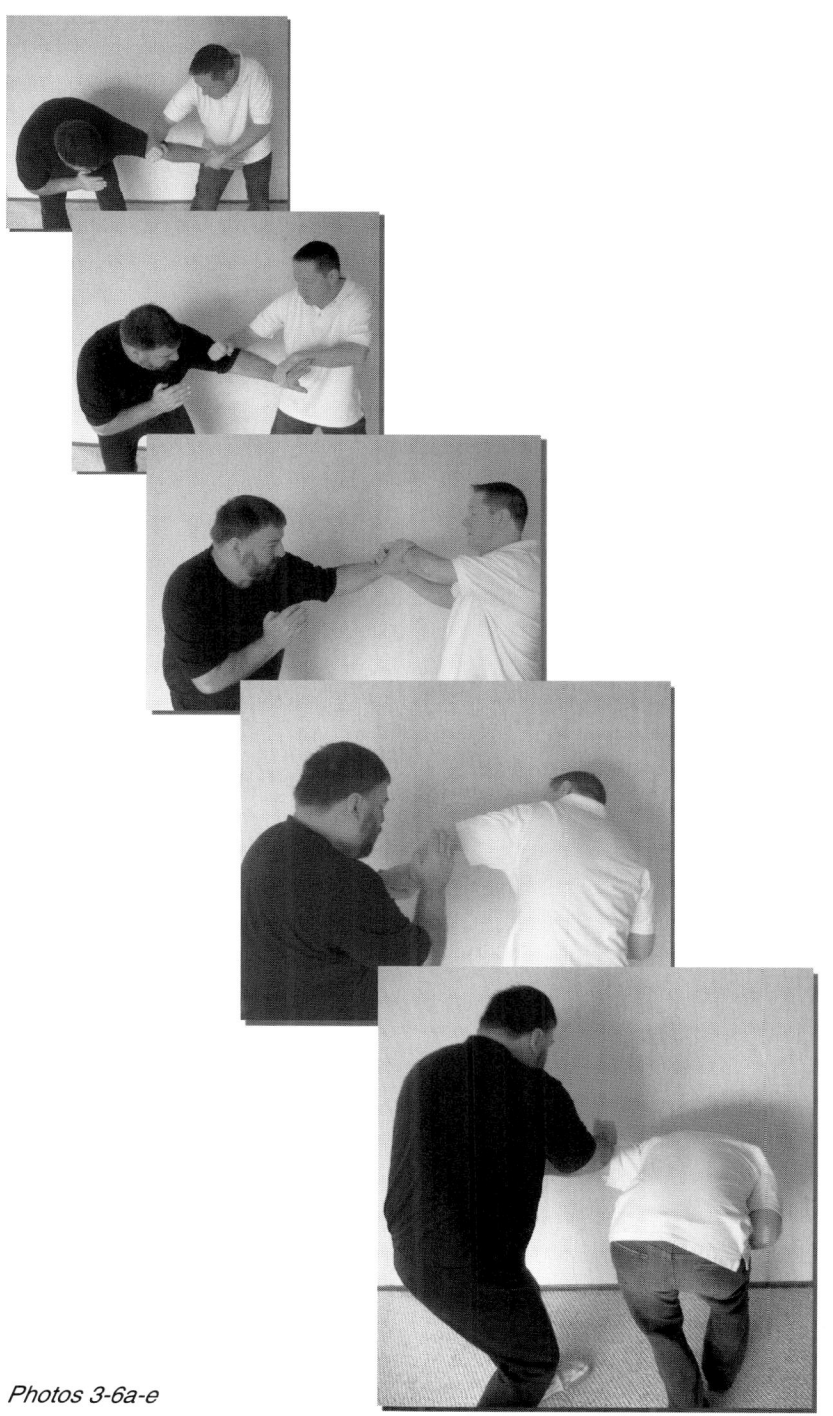

Photos 3-6a-e

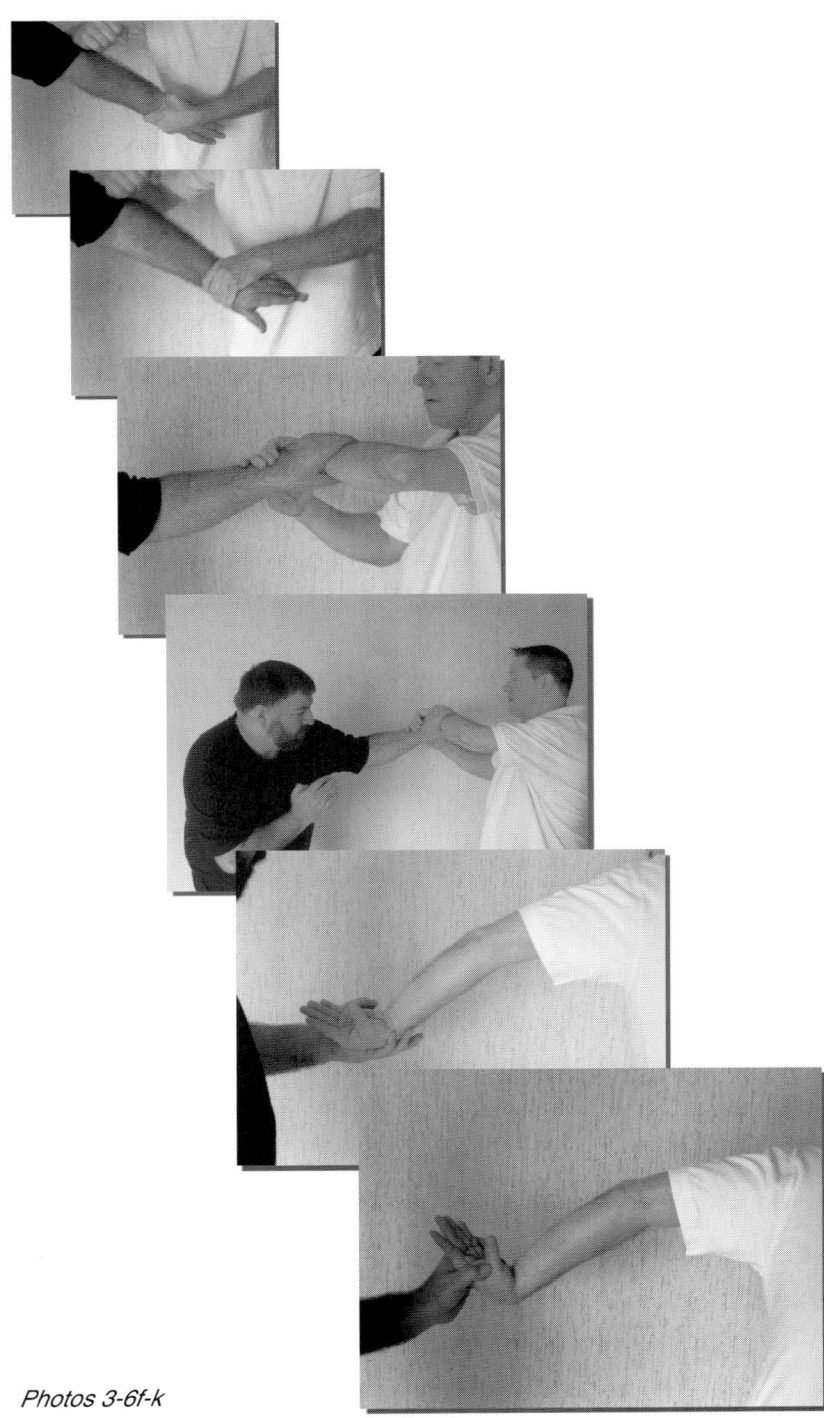

Photos 3-6f-k

On the previous page, I inlcuded the Wrist-Grab-Reversal sequence again, focusing on the rotating hand (photos 3-6f-k).

Even though Photo 3-6j looks like I have released pressure, I haven't. Be sure to maintain pressure.

Also, keep in mind, your other hand would be exerting downward pressure above your opponent's elbow. (My right hand has been removed for the photo.)

It's time to feel for your "point of no return."

When the opponent pushes down on your arm with sufficient force, you won't be able to wiggle your body around to grab his wrist in the reversal.

Grab the opponent's wrist before your shoulder drops below the level of your own trapped wrist.

In this case, the critical point comes just about when the arm (the "line" between the wrist and the shoulder) is parallel to the floor.

Now that you have two reversals, add variety to your arm-bar workout.

When an arm bar is snapped on, you have two options for a reversal, as does your partner in response to your reversal.

Let's add a third reversal to the game.

Arm-Lift Reversal

Again, you start as the recipient of the classic arm bar. Reach up and grab the arm that is pressing your triceps.

Pull it forward to release pressure, the way you did in the first reversal (photos 3-7a, b). Except this time, turn your partner's arm palm up and your arm palm up (photos 3-7c, d).

Apply pressure with your arm by lifting it into your opponent's arm. If your opponent raises up onto tip toes, it shows that you have executed the move correctly.

By now, you know that once you can perform the technique with some facility, it's time to look for the *critical* point.

You will experiment with pressure to find at what point you can no longer pull your opponent's arm off yours or raise your arm.

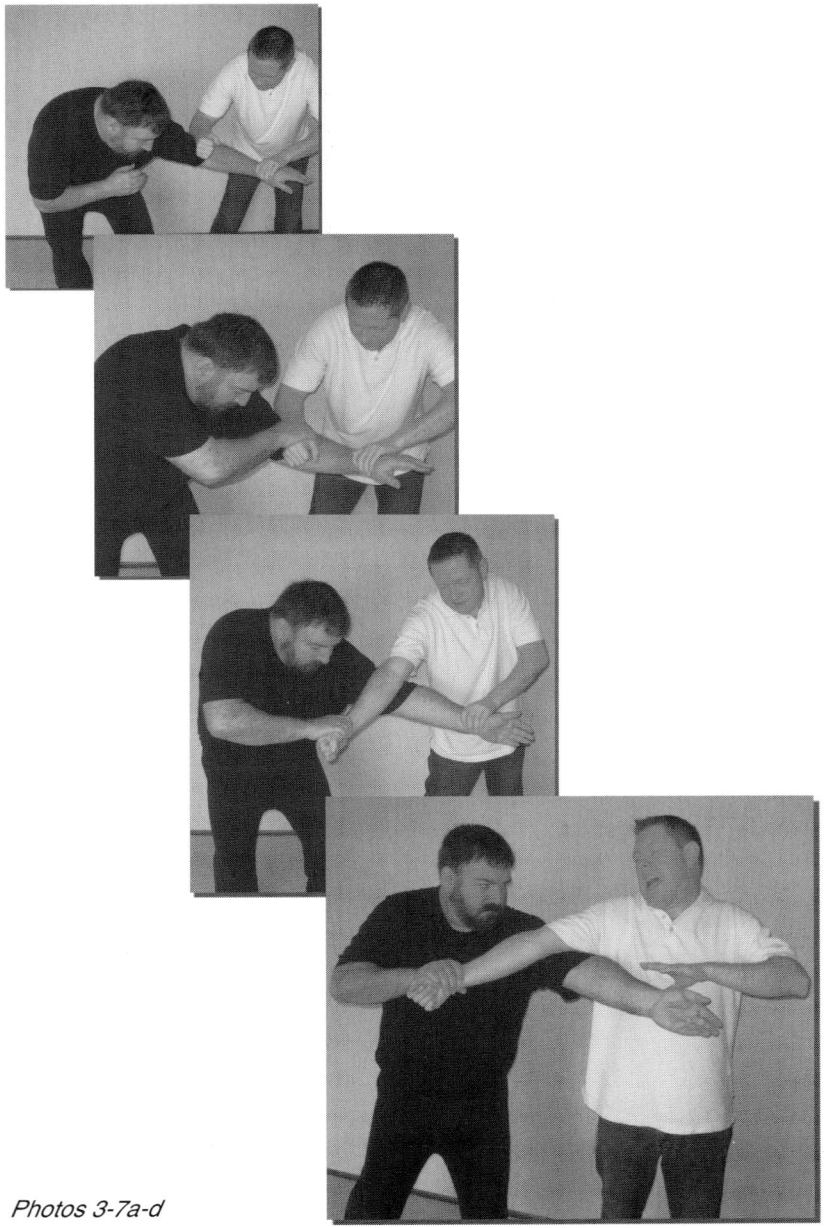

Photos 3-7a-d

There is also a follow-up to this move:

Remember how you rotated your arm back on top, at the end of the Pressure-Release Reversal?

You can use the same rotation here.

After lifting into your opponent's arm, rotate your arm into your body and up (photo 3-7e), while using your other hand to turn his arm, elbow-up.

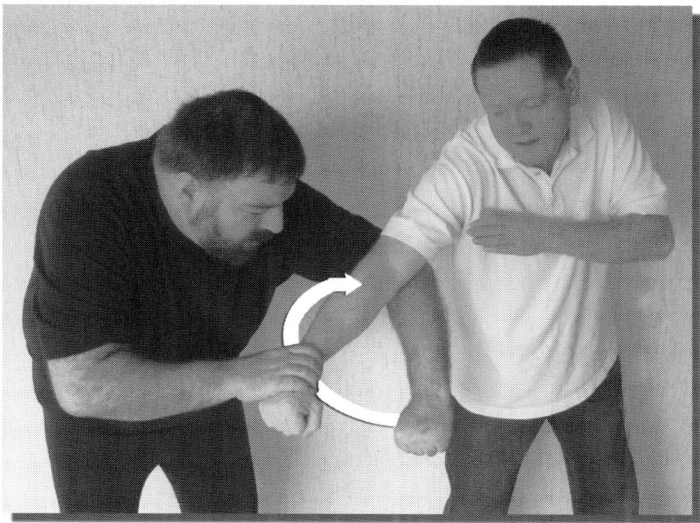

Photo 3-7e

Then you put another arm bar on your opponent.

Of course there are oodles of other locks that you could use as follow-ups, too. Keep experimenting.

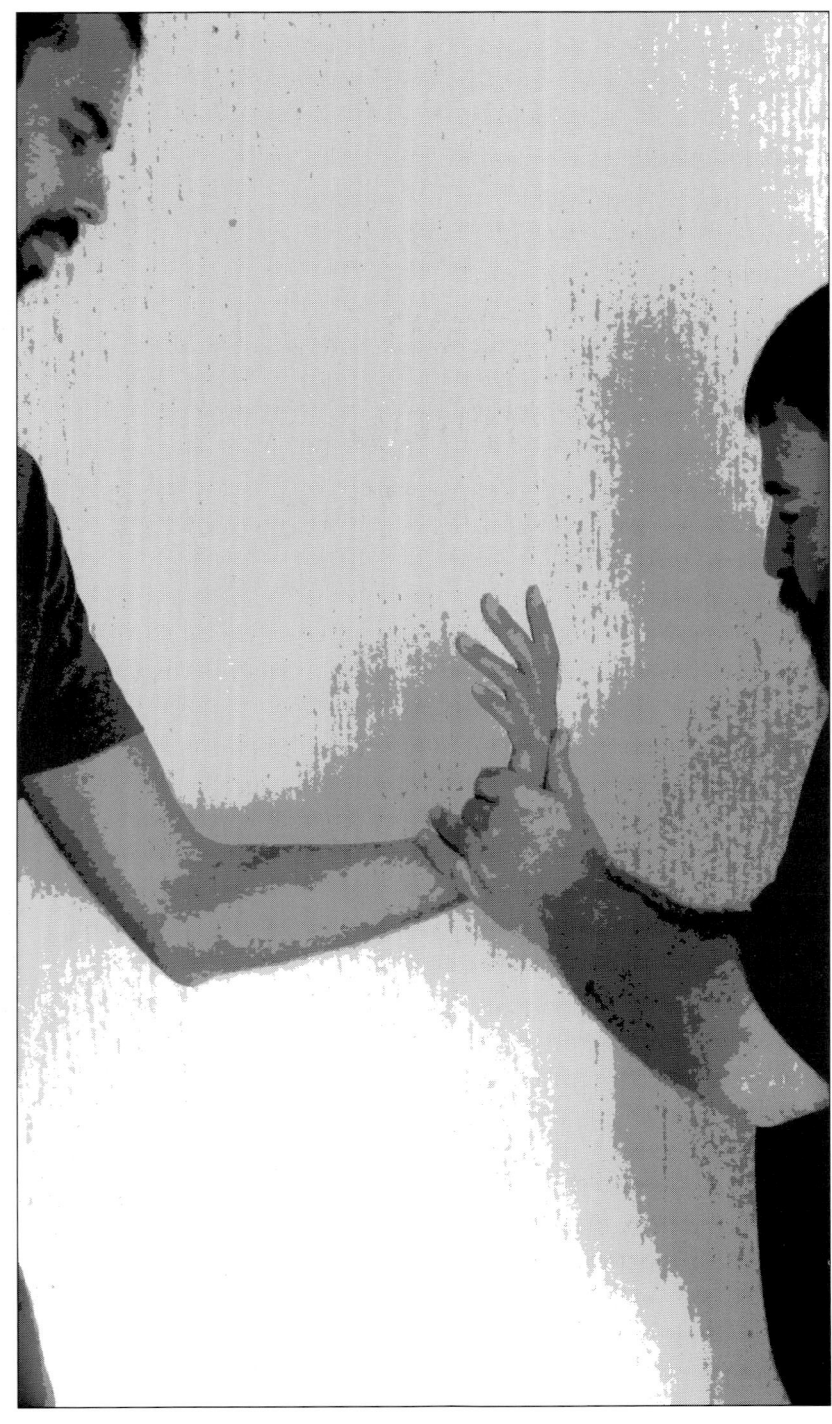

4
A Dozen Super Techniques to Promote Thought

Even though there are only a limited number of directions to *tweak* the fixed number of joints in the human body, variations abound. There really are hundreds of wrist and joint locks.

The following baker's dozen were carefully chosen.

There are easy locks and hard ones, long routines and short "instant" locks, wrist locks and arm bars, common locks and some weird ones, mundane and fancy.... I have tried to give you a variety.

More than just a random collection of locks, I chose each lock because it illustrates a principle that is important for you to learn. It's up to you to glean the important points of each lock; what's important to me may be something different to you.

As you learn each lock, generalize for different situations. What attack would cause you to choose one lock over another?

Can you get to these locks from different attacks?

Can you modify these locks to suit your own needs? What is the most important aspect of each lock?

#1: The Basic Lock

It seems that just about everyone is familiar with the Basic Lock.

I've seen police use it. Although it's illegal in many wrestling arenas, wrestlers sometimes use it. And it's used all the time in the movies.

It's used everywhere; yet 80-90% of the people out there using it, are doing it incorrectly. Some give up on the move before really perfecting it. Others don't seem to get the right force and motion; their opponents are easily able to struggle out of the hold.

I've seen pitiful attempts at what should be a very effective wrist lock. You won't make their mistakes.

I've taken a lot of space describing this lock and its variations.

Let's put it this way: you can't call yourself a wrist-lock expert and not know this wrist lock. Not only are you going to learn this lock inside and out here, you will start the two patterns in this book with the Basic Lock.

The patterns will allow you to easily flow into different holds and train the body to know where to go in a real encounter.

You will learn to execute the lock from a two-hand grab (page 57). You will learn the correct *energy*, so that the lock will solidly hold your opponent.

You will learn a thumb-grab variation.

You will learn two techniques to overcome those who resist with the Small Fist Circle.

Follow my directions, practice with a partner, and you truly will be an expert at this wrist lock. You'll amaze yourself and others.

You will eventually need to learn to generalize this lock to other opponents (Chapter 7). But first, here's the basic technique.

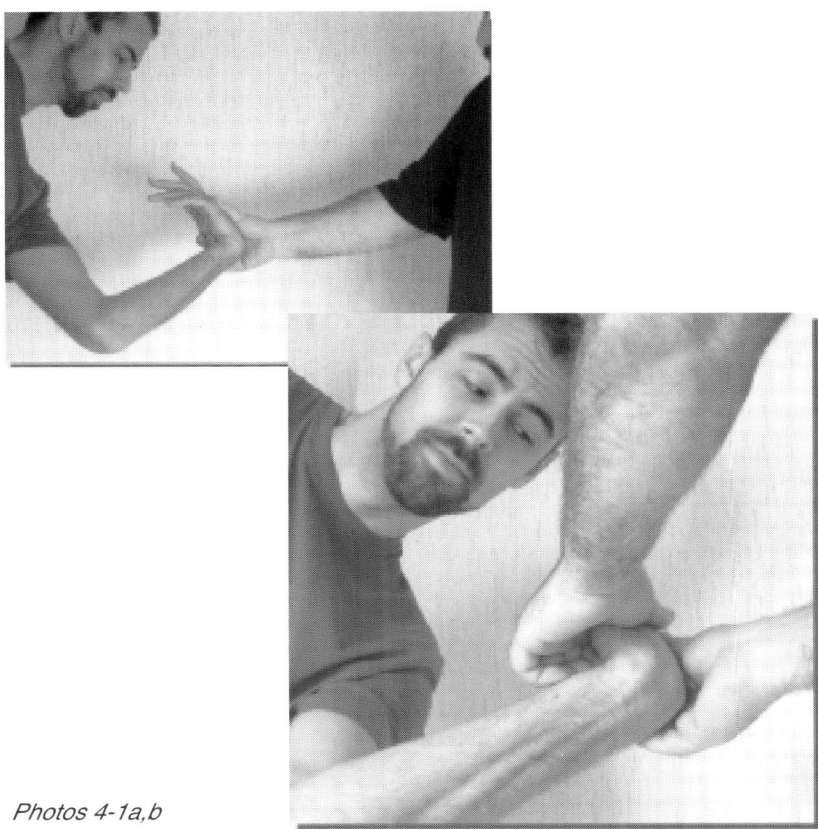

Photos 4-1a,b

This lock can be executed with one or both hands (photos 4-1a and b).

If you perform the lock with only one hand, only your thumb on the back of your opponent's hand, then I recommend that you either work left to right hand or right to left hand. In these photos, grab the opponent's left hand with your right.

Here is the Basic Lock in detail: the opponent's hand hangs down. Grab your opponent's hand as in Photos 4-2a and b.

Rotate the hand up, matching Photo 4-2c. Pause here. When you're actually performing the lock, there won't be any pause; you'll just flow right into the correct pressure. The pressure will change, as you smoothly flow the wrist almost to the point of no return. At the last instant, you'll apply a more forceful pressure.

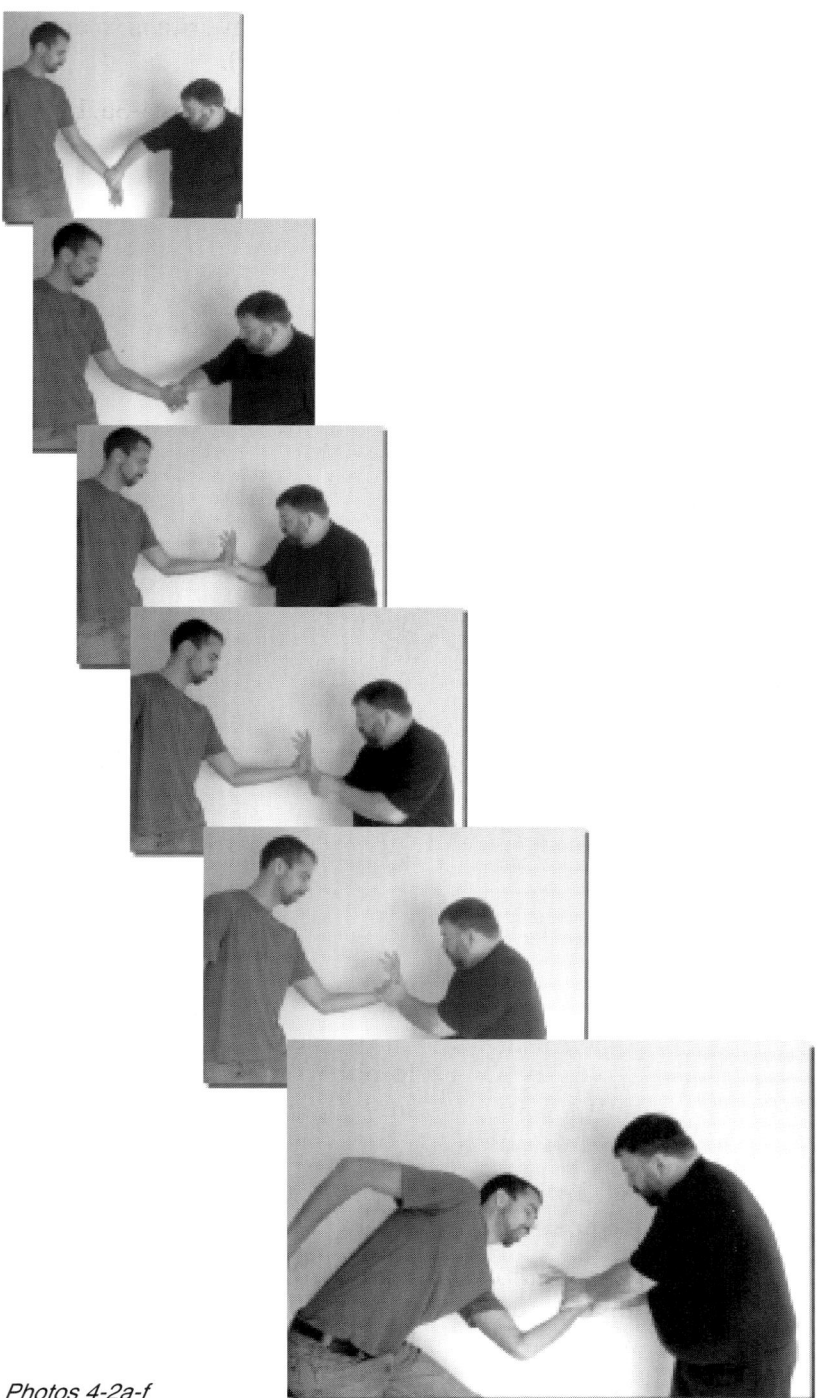

Photos 4-2a-f

At this point, you have several options. My favorite is to apply a lot of pressure straight down (photos 4-2d-f).

You could even open-hand punch his wrist (photos 4-3a, b); don't punch your practice partner with force.

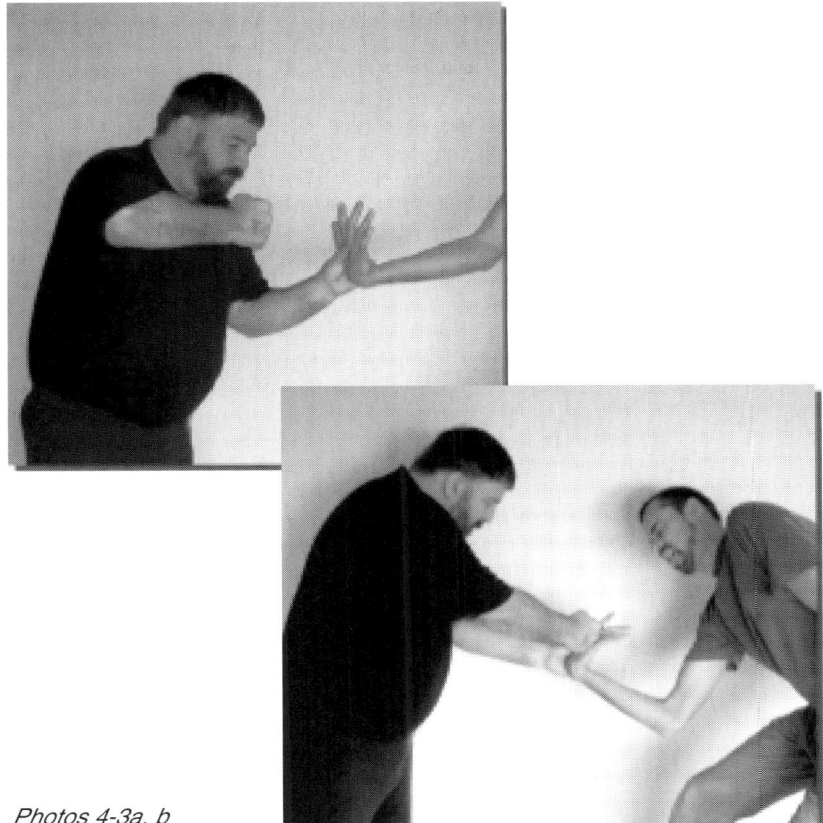

Photos 4-3a, b

You could use your open hand to put pressure on the inside of his forearm, while putting pressure directly onto the back of the hand (photos 4-4a and b).

How about a similar idea with pressure right below the inside of the elbow (photos 4-5)?

Try both of these variations with and without your extra hand applying limiting pressure. The extra hand helps you find the proper pressure with the other hand.

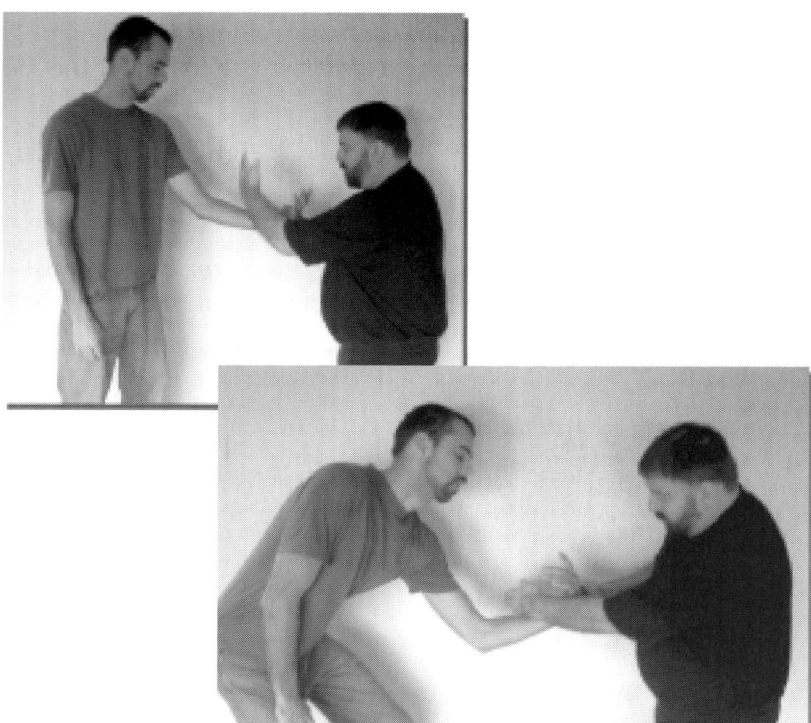

Photos 4-4a, b

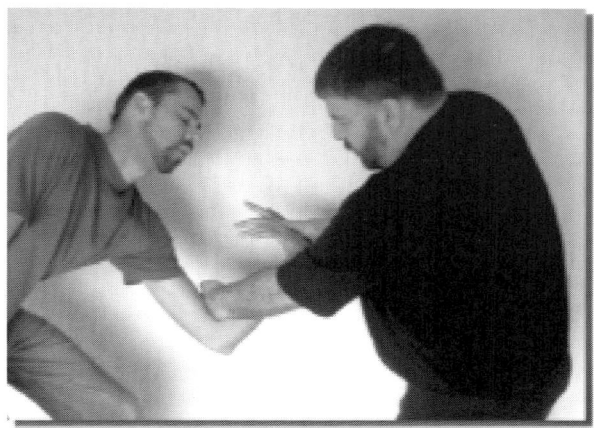

Photo 4-5

Try the same lock with a thumb grab as in Photo 4-6a. The principle is the same, but you're going to have to adjust the pressure. It's more of a pull-down pressure.

You should be trying to drag his thumb straight down. Experiment with variations; it all depends how you grab the thumb – right to left or left to left (photos 4-6b, c).

It takes a minimal amount of force. Even the weakest of wrist-lock experts should be able to cause a great deal of pain to an opponent's thumb.

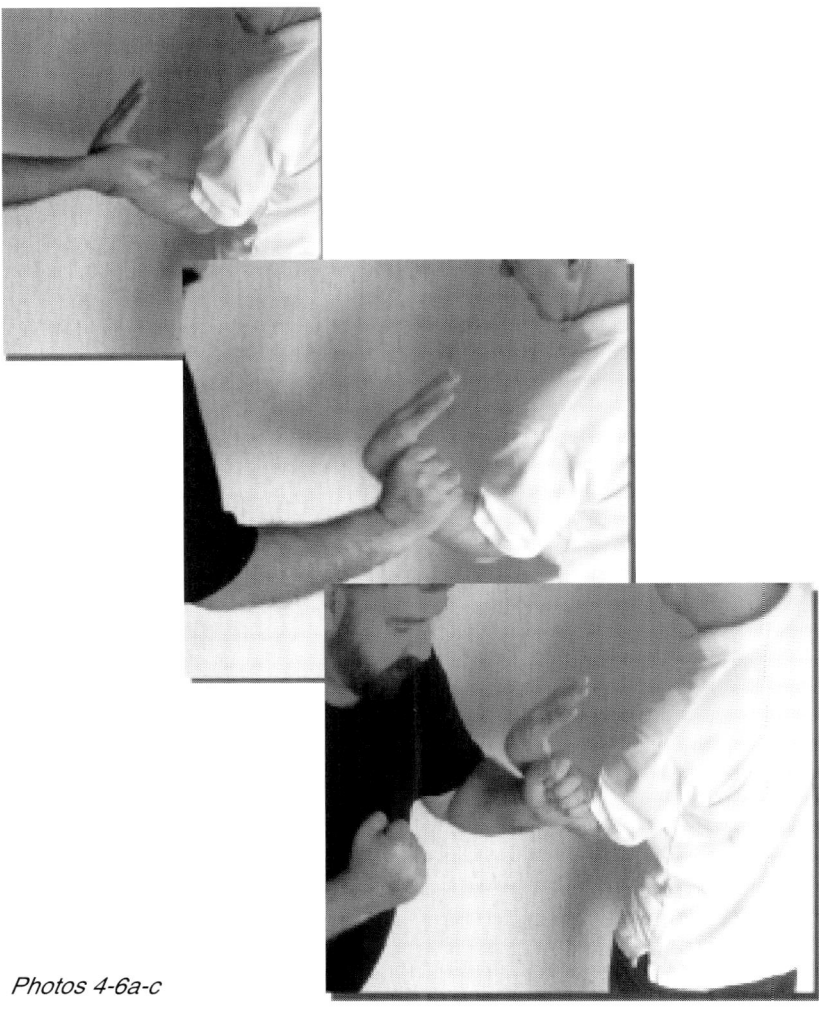

Photos 4-6a-c

Go back to the regular wrist lock with your thumb on the back of his hand. Have you found *the point of no return* on this lock yet?

It's especially important to know the point when the lock is being put on you. Can you feel it?

I'll give you a hint. Study the relationship between your wrist, your elbow, and your shoulder. When your wrist gets lowered, what naturally happens to your elbow? Yep. It starts to rise. Hmmm. Just how low does that wrist have to be? Don't forget to consider your shoulder.

The Pickpocket

For those who haven't experienced the *Tube,* it's the very sophisticated subway system found in London, England.

One summer in the early eighties, I had the occasion to use the Tube. I was waiting on a platform at Bayswater Station on my way to Foyles Bookstore, the largest bookstore in the world.

While I was waiting, a pickpocket tried to lift my wallet. He reached my back pocket and grabbed (photo 4-7a). I rotated his hand, and– lo and behold (photos 4-7b-e) ... I had him in a perfect lock.

So, did I punch him (photo 4-7e)? Actually, no. He was surprised, and so was I. I had effected the lock without thinking, so it surprised me, too.

He pulled loose and ran away ... without my wallet.

Anyway, this is definitely a sequence to practice. You never know when someone is going to grab you or your wallet from behind.

How could you modify this, if the attacker were to grab your shoulder?

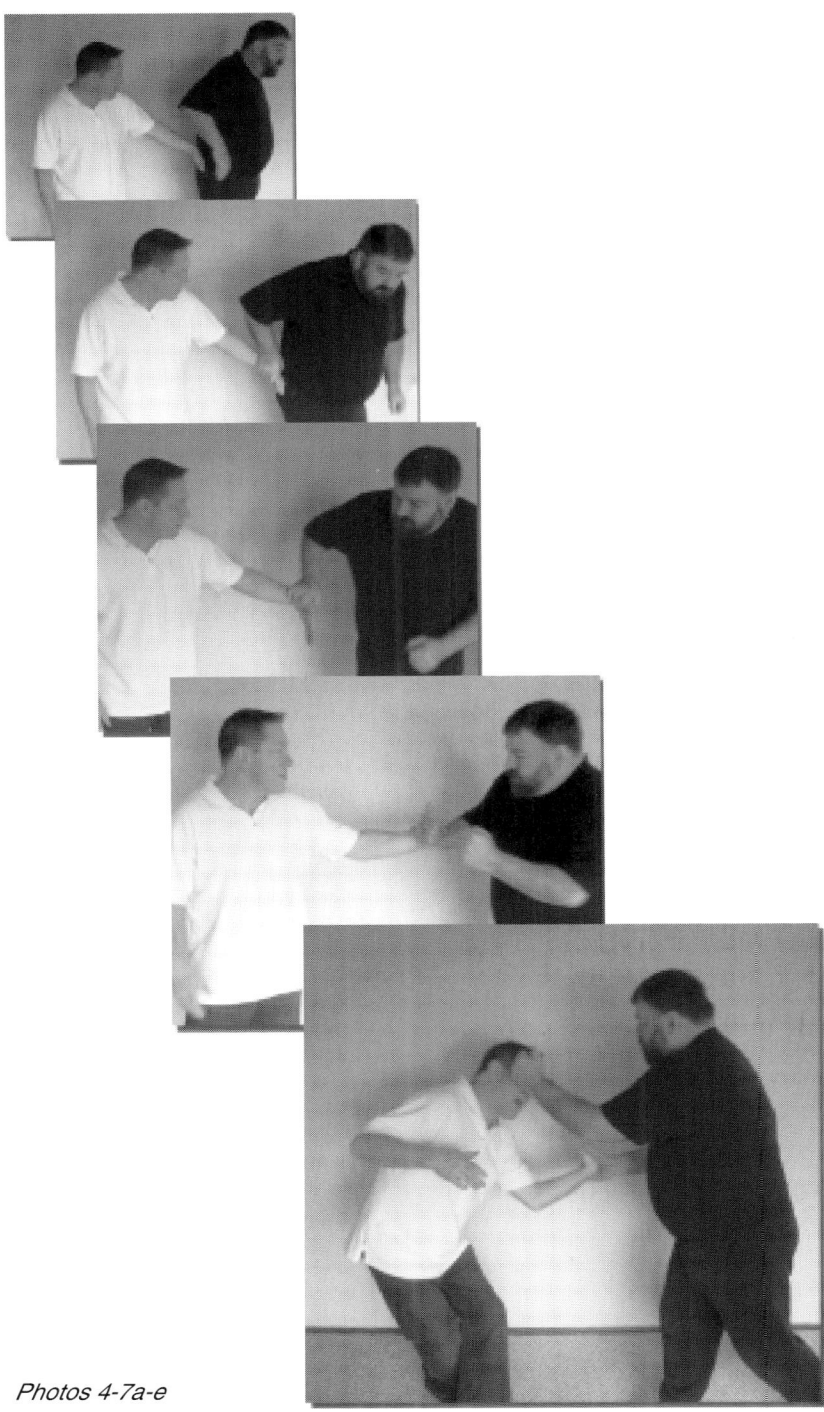

Photos 4-7a-e

Pickpocket Tip: If you rotate to face your opponent, the lock flows nicely at the same time; both his (or her) arm and your body rotate at the same time (photos 4-8a-c).

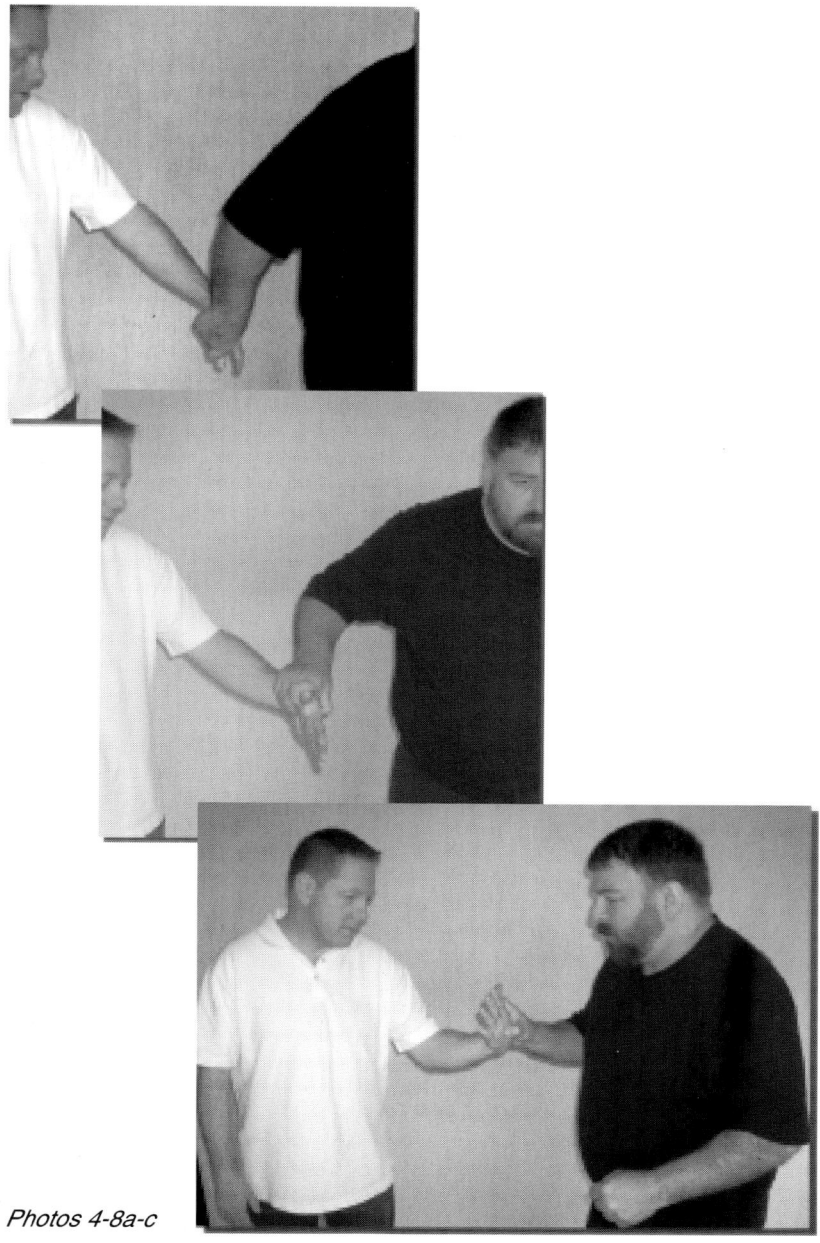

Photos 4-8a-c

The Two-Hand Grab

This is a sequence that could definitely enhance your reputation. It's a great demonstration.

Your opponent grabs your hands as in Photo 4-9a.

Photo 4-9a

Rotate your palms up and start to put his (or her) wrist into the palm of your hand (photo 4-9b).

It doesn't matter which hand goes into yours, because you're starting out with both hands grabbing yours in the same way. Rotate either hand to the top position; it's your choice.

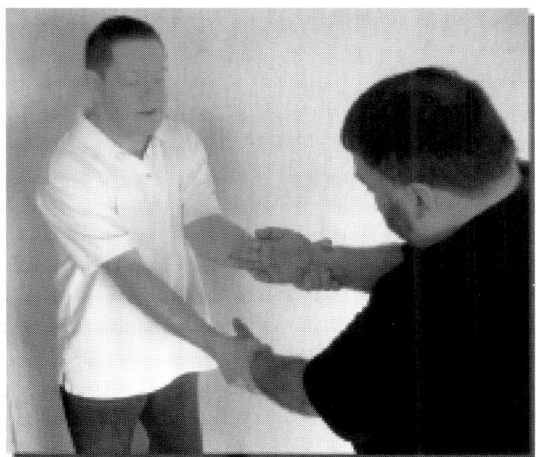

Photo 4-9b

Once you've rotated your attackers wrist into one of your hands (photo 4-9c), firmly grasp that wrist, and rotate your upper hand palm down, and in toward your body, escaping the grasp (photo 4-9d).

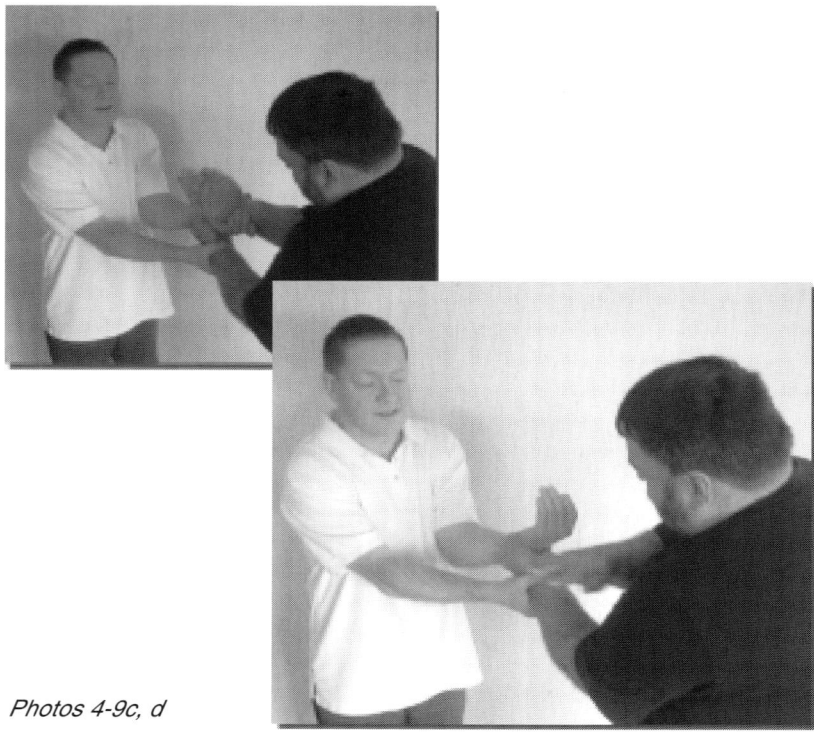

Photos 4-9c, d

As soon as your hand is free, and it may take a lot of pull to free it, come back with the edge of your hand against the back of the opponent's (photo 4-9e).

Now, turn the pressure of your knife-edge hand-position downward, and continue putting pressure on the wrist lock (photo 4-9f).

If you feel control slipping, flow into another lock, or reapply the knife-edge hand. Also, apply more pressure.

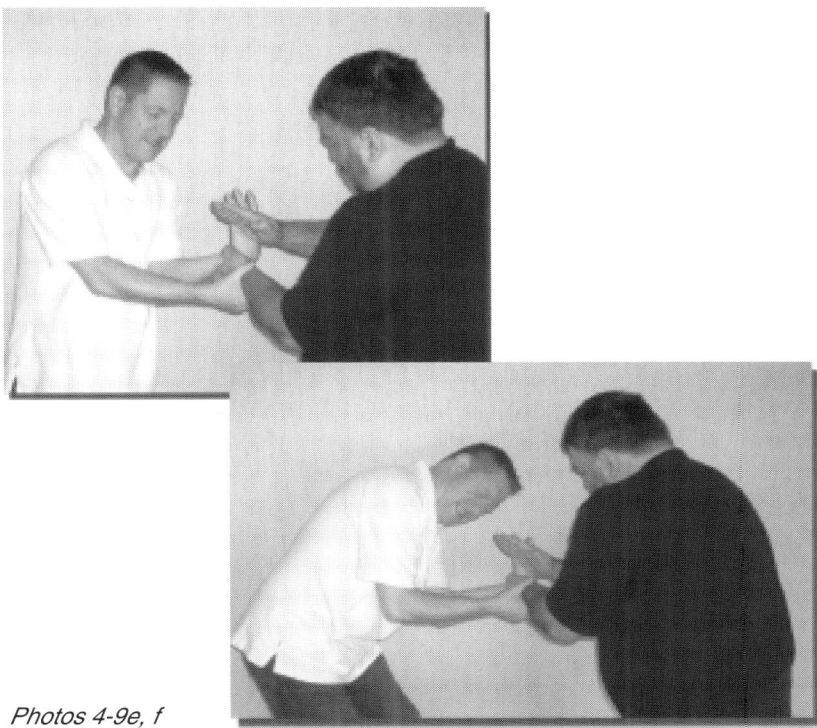

Photos 4-9e, f

Try this little tip: When you first feel the two-hand grab, exert a little force outward. This is the opposite direction of the lock.

If your opponent resists, you'll feel force countering in the opposite direction.

Perfect ... use the force to effect your Basic Lock (photos 4-10a and b, below).

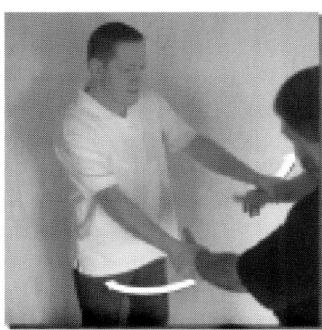

Once you have the lock applied, you have many options, from hitting and kicking to flowing into another lock. Why another lock?

I almost always flow into a different lock, because I personally don't feel as though I have *the best* control in the knife-edge position. Sometimes, I just adjust my hand position to the more familiar thumb on the back of the opponent's hand. (I really do have a lot of control with the knife edge, it's just not my favorite position for "complete" control.)

When you're in an adrenalin-pumping situation, it's always better to control with a "favorite." You'll feel more confident and have the upper hand.

Now you can put on the Basic Lock either from a full two-hand restraining grab by your opponent, or a single grab that you initiate with either one or both hands.

You're fairly consistent in your technique.

Now what?

What do you do after you initiate the lock?

You actually have quite a few possibilities. We'll discuss three or four here, and then give you some ideas on how to further your search (or should I say research).

Idea #1

Put The Basic Lock on your opponent and then ... hit. That's right.

You should know by now that I go for the simplest, most direct route when I'm in a confrontation. Yes, a straight hit counts as a direct route. Don't you think?

It's obvious: you pick the target. In other words, look for a good opening. And practice and plan timing. I usually hit right when his body starts to torque.

This all happens right before I reach his point of no return (discussed in Chapter 3). I like to believe that my punch helps him on his way to that critical point where he can't fight back.

You have different possibilities, as long as the hit is efficient -- direct (photo 4-11).

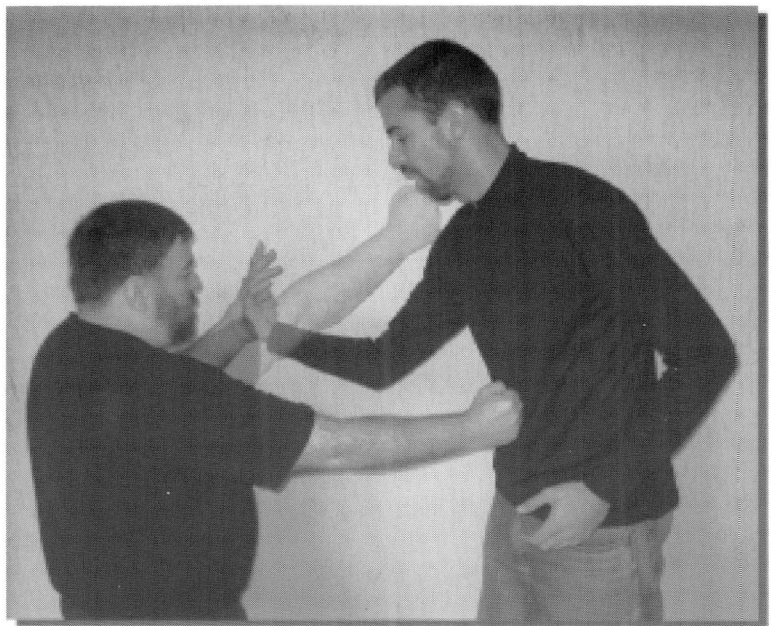

Photo 4-11

Idea #2

In my travels through different martial arts schools, I have had more than one expert claim that the wrist won't break on the Basic Lock, no matter how hard it's applied. I don't believe it!

Be careful!

Photo 4-12

I also haven't had the guts, nor the volunteers, to experiment. Those esteemed experts claim that if you really torque the wrist, and put the lock on with full force, then the body will flip right over in the air, rather than allow the wrist to break.

Again, I don't believe it, especially since I really do whip the pressure back in a straight line toward the wrist. Most practitioners exert pressure in a circle, which might allow the body to flip.

Anyway, idea #2 is that you snap the lock on hard. I mean with full force (photos 4-13a-d). Think of it as an experiment. Will your attacker's body flip into the air, or will you end up breaking his wrist? (If you are practicing with a partner, I am kidding; if you are really defending yourself, it *might be* the perfect time to test your theory.)

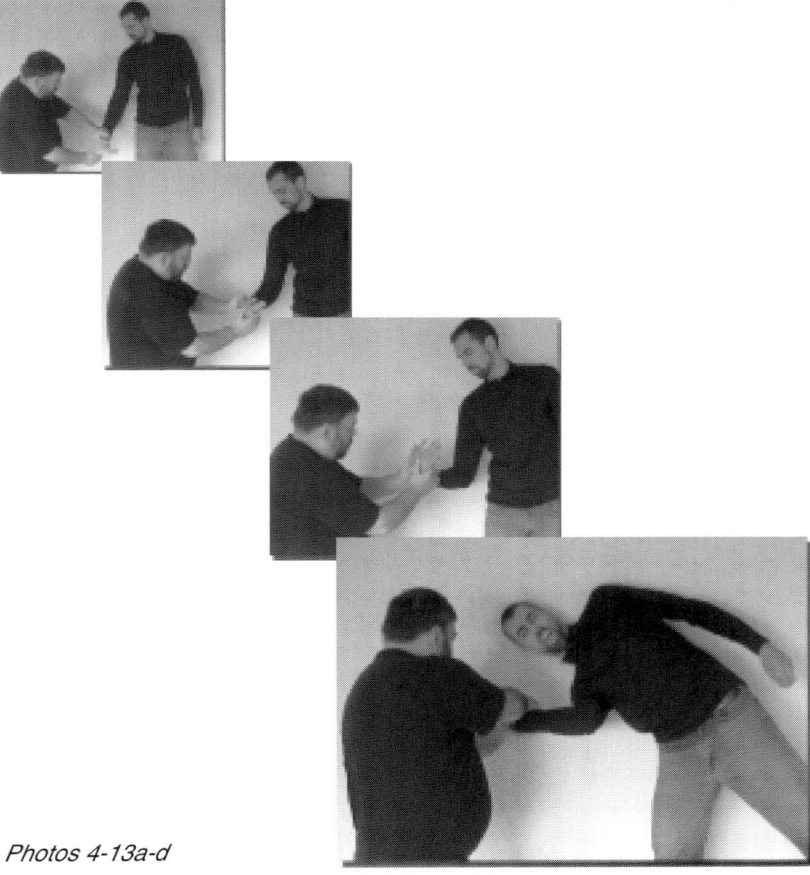

Photos 4-13a-d

Steve Golden says, "A martial arts person will flip, but a person off the street may not, because the fear of falling is so great."

Save this *experiment* for a real attacker. With either outcome you'll probably have to deal with some aspect of the law, either filling out reports, or some form of litigation. In other words, don't take the risk, unless you have to. (May you never have to!)

Idea #3: Chicken Wing Plus

Go from a Basic Lock into another lock. An alternate explanation for the Chicken Wing is embedded in Pattern #1 on page 124.

A Chicken Wing works beautifully on tall opponents. (Take a look at my almost-seven-foot practice partner in the photos.)

Start with a Basic Lock. As you apply pressure, lift the wrist and arm up a bit (photo 4-14a).

Photo 4-14a

Reach past your partner's locked arm and up with your free hand (photos 4-14b-d).

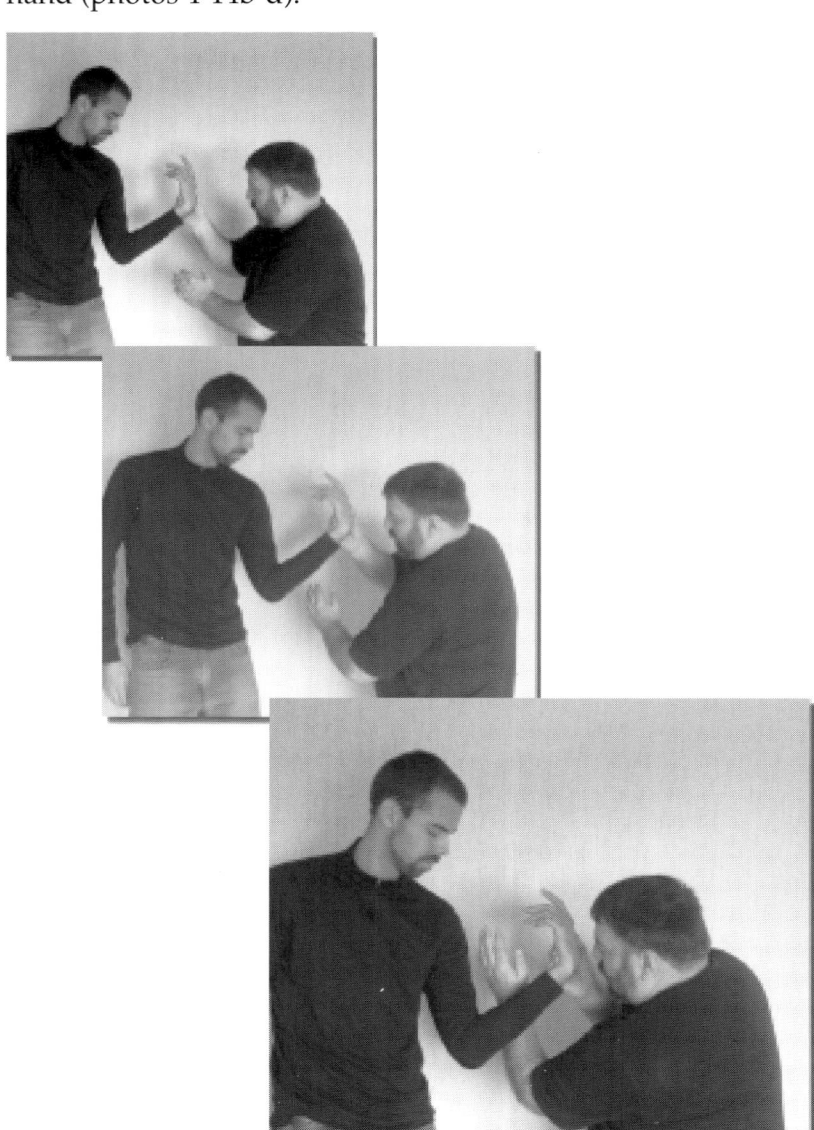

As you reach up, grab the back your partner's hand. The lock pressure is about the same; you have to switch the hand that does the locking (photos 4-14e-g).

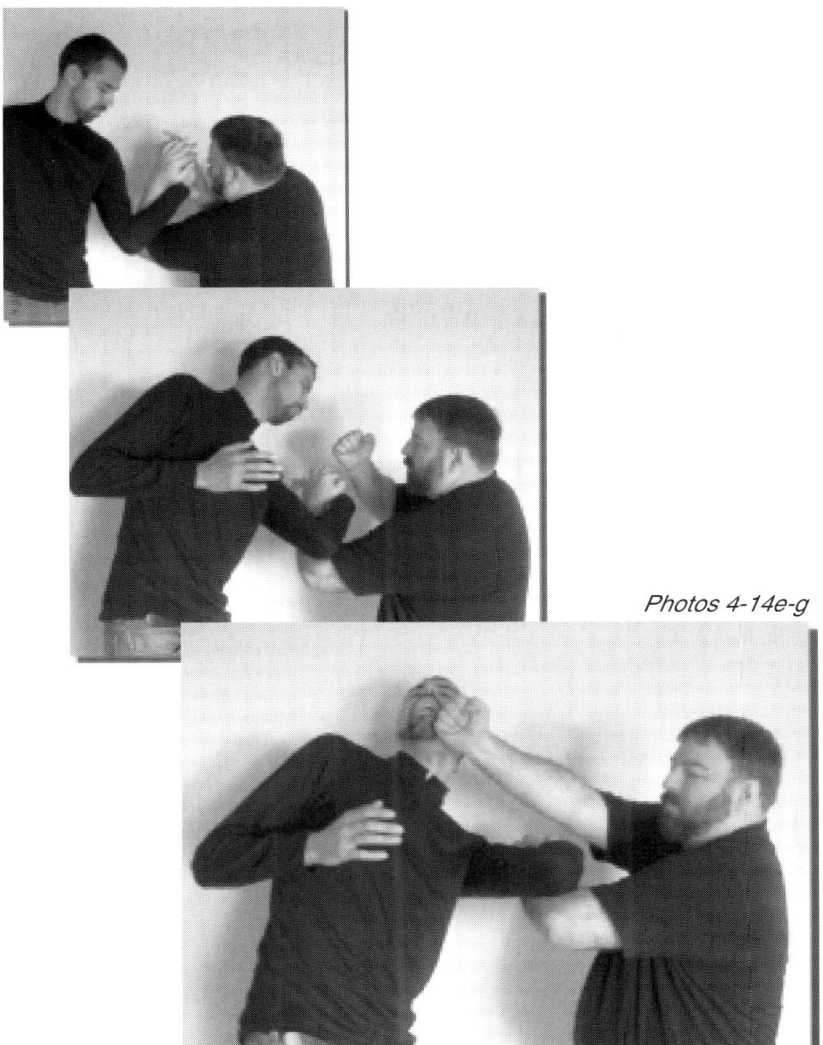

Photos 4-14e-g

You could switch to a thumb variation of the same lock. It's described earlier in this chapter, on page 53.

You could go into straight-arm techniques, flow into other patterns, or take your opponent to the ground.

This is one lock that should definitely be included in your experiment sessions.

#2: The Step-Through

The other lock that has many variations is the Step-Through. We'll take ours from a handshake position. (It could be a wrist grab instead of a handshake, or you could also do variations by grabbing the other hand, but we'll start from a basic handshake position.)

Let's learn to do this lock correctly:

Instead of going straight in for a normal handshake, I want you to hesitate with your hand for an instant; you may even want to draw your hand back ever so slightly.

Even though it's hard to practice for this, when your partner knows your objective, the goal in this hesitation is to get your opponent to reach forward.

You want him (or her) slightly off balance by having to extend, to reach you, when performing the technique (photo 4-15a).

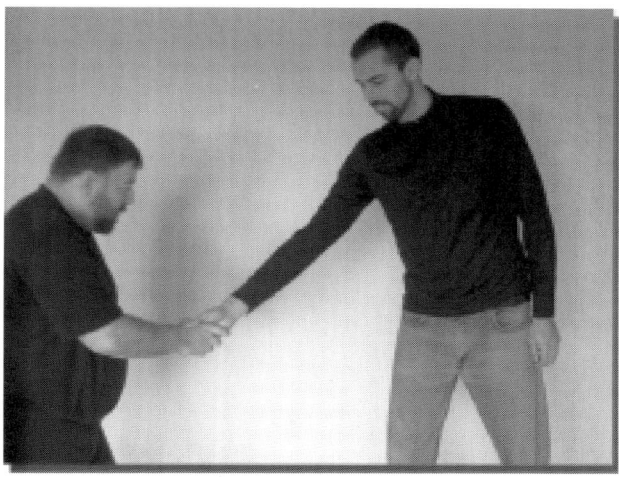

Photo 4-15a

Now, as you grab the hand step through the opening between the grabbed arm and the body (photos 4-15b, c). As you step through, take the hand with you and apply pressure behind the back (photos 4-15d-f).

An important point is the hesitation. Another reason you want your opponent off balance is to draw the body forward and low; you definitely have to duck to get through the opening.

If you were to do this move with your opponent standing completely erect, you might find yourself locked in a reversal. Remember, duck, to avoid reversals.

Experiment to discover how low your opponent really needs to be. Is it the same for every opponent? What about the position of your shoulder in relation to your opponent's?

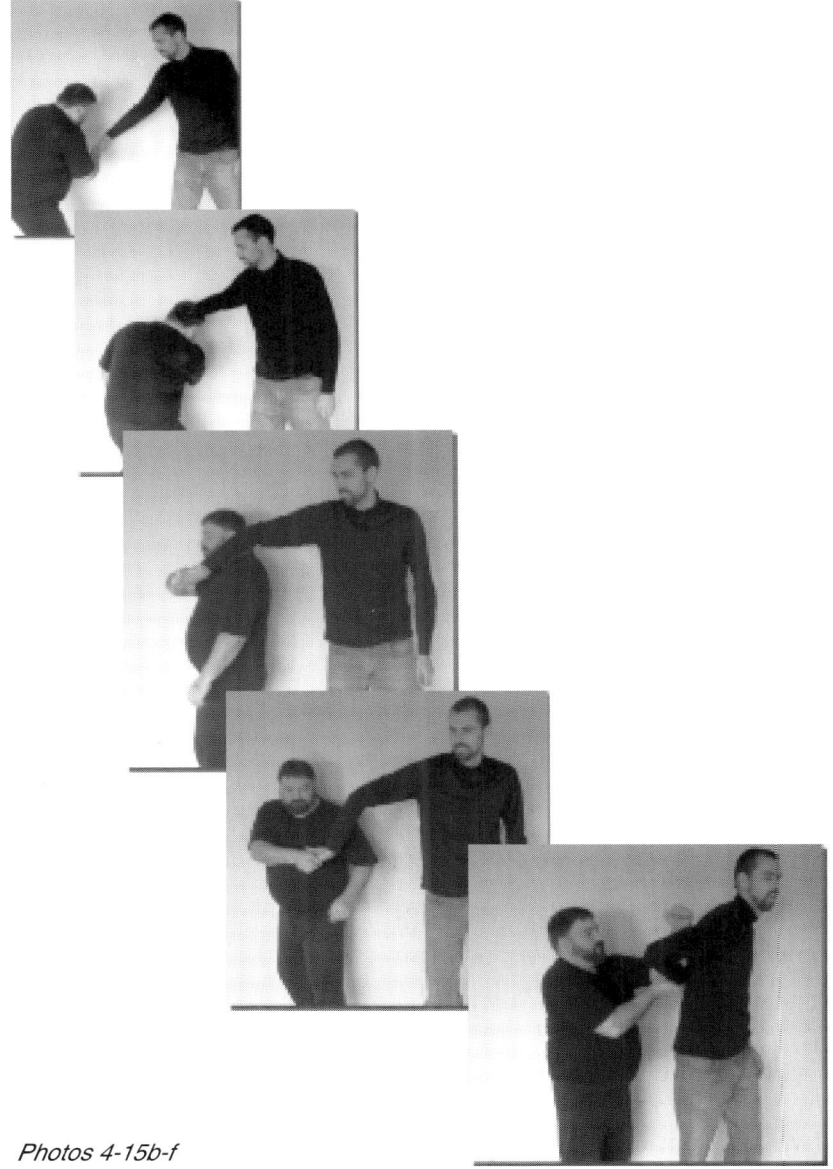

Photos 4-15b-f

Once you get the arm firmly held behind the back, you should experiment with fingerlock positions. (See the end of Pattern #2, page 148.)

#3: Ground Control to Major Long ... Time

This next one is an easy-to-learn, versatile move.

If you ever take someone down to the *ground*, with an arm bar, like the Step Through Lock, or any other lock, you might want to consider how you're going to maintain *control* for a *long* period of time.

When your opponent is flat on his (or her) face, pull the locked arm straight out, perpendicular to the torso (photo 4-16a). Bend your partner's wrist absolutely straight up and apply pressure into the wrist, bending the fingers toward the arm (photo 4-16b).

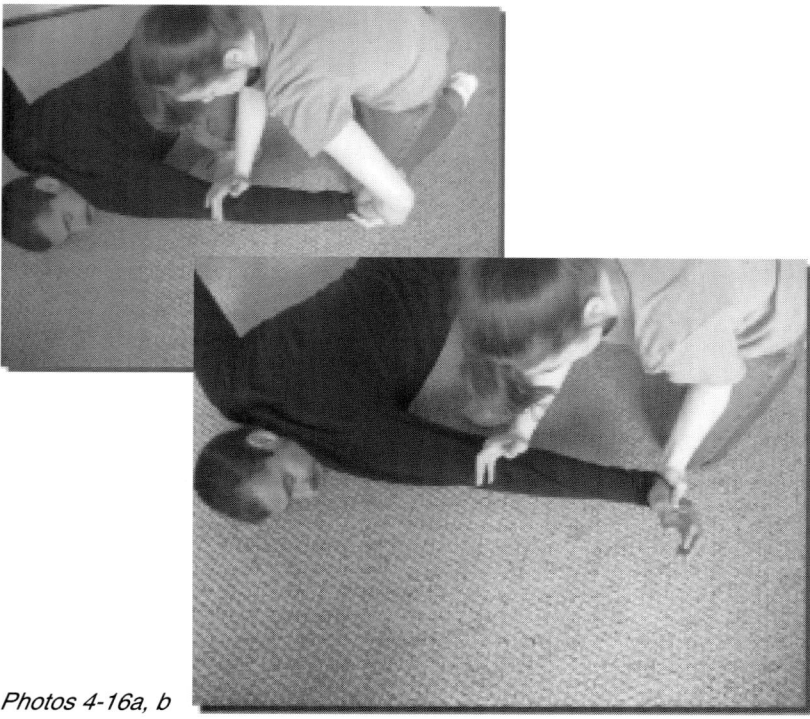

Photos 4-16a, b

Where can you go from here?

There are a variety of possibilities that my teacher, Steve Golden, taught me. These two tickled my fancy.

I like the first one for its simplicity, and I like the second one because it's fancy, but still easy to get into.

The first continuation is nothing more than making use of a stray stone to cause pain. You slam the wrist down on a small rock on the ground or maybe a set of keys (photos 4-17a, b). Steve causes a little pain, then commands, "Don't move!" They tend not to move.

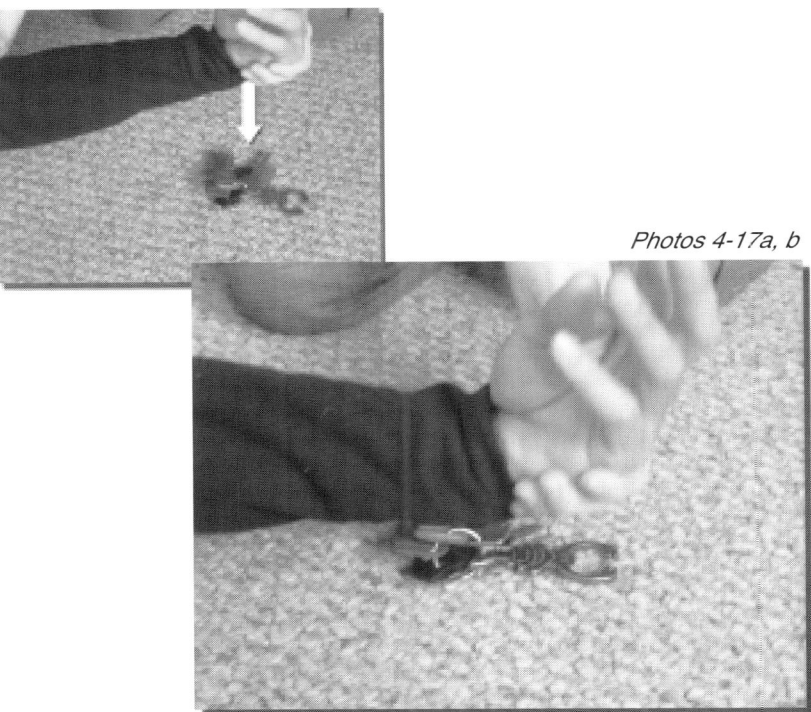

Photos 4-17a, b

For the second continuation technique, you're going to sit on him (literally) for awhile. From the outstretched-arm position, lay your leg on top of his arm as in Photo 4-18a.

If your opponent's left arm is outstretched, you use your right leg, and if it's the right arm, you put your left leg on top. Bend your opponent's arm back up over the same leg that's on top of the arm (photos 4-18a-c). With the proper twist to the arm around the leg and pressure on the wrist, even a small person can hold a larger brute until help arrives.

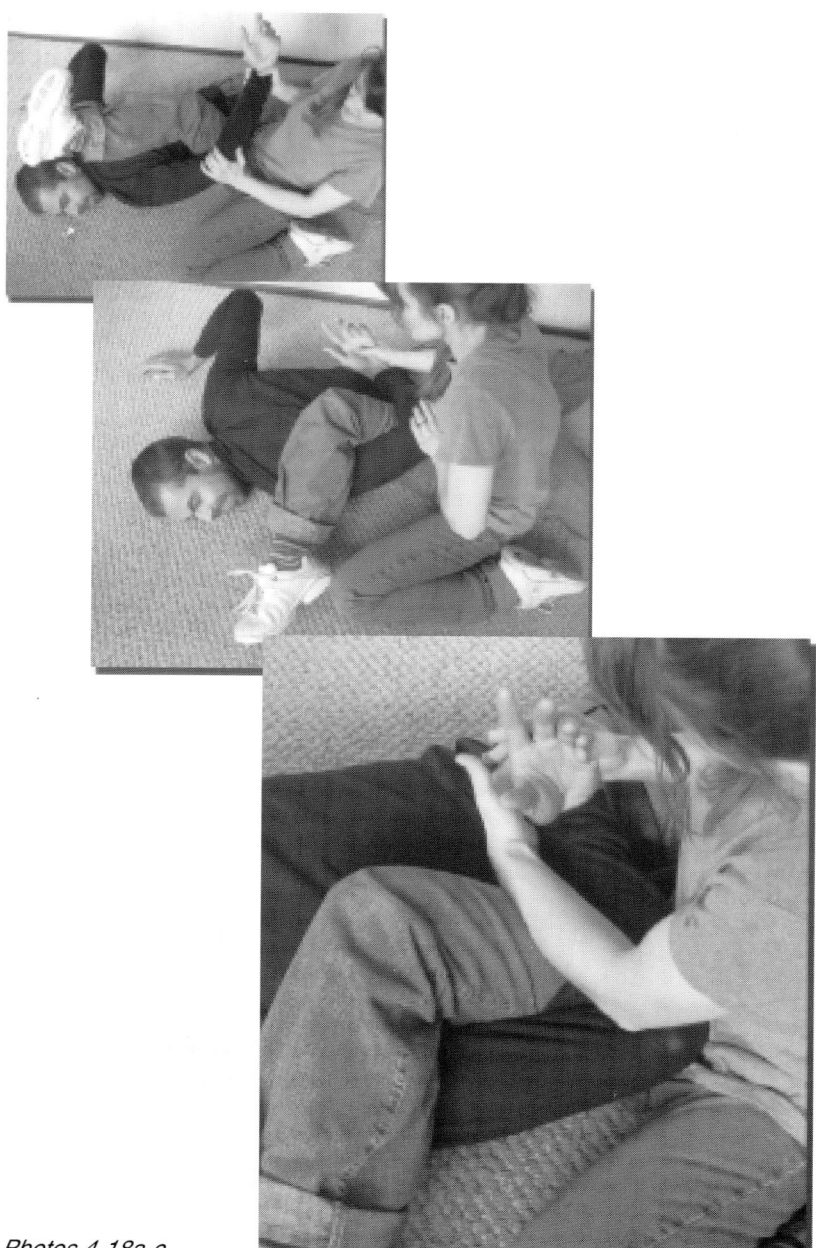

Photos 4-18a-c

#4: Shoulder-Shove Arm Bar

The next is a variation on the arm bar, with more of an Aikido feel to it.

The difference is that you exert control with your body, instead of your wrist. For an explanation of the arm bar and its variations, refer to pages 32-45.

To start this arm bar, grab your partner's arm, and pull it out straight.

Stand slightly behind your partner; grab his right wrist with your right hand (photo 4-19a)), or you could grab his left wrist with your left hand.

Photo 4-19a

Rotate his wrist, so that it's facing back toward you, with his elbow touching the front of *your* body (photo 4-19b).

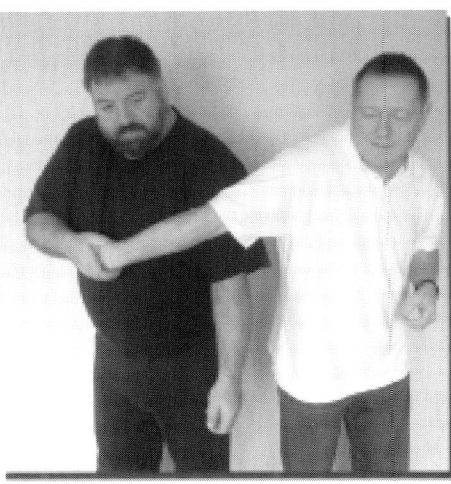

Photo 4-19b

Now, by pivoting around in a tight circle, away from your opponent, you will put pressure on your opponent's elbow (photo 4-19c, below).

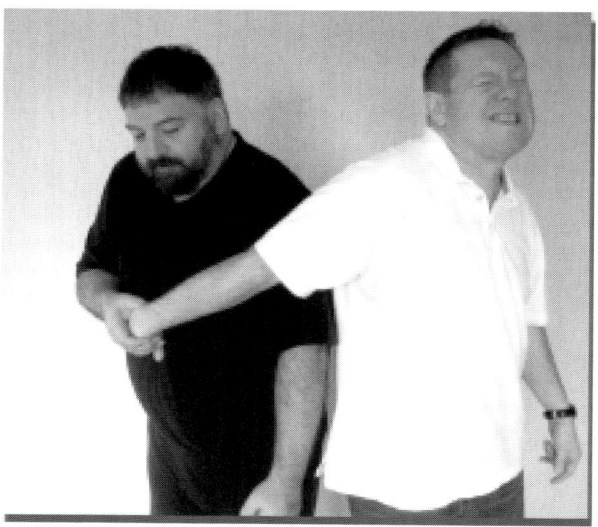

If you put a lot of pressure on the elbow, it will force your opponent to try to speed up to ease the pain. This is exactly the response that you want in order to execute your next move....

Note: If you have your opponent's right arm, turn clockwise; if you have your opponent's left arm, turn counterclockwise (photos 4-20a, b).

As he speeds up, he makes a bigger circle around your tighter rotation.

He is reacting to your small circle with bigger steps. Now, cut his big circle short with *another smaller circle* of your own, twisting in the opposite direction. This smaller circle develops into the Basic Lock. Even if it sounds complicated now, I'll help you figure it out.

Let's start with the shoulder shove (photo 4-21a). As you shove, your partner speeds up, breaking contact with your arm (photo 4-21b).

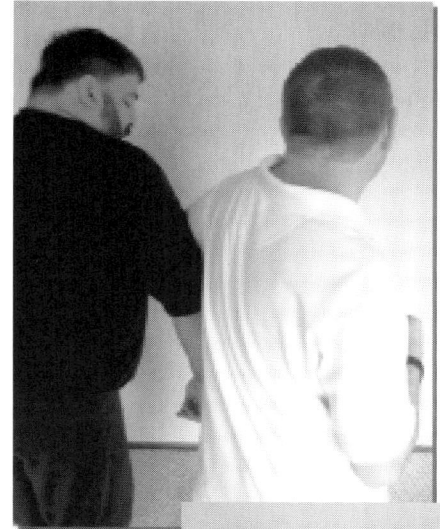

Photos 4-21a, b

As you feel the release of the pressure against your opponent's arm, raise your hand along with his held hand (photo 4-21c, d). It helps if you think about rotating your hand to a thumb-down position.

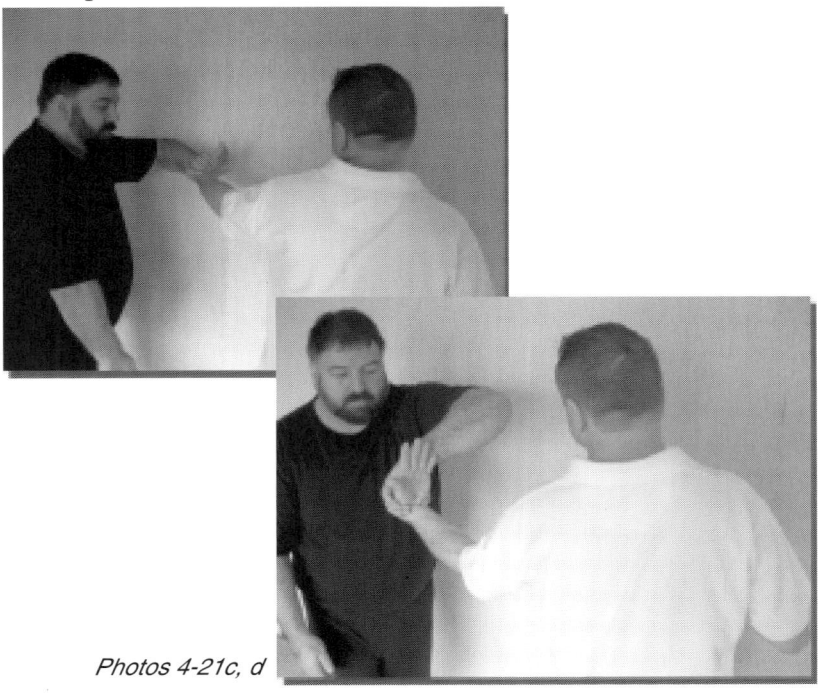

Photos 4-21c, d

Photos 4-21e and 4-21f (below) continue the pressure back in the opposite direction. The more speed that your opponent has going in the first direction, the more it's going to torque his wrist when you change directions.

Photos 4-21e, f

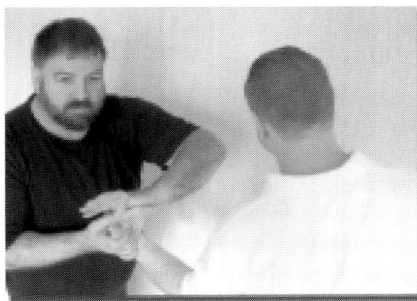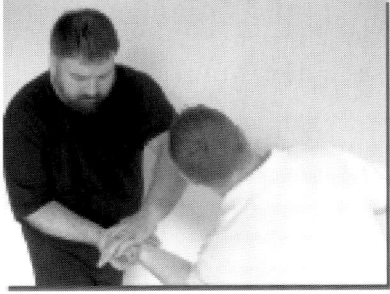

If you noticed that your elbow passes very close to your opponent's head, good for you. Definitely take advantage of the opportunity. Switch the Basic Lock to the other hand, as you continue with an elbow strike (photos 4-22a, b).

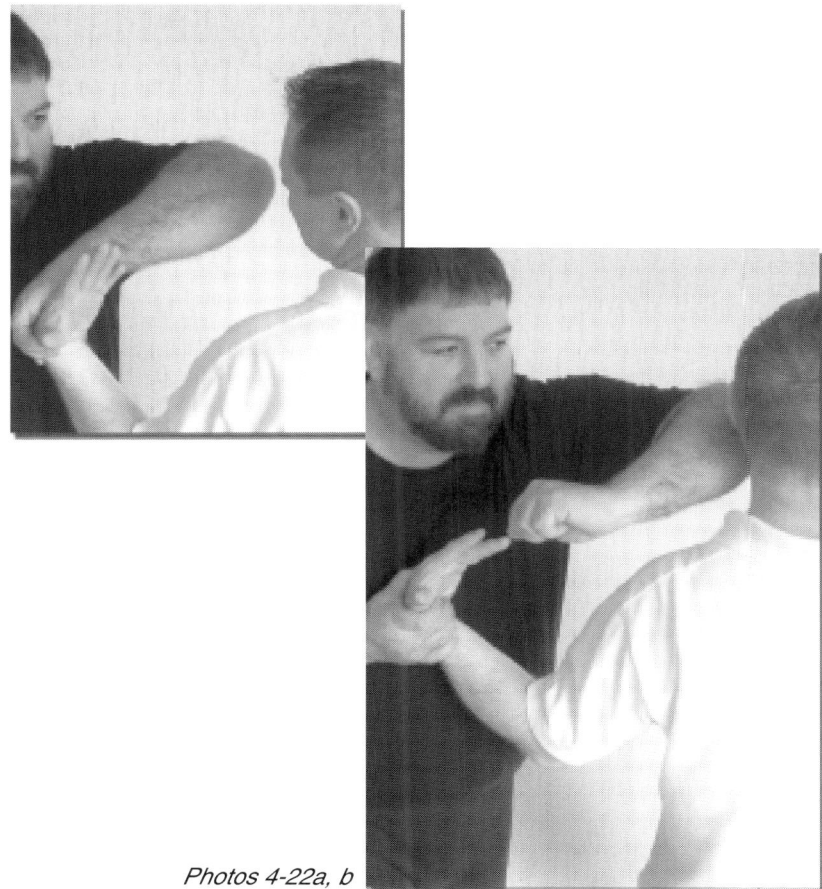

Photos 4-22a, b

An alternate follow-up off the initial pressure exerted by the shoulder, is to go into a head lock.

Reach up under his arm as in Photos 4-23a-c.

Put your hand on the back of his neck (photo 4-23d).

Now, there are several different pressures you should experiment with. You could pivot his head inward.

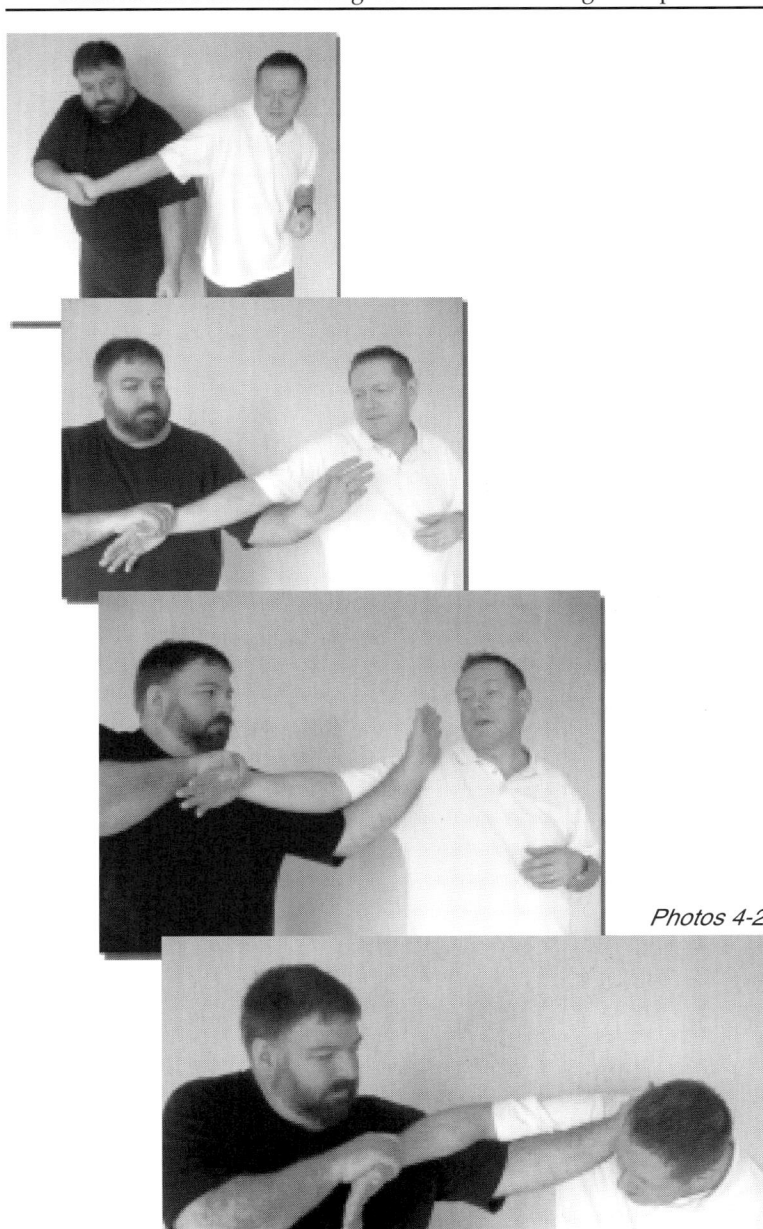

Photos 4-23a-d

You could press down and forward to drop him to the ground, or to try a throw. (Always be careful with the neck, head, and spine — especially when throwing someone.)

From here, experiment with your own variations.

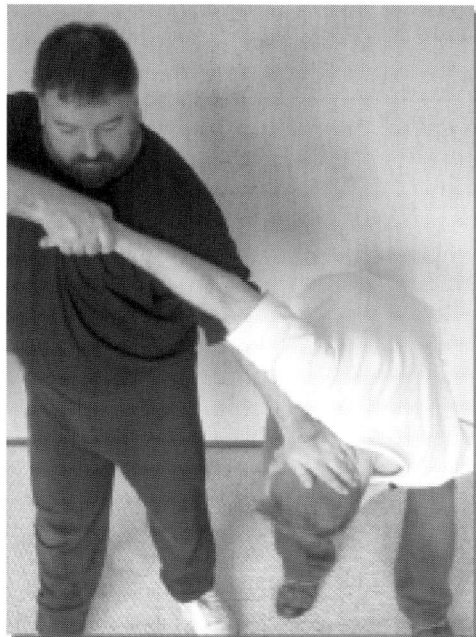

Photo 4-23e

#5: A Weird Lock With No Name

An *alternate to the alternate* is a completely different lock.

It's a little weird, but I like it. And, I have found it very useful over the years.

Use it when your opponent bends the control arm, making your pivot impossible.

Use it when you find your arm stuck on the inside of your opponent's guard.

Use it when your arm bar gets *interrupted*.

Start from the arm-down arm-bar position (photo 4-24a). Reach up on the inside, but instead of reaching up to the head, you're only going as far as his biceps.

As you reach up to grab his biceps, you bend his forearm in toward his body, hand down at the wrist (photo 4-24b). You can get several different controlling pressures with this lock.

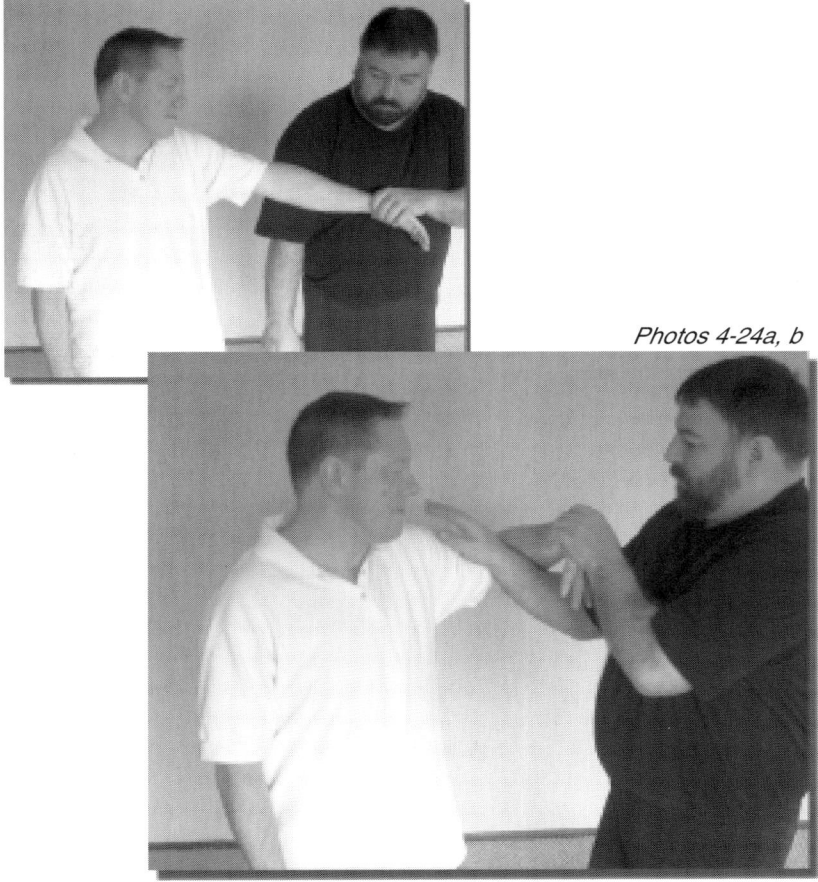

Photos 4-24a, b

First, you cause pain by bending the wrist down and in (photo 4-24c). You also cause pain by the fact that your arm is wedged in between his forearm and his biceps. Some people can even add more pain by twisting the biceps (photo 4-24d).

Don't worry if you're not getting all the pain spots. Any single point of pressure should be enough to control your opponent.

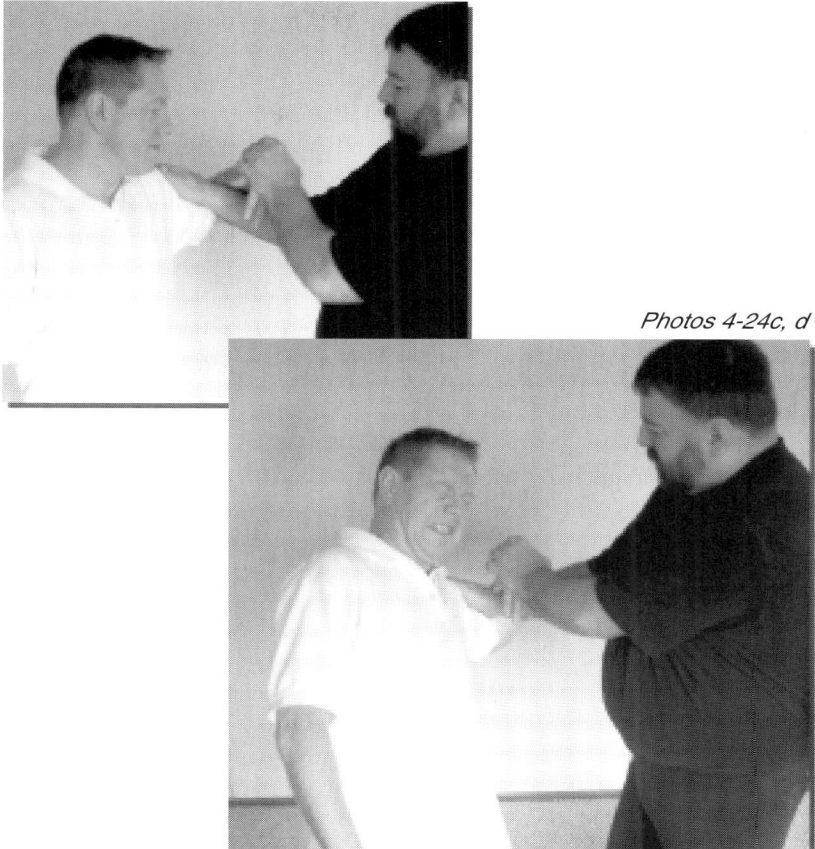

Photos 4-24c, d

#6: Kickstart

I call this lock the *Kickstart* because of the little finesse that you get to pull at the end of the sequence.

This technique is similar to the Double Ninety-Degree Lock, except one of the angles is in the opposite direction. (See the Double Ninety-Degree Lock on pages 119-121.)

Also, the Kickstart has interesting controls with the various pressures against the small finger and knuckle.

You would naturally try this lock any time your opponent's hand is thumb down. You could also grab the hand in a thumb-up position, and rotate it, so the forearm is parallel to the floor, and then the thumb points down (photos 4-25a, b).

Your opponent could be reaching in to you across your body. If he's a wing chun artist, he could have just performed a *bong sao*.

He could be blocking in front of his face, with the palm of his hand facing you.

Grab his hand in an upside-down handshake (photo 4-25a, b).

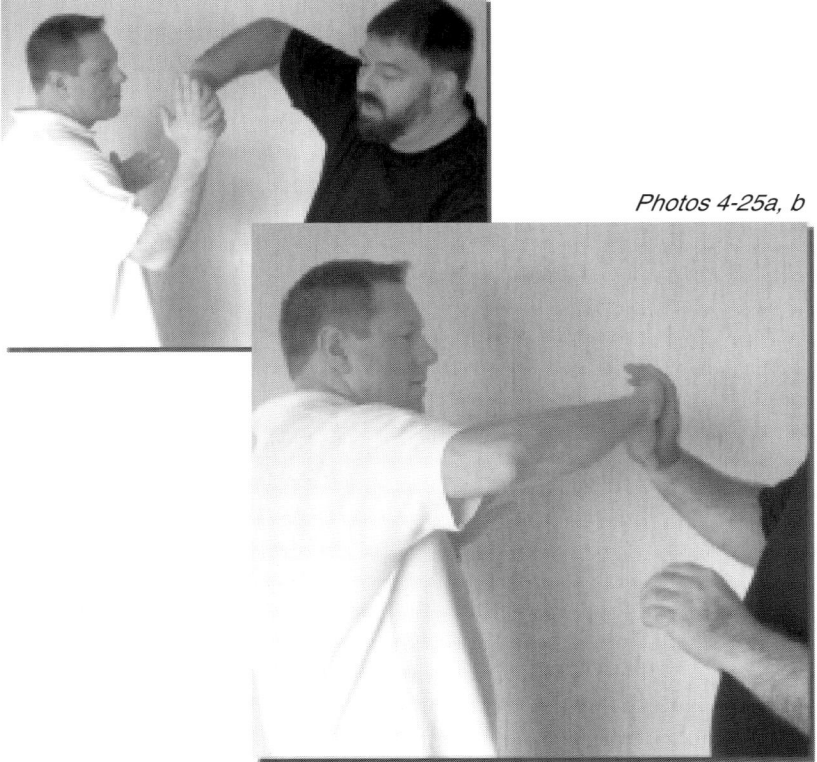

Photos 4-25a, b

Rotate your practice partner's arm to a horizontal position (photo 4-25b).

In the first edition of this book, I had you reach across the elbow with your free hand. The hand came up over the top of the arm, and reached to the inside of your partner's elbow joint. By pulling in toward your own body, you'd bend his elbow to a ninety-degree angle.

Since then, I have found that your opponent will naturally bend at the elbow in an attempt to avoid the lock. Perfect -- your enemy does the work for you.

With your "handshake hand," push your partner's hand back toward the bicep (photo 4-25c, below).

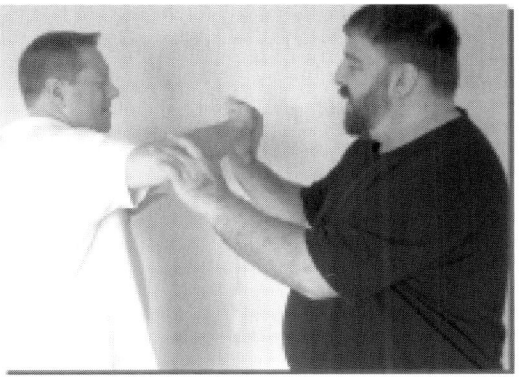

Keeping his arm parallel to the floor, you lower him with complete control (photos 4-25d, e). Great move! It gets better.

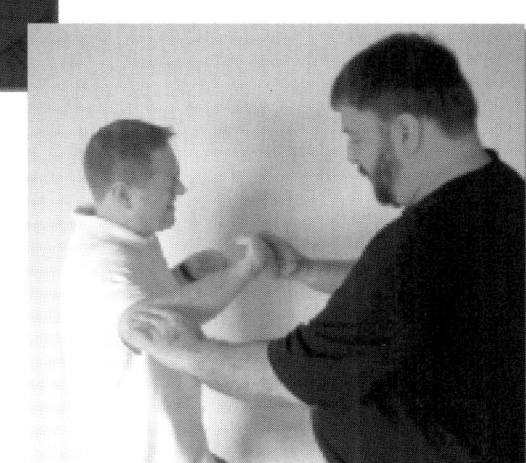

Photos 4-25d, e

If you push his little finger even further toward his biceps, you will have a lot better control. This is the *kick-start* part of the move.

You control through added pain (photo 4-25f).

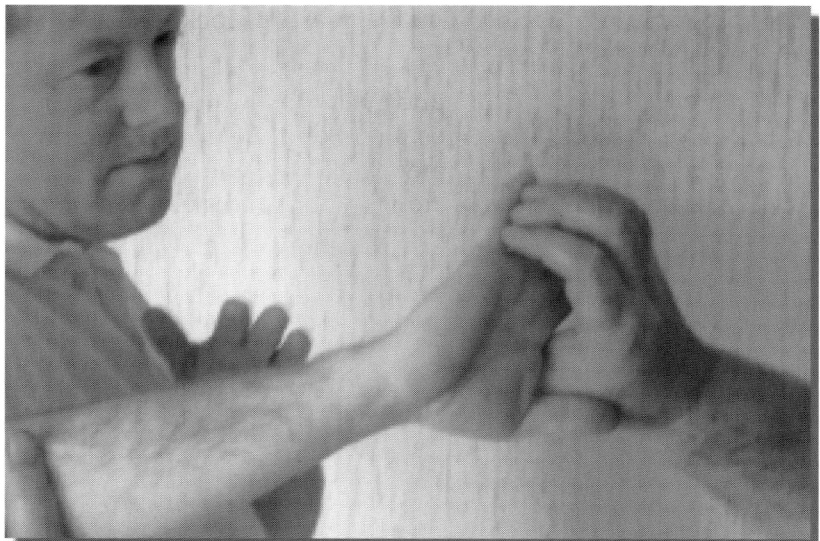

Photo 4-25f

Note: My students and I were playing with this lock during the photo shoot for this book. They found that they could cause a lot of pain by crushing the little finger into the third finger at the knuckles.

Roll the little finger over and into the next one. A wincing face on your partner will indicate whether or not you have the correct pressure.

#7: Kickstart with a Vertical Twist

This lock is a natural to learn after the Kickstart.

You are going to take the regular kickstart into a vertical position and use a different torque to "cause pain."

Start from the control position in the previous lock, The Kickstart (photo 4-26a).

Take your hand off his elbow, and grab either mid-forearm or closer to the wrist. In the photos, I grabbed the upper forearm, but if you are having a hard time controlling your partner's body movement, then you'll find it easier to grip closer to the wrist. Experiment.

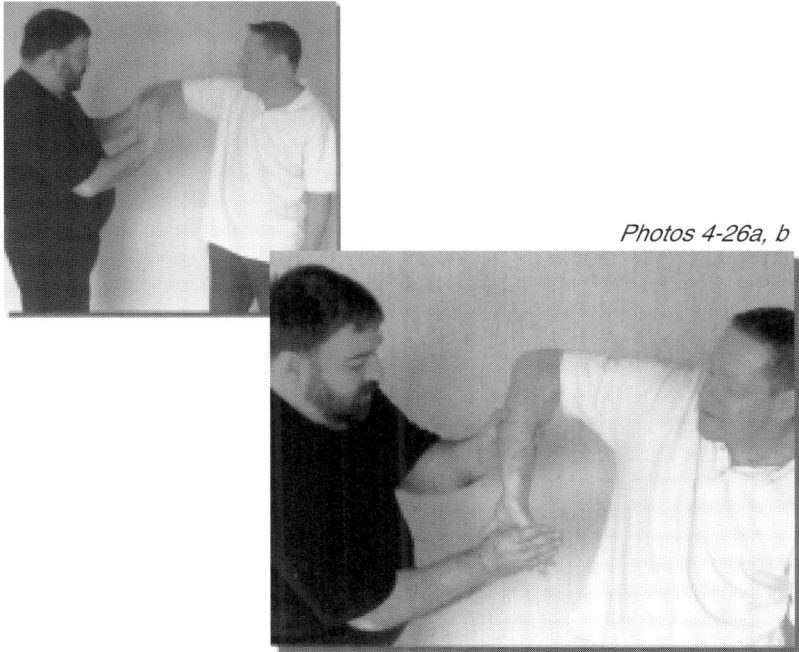

Photos 4-26a, b

When you grab the wrist or forearm, make sure your thumb on is on *the inside*, close to your body, and your fingers on the outside, closest to your partner's body (photo 4-26b).

As you're grabbing, rotate the gripped hand to a vertical position (photo 4-26c).

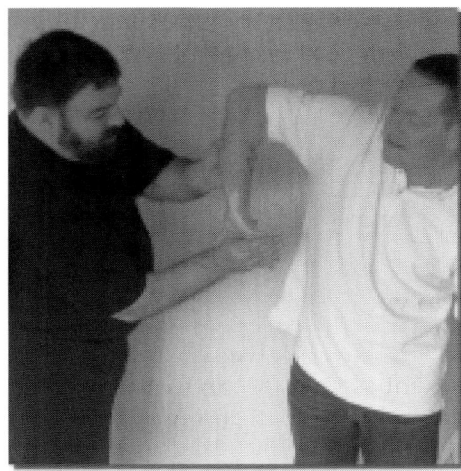

Photo 4-26c

Now is where it gets a little tricky. While holding the wrist or forearm firmly in place, you twist the hand around as in Photos 4-26d and 4-26e.

Work to control your partner's body, and keep it from swinging around into your side by exerting tension on the wrist.

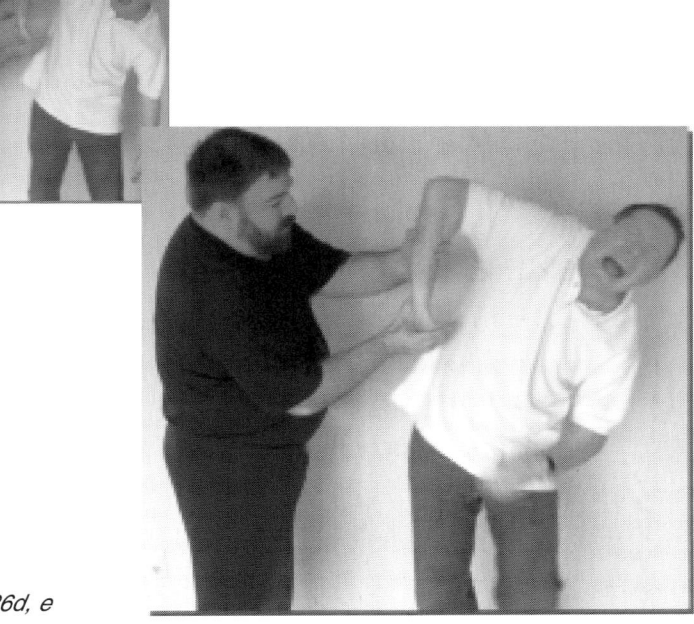

Photos 4-26d, e

You'll have to experiment with the tension to come up with a limiting control. Don't worry if you can't quite get the right technique.

I have a good cover to offer.

If, when you torque the hand, your partner's body starts to pivot into your side, lift the elbow of your hand that has the wrist.

As the body whips around into your side, let it slam full force into your elbow. Ouch!

You can even help your opponent along with an extra twist. For a little more assertion of your control, see if you can cause your partner to raise up on tiptoes.

You could always end this routine by going back into the original position of Lock #6.

Just back out of it the way you got into it.

It's almost as if you digressed for a second, and now you're back on track.

What better way to strut your stuff, than by fading into an alternate move for a minute (#7), the whole time keeping control of your opponent, and then fading back into your original lock!

You can move your opponents around at will, and there's nothing they can do!

#8: Take a Bow

Are you ready to take a break with an easy lock?

If you ever find the flat of someone's hand on the front of your body, you can do a variation of this lock.

Your opponent puts his or her hand onto your chest (photo 4-27a). Someone wants to put a hand on you. And you let him!

In fact, you help. You lock his hand into your body (photo 4-27b).

Then all you do is bow. Yes, that's right—you bend forward (photo 4-27c). That's it. You should easily be able to cause pain. (Take a step back, to avoid clunking heads together.)

You might want to lower your opponent even further by dropping to one knee. Experiment slowly with this one; you don't want to break his wrist, or vice versa, when it's your partner's turn.

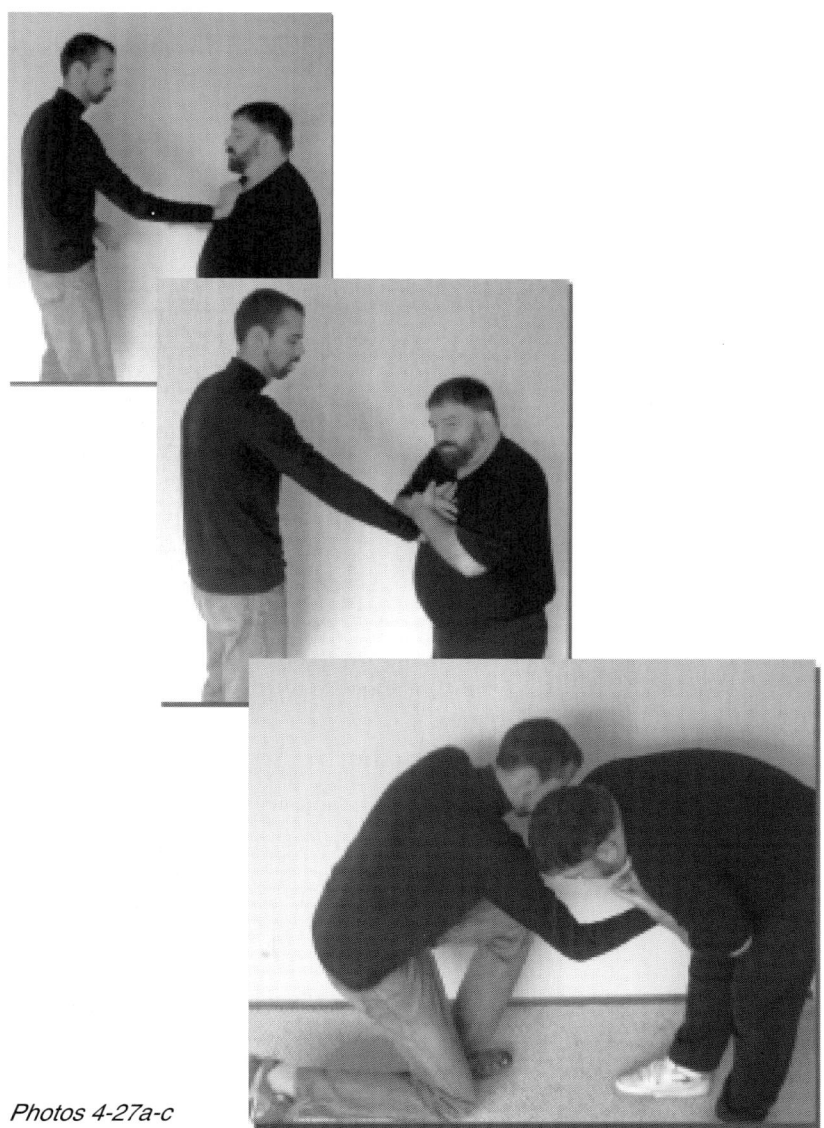

Photos 4-27a-c

#9: Arm Grab

Here's another easy one. Start with a wrist grab, right to right as in Photo 4-28a. Or you can go directly into the lock with left arm snaking between your partner's right arm and torso (photo 4-28b).

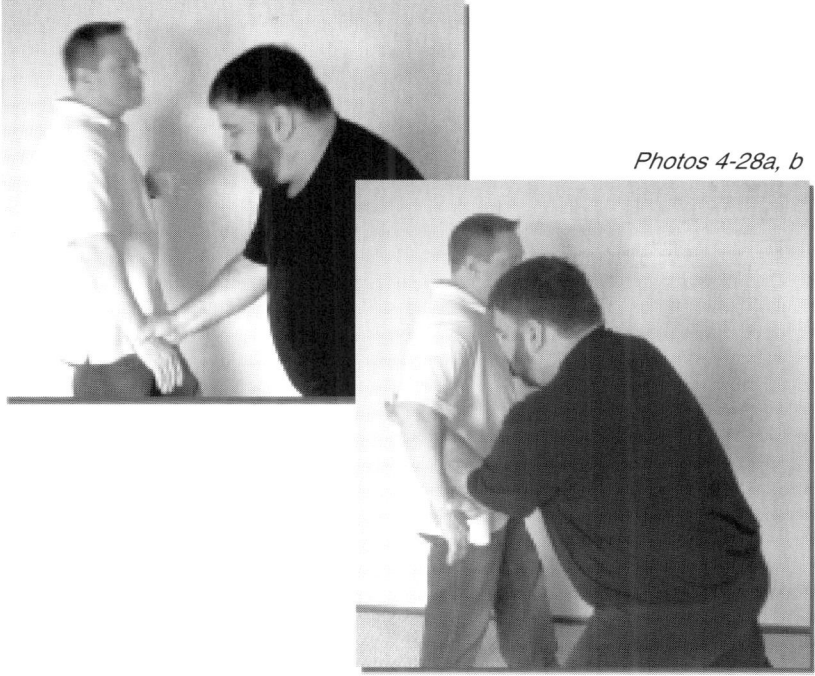

Photos 4-28a, b

With your right hand to your opponent's right triceps or left hand to left triceps, grab almost behind the triceps. Rotate the triceps toward you (photo 4-28c). (Snake your arm in closer to the *shoulder*, if your opponent is shorter than you.)

Photo 4-28c

While you're rotating the triceps, lift your other arm, between your opponent's arm and body, towards the head, into an arm lock.

Bring your forearm up, over your opponent's shoulder, and apply pressure downward (photo 4-28d).

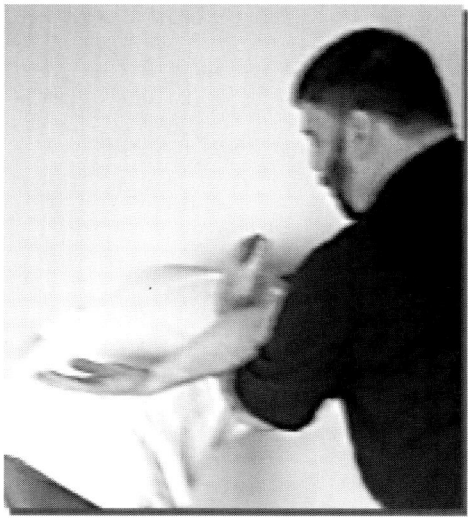

Photo 4-28d

Once you have the arm locked, you can cause even more pain -- I mean exert more control – by twist the wrist of the locked arm. As a bonus, you can torque the wrist in either direction (photos 4-28e, f).

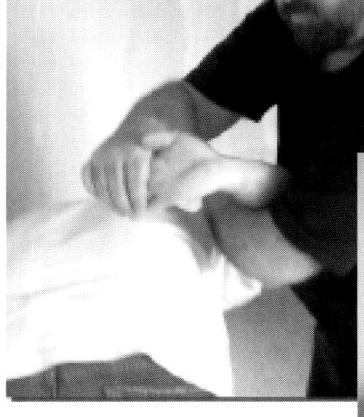
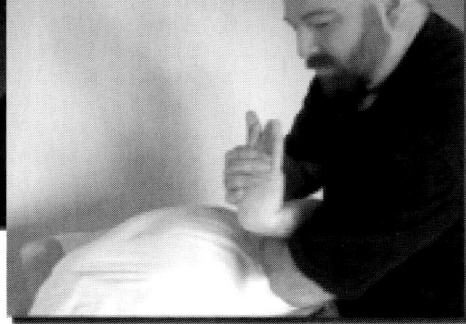

Photos 4-28e, f

#10: Uncle Fred

It's time for Uncle Fred. Are the names of these locks getting weirder, or what?

I really don't know exactly why we call it Uncle Fred, but it has something to do with the progression from a nonviolent hold that you might place on a relative who had imbibed a little too much and needed to be controlled, to a lock filled with many strikes.

It just seemed so ludicrous, because you'd never actually go through a progression like this on relative.

Your opponent grabs the front of your shirt with both hands (photo 4-29a). You swing one hand over and lock it onto both of his; you keep your elbow bent as you lock on (photos 4-29c).

Did I mention that you get a free eye jab on the way to grabbing the arms (photo 4-29b)?

Photos 4-29a-c

Your other hand swings over his two hands (photo 4-29d), and comes down to your side, locking both his hands into your armpits as you turn your body, so your back is to him (photos 4-29d-f).

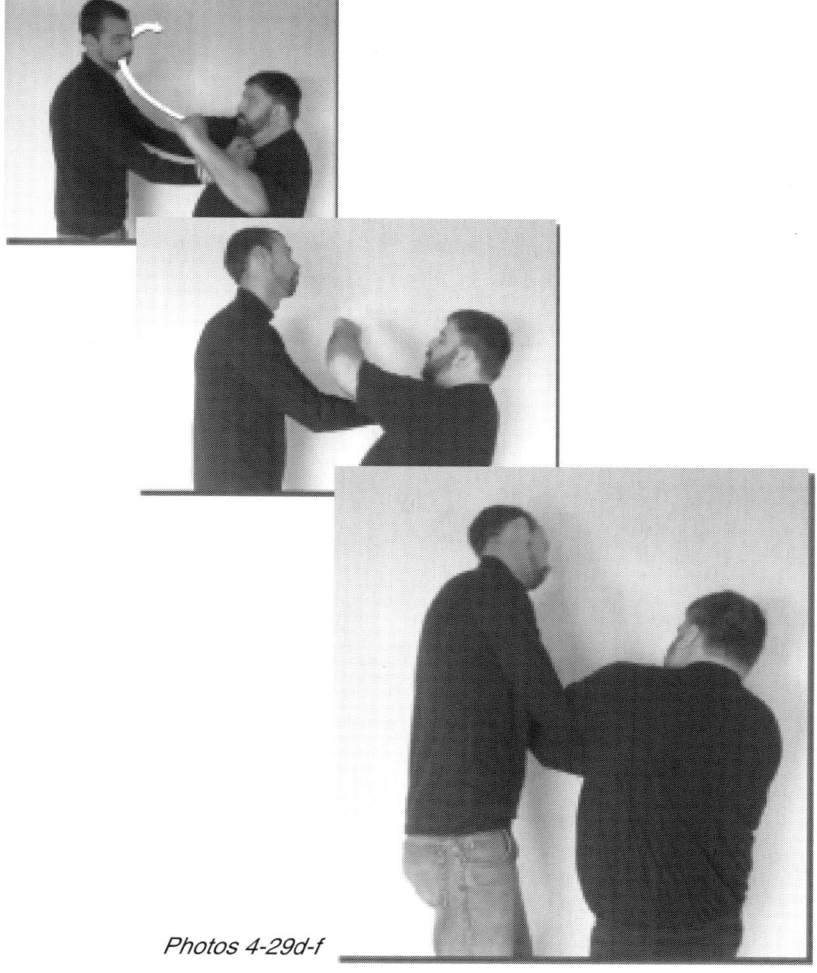

Photos 4-29d-f

Are you concerned about taking your eyes off your opponent? Bruce Lee advised against it. In this one instance, with both hands tied up, let's risk it, OK?

Once you have turned your body, locking the arms under your armpit, you are set up for a perfect elbow strike to the jaw (photo 4-29g).

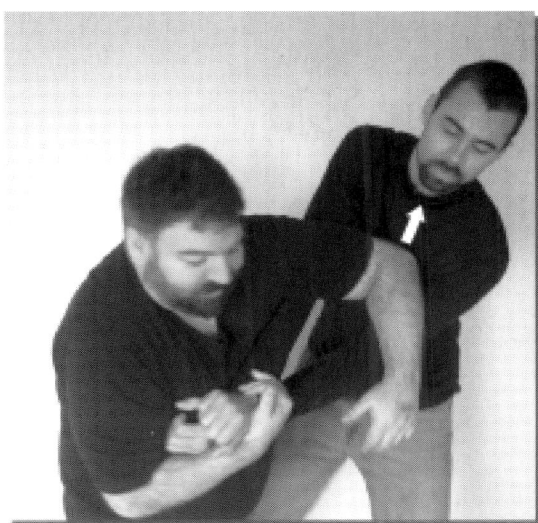

Photos 4-29g

This sequence alone is really fun to do, and effective. It can become a work of art (original artist for this set, Steve Golden — insipred greatly by Ed Parker), if you add in even more strikes. Are you ready? OK, here we go, starting with a re-cap....

As you began the sequence, the hand that came across over his two arms eye-jabbed him. As that hand locked on, you took an elbow-jab to his face. (If you missed that elbow jab, pretend it was between Photos 4-29b and 4-29c.)

The other hand that came over had a free hit, too.

I usually wait until my back is to him before I use that second elbow for a hit to the face (photo 4-29g).

Whew! All caught up. Now ...

You are also in position to lift one of your heels right into his groin (photo 4-29h).

Can you find any extra hits? Maybe after the groin kick, as in Photo 4-29i on the next page.

You're becoming a fighting machine.

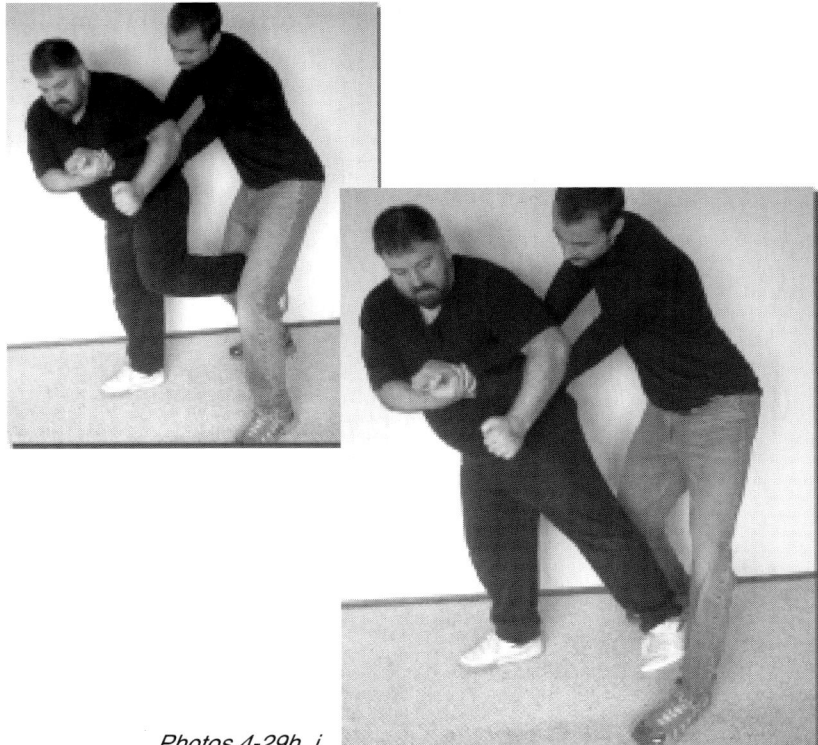

Photos 4-29h, i

#11: Live Long And Prosper

In the first edition of *Wrist Locks,* you learned The Nast Hand-shake (photo 4-30). Since then, I have covered that particular lock in more detail in a different ebook. As a new variation, I have decided to turn the handshake ... upside down.

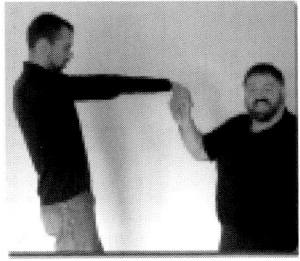

Photo 4-30

Grab the fingers, when they are pointed toward the ceiling. If you were to try this lock with the fingers pointed toward the floor, then ... you are back in The Nasty Handshake.

I call this lock *Live Long and Prosper*, because I imagine grabbing someone starting to make the Vulcan sign from one of the incarnations of *Star Trek* (photo 4-31a). (Hey, it was 50-50. I could have called the lock *The Sign of the Kohanim*.)

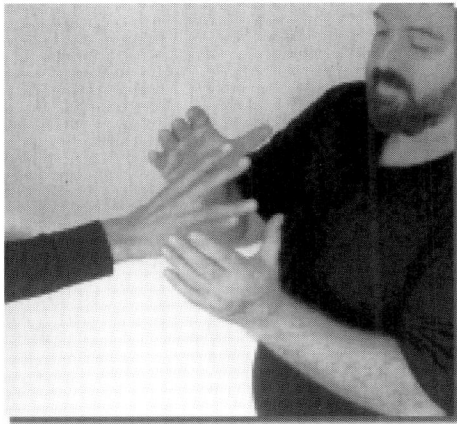

Photo 4-31a

Grab the fingers, a couple with each your hands. If, by mistake, you grab three with one, and one with the other hand, that's OK. For symmetry, I like two in each (photo 4-31b).

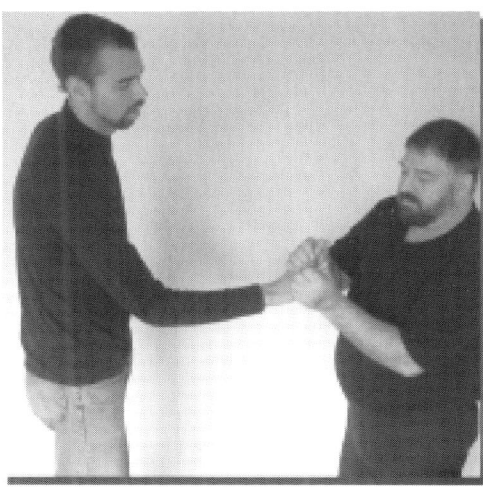

Photo 4-31b

Once you have the fingers firmly grasped, slowly bend them towards the back of your partner's wrist. Emphasis on s-l-o-w-l-y (photo 4-31c).

If you are looking for a little frosting on this cupcake of a move, drop the hand and arm quickly, straight down. Use a lot of pressure to shove your enemy's elbow into and through the floor (photo 4-31d).

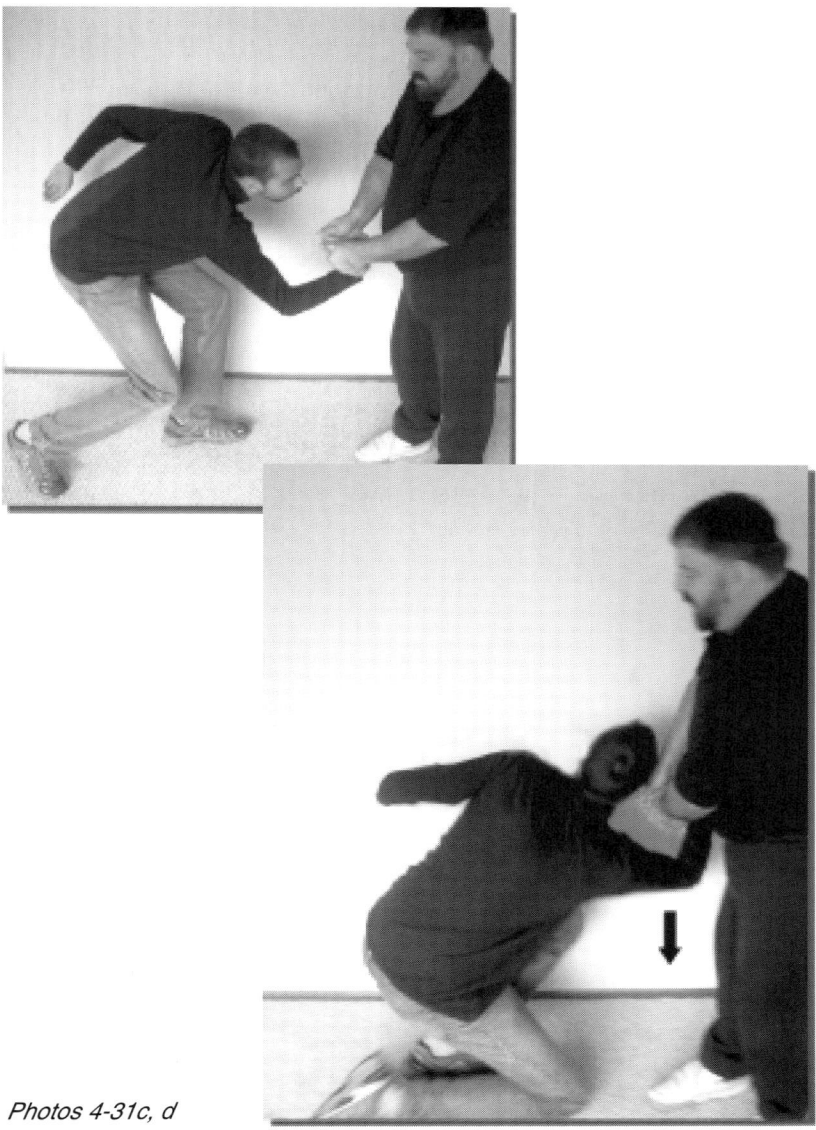

Photos 4-31c, d

#12: Revving the Motorcycle

This particular lock is very cool.

When done correctly and with a little extra force, it can cause a lot of pain. It is particularly impressive when a smaller person performs it on someone considerably larger and stronger.

As with all of the locks, I want you to really master this. It is always more than just memorizing a series of movements.

In the case of this lock, you should be able to feel exactly how far to rev your opponent's arm. Also experiment with lowering your opponent's arm. I advise lowering the arm parallel to the floor, but you should certainly experiment, to see what works for you.

I also suggest lowering your own body as you lower his arm. Try lowering his arm by pushing down on the wrist as you stay upright.

It's a different feeling from lowering your whole body. Which gives you better control? Which lends itself to better balance? Maybe your next step after securing the hold will determine which body position to effect.

The opponent grabs your wrist across, either right grabs right or left grabs left, as in Photo 4-32a.

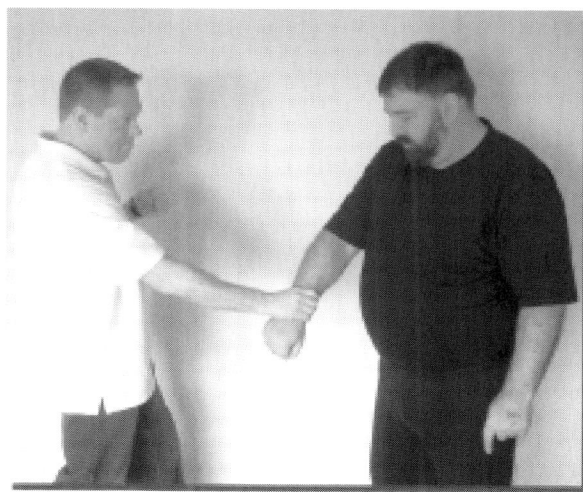

Photo 4-32a

The first thing to do is use your free hand to hold his fingers against your wrist (photo 4-32b). Yes – you want him to hold on. In fact, now he can't let go.

Now, reach up with your trapped hand and grab the wrist (photo 4-32c).

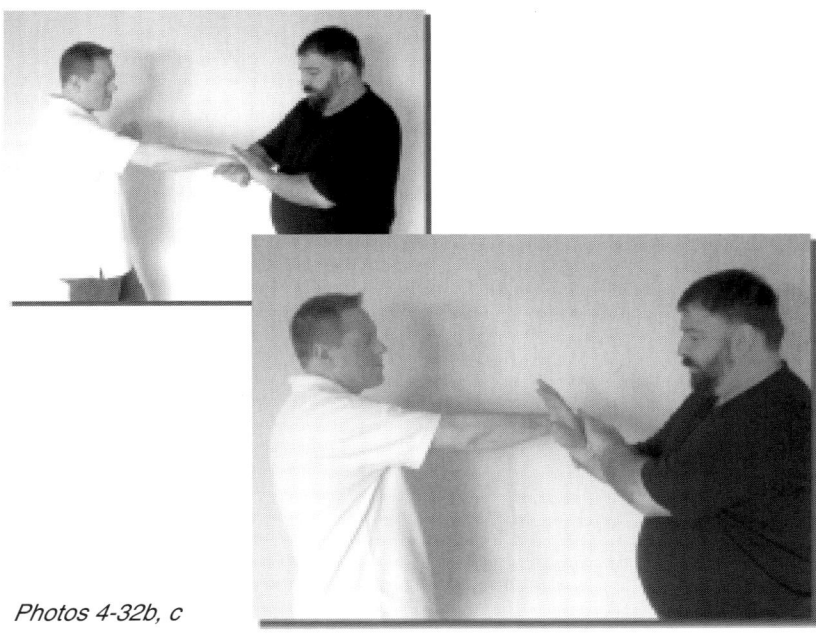

Photos 4-32b, c

With a firm grip, rotate his wrist and forearm forward as if pantomiming the revving of a motorcycle (photo 4-32d).

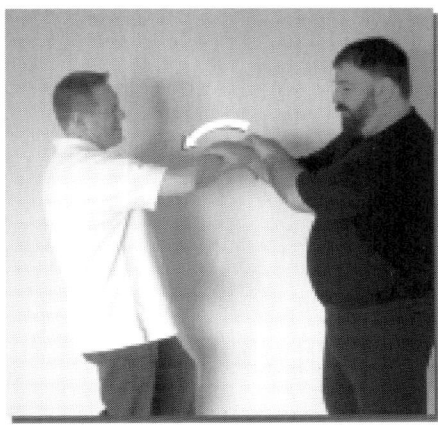

Photo 4-32d

When you can't turn the wrist any more, lower your partner's whole arm with the forearm parallel to the floor (photo 4-32d).

If you've got the right "feeling," your practice buddy's body should be dropping to the floor (photo 4-32e, f).

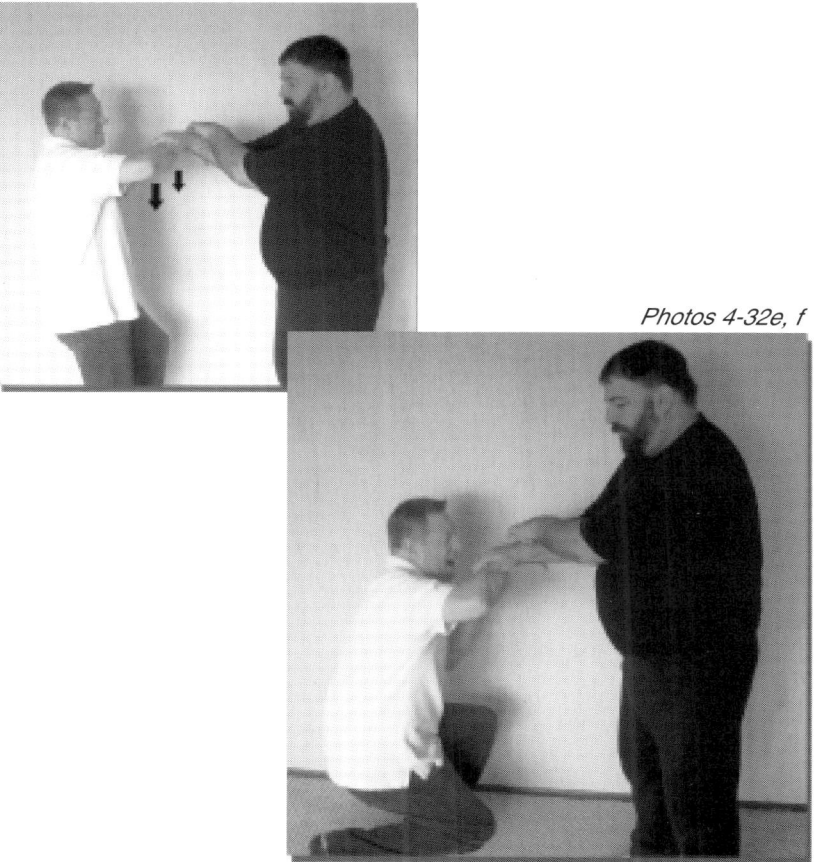

Photos 4-32e, f

This is one you're going to have to play with.

Make sure you have enough torque on the arm to drop the body, but not so much that your opponent starts to turn out of the hold even before you start lowering the arm.

Once you get the finesse of the move, it won't take much effort to effect the lock.

—A Baker's Dozen—

#13: Oops! Revving the wrong wrist

This is a mistake that a lot of amateur wrist-lockers make.

They learn the rev technique, and they love it. Then one day, someone grabs them. They try to execute the move, and nothing seems to work. It's all wrong, and they can't figure out why.

The explanation is simple, (and so is the new wrist lock). Your opponent grabbed the wrong wrist. Instead of grabbing across the body, he or she grabbed the same side, from the bottom, instead of the top (photo 4-33a).

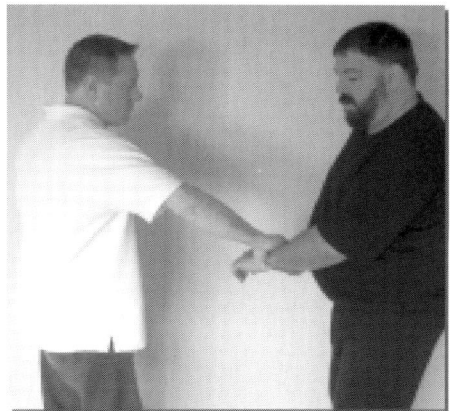

Photo 4-33a

Don't worry about it. Clamp down on his fingers just the way you did when "revving" (photo 4-33b).

Rotate your elbow over his forearm (photo 4-33c) and continue the motion down and into his body (photo 4-33d-f).

You can drop your knees quickly in a squat, to lower him even further.

This lock flows well into other locks.

For example, do you see the relationship between the ending position of this lock and the "L" of the Double Ninety-Degree Lock found on page 121?

Can you flow from one to the other with a minimum of hand movements, and without letting up on the pressure?

After all, you don't want to give him a chance to escape.

Good luck. This is a very workable lock.

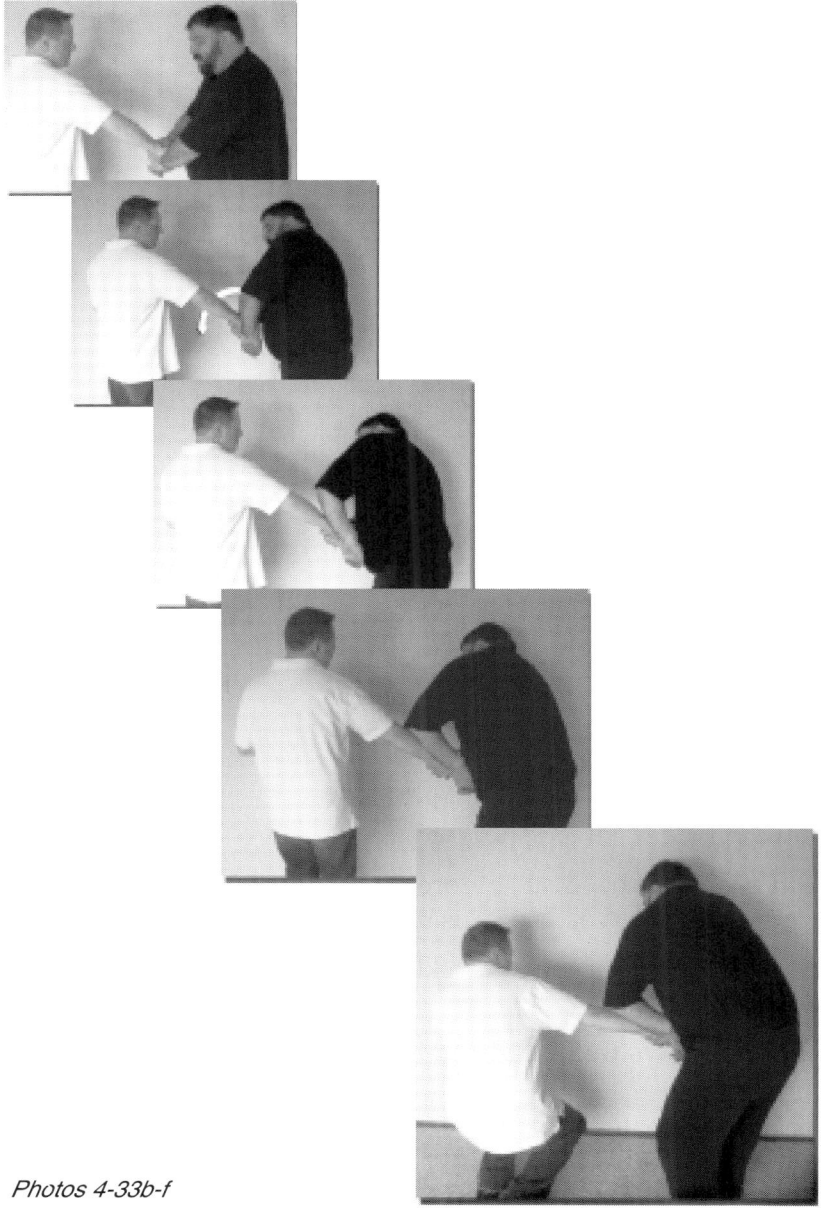

Photos 4-33b-f

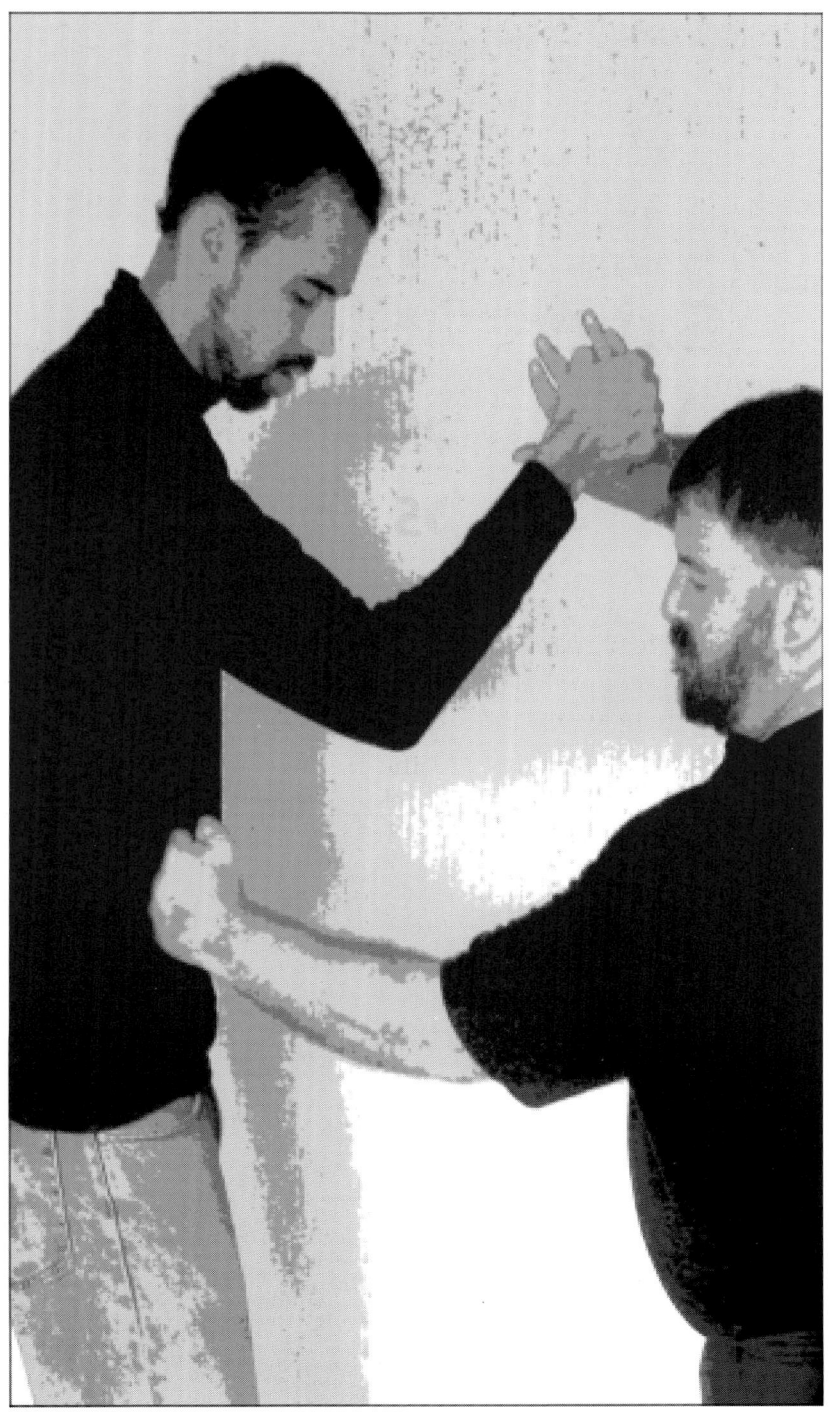

5
Expert Responses When Someone Grabs You

Responding to a grab with a wrist lock is a natural.

There are a lot of grab techniques already dealt with in this book, and there are more yet to come.

If you're looking for some specific techniques, why don't you try Chapter 4, **A Dozen Wrist locks to Stimulate Thought**? Specifically look to *Take a Bow* (#8), *Uncle Fred* (#10), *Revving the Motorcycle* (#12), and *Oops!*(#13).

After this chapter, you'll study Chapter 6 on patterns. See if you could reverse engineer each lock back to a start from a grab.

Look for familiarity in the starting positions for the various locks.

Are your opponent's hands in similar positions, except they're wrapped around your body?

If, for you, wrist locks are the answer to grabs, then you'll appreciate Chapter 11. From *Let Me Get You Started*, to *Knuckle Rubs*, there are a lot of ways to take grabs.

Now that we've highlighted some spots for addittional grab responses, I'll deal with general principles of what to do when someone grabs you.

We'll stay fairly general, so you can apply these lessons to your own specific situation. After reading this chapter, I encourage you to look into some of the materials listed in the resource section.

Remember, to become an expert, you have to go beyond one book. Learn as many responses to as many grabs as possible. Make these responses work on opponents of all sizes. Learn to adapt to big, muscle-bound brutes.

Also, don't be disappointed that the rest of the chapter focuses on what seems to be unrelated to wrist locks. The connections are there. Call these the warm-ups.

Escape and cause pain, then lock. First, let's deal with the pain that your opponent is exerting on you....

Your Opponent Causes Pain

Your opponent has a hold of you in a way that causes pain (photo 5-1a).

This could be a twisted arm, bent fingers, or even a hair pull.

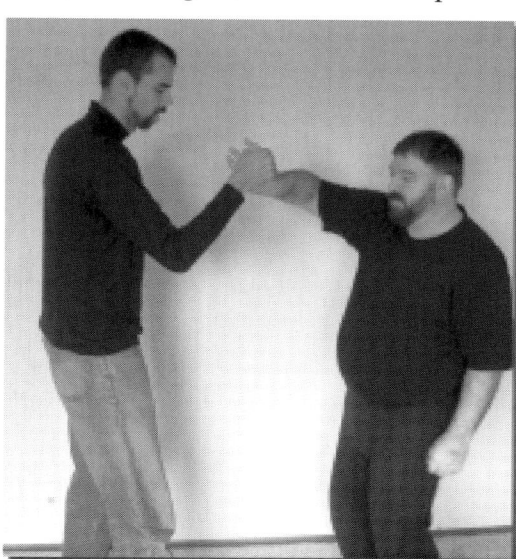

Photo 5-1a

Let's assume your opponent has not yet gone beyond your final tolerance threshold, where no response is possible.

If the pain is so great that you absolutely can't move any part of your body without breaking something, then you'll either break it or you won't respond. But if you still have some "kick" in you, I would suggest the obvious – *get rid of the pain*.

How you stop the pain is an interesting question.

I tend to release the pain I am feeling by causing instant pain on my opponent.

Reversals and counters are fine, if you have time before the point of no return, or if you can feel the direction you need to go.

When you're already feeling pain, it's sometimes hard to get to a joint or limb on your opponent, before he snaps the move on so hard that you can't even attempt an escape.

I find that a direct hit or kick to a pain center does wonders.

A kick to the shins or knee cap tends to get your opponent to release his hold (photo 5-1b). It's much easier to throw a lock on him afterward, while he's reacting to the pain of your initial counter.

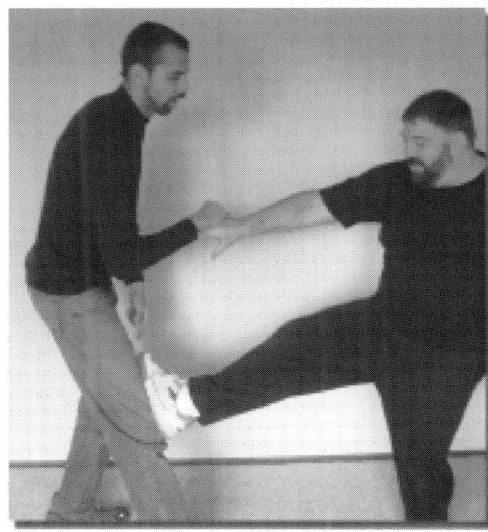

Photo 5-1b

Hits and eye jabs are especially effective to release pressure causing you pain (photo 5-1c). Make sure your hit is more than just an annoyance. You want an immediate release of pressure.

When practicing, wear protective eye gear, or eye jab above the eyes. Maybe agree on forehead taps, to simulate an eye jab (photo 5-1d).

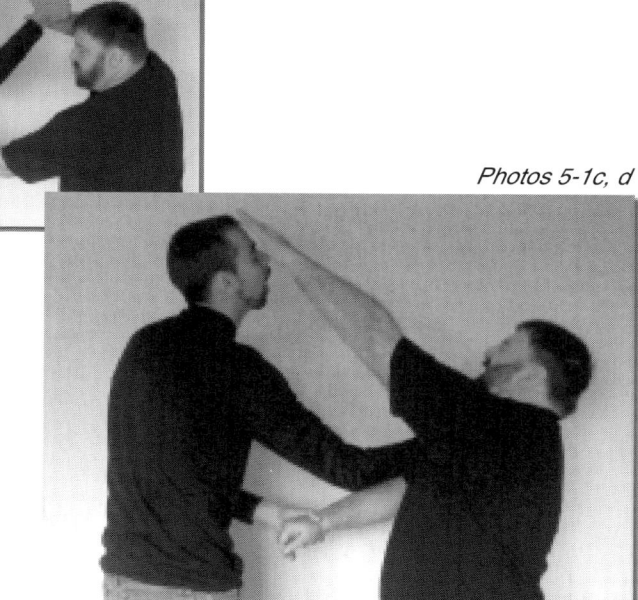

Photos 5-1c, d

If you can't or won't hit, you have to release the pressure some other way.

Could you grab some fingers and twist, as in Photos 5-2a-d? A typical reaction to a painful hold being applied is to fight to release the pain being applied. It's human nature.

You feel the pain of a bear hug, so you try to peel fingers. Make the finger wrenching your second line of counter attack.

Retrain yourself to react instantly by causing pain to your opponent, first.

Sometimes this can be accomplished with a counter hold; sometimes it takes something more direct.

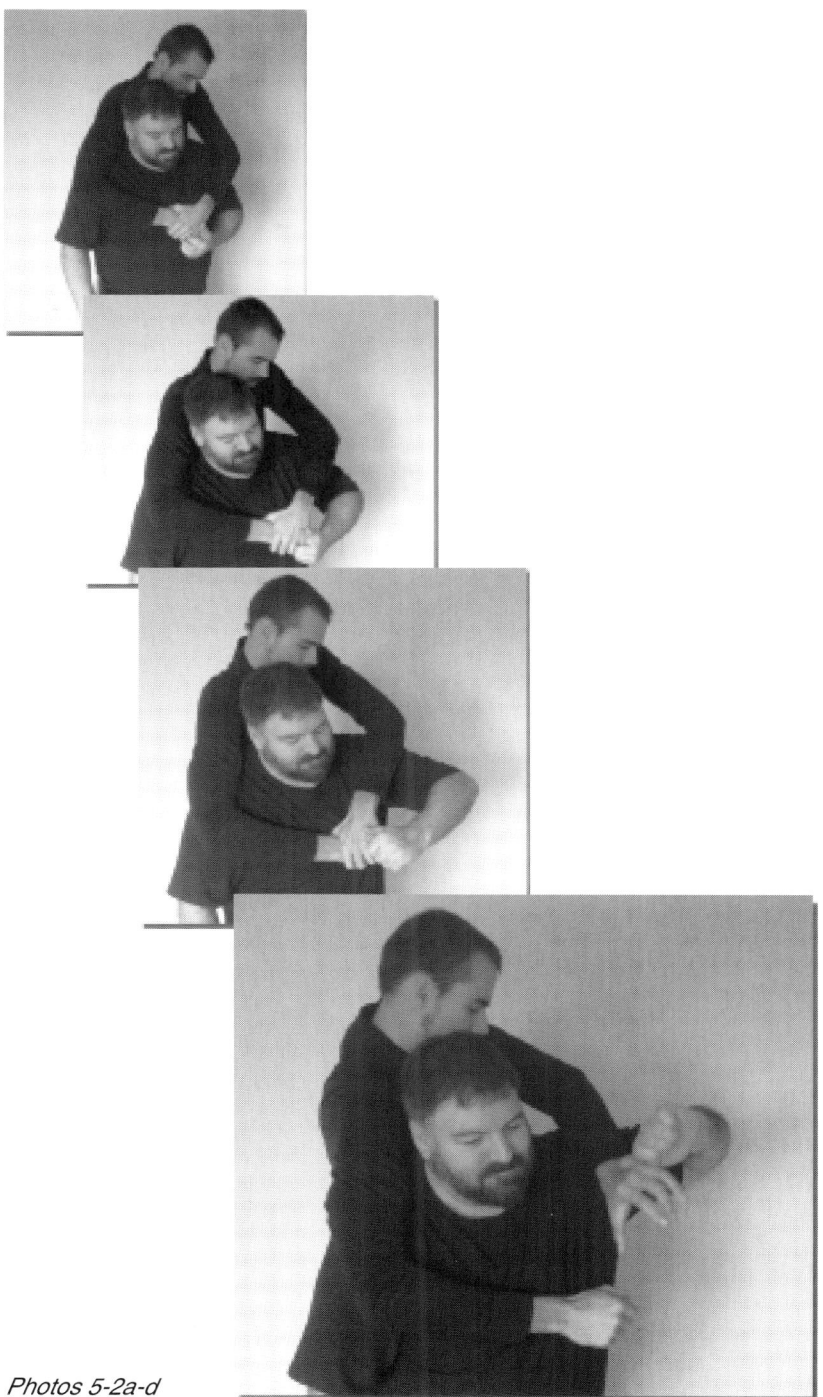

Photos 5-2a-d

Grab From Behind

Again, if you're going for instant pain, I recommend kicks to the shins, knee kicks, a head butt to the nose, and so on (photo 5-3a).

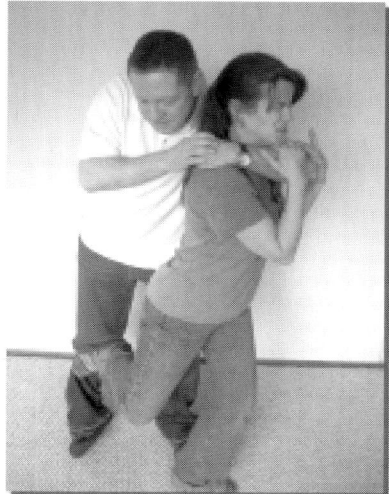

Photo 5-3a

A groin shot is nice, if at least one of your hands can get back there (photo 5-3b). I also favor an elbow to the ribs. How about grabbing the hair (photo 5-3c)?

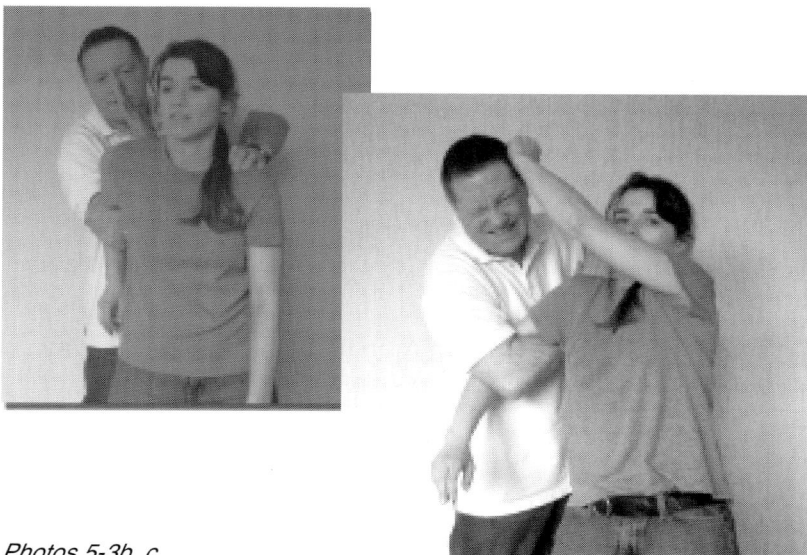

Photos 5-3b, c

For a slightly more passive response, try knuckle rubs already mentioned in this chapter (photos 5-3d, e). Or you could pull at one of his fingers.

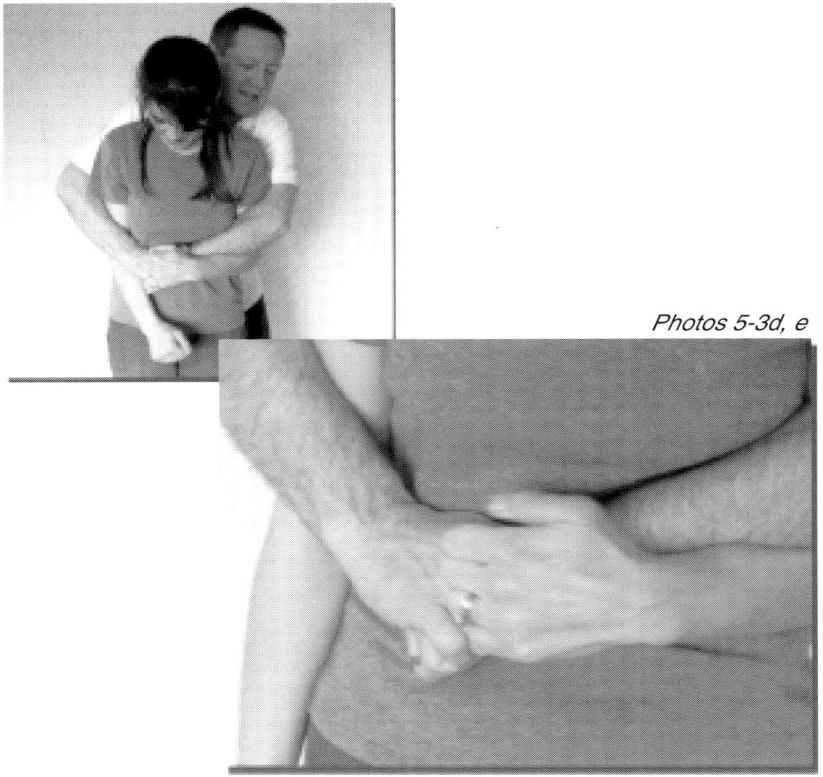

Photos 5-3d, e

If you can somehow swing your hips behind your opponent's, you can stand up straight and break his hold.

From there, all sorts of hits are possible.

Lifting an arm off you by means of a finger control (or maybe even a pressure point) is a good way to start a release.

If it were a real situation, I'd probably be hitting all the way through my release from my attacker.

Of course, there are risks involved with going berserk in a fight. You are legally responsible for your actions.

Know your limits.

Nelsons and Other Wrestling Moves

It's beyond the scope of this book to make you a wrestling expert. And that's not its goal either.

The little piece of advice that I will give has to do with timing.

A lot of the wrestling holds don't work, if you counter early enough. You can start playing by having a partner slowly put a hold on you.

As you feel an arm snake through your arm or leg, (or even around your neck), see if you can stop its progress. Can you release your appendage and get to a position that is familiar to you?

As you slip holds, don't forget you have elbow strikes, face hits, hard slaps, and eye jabs.

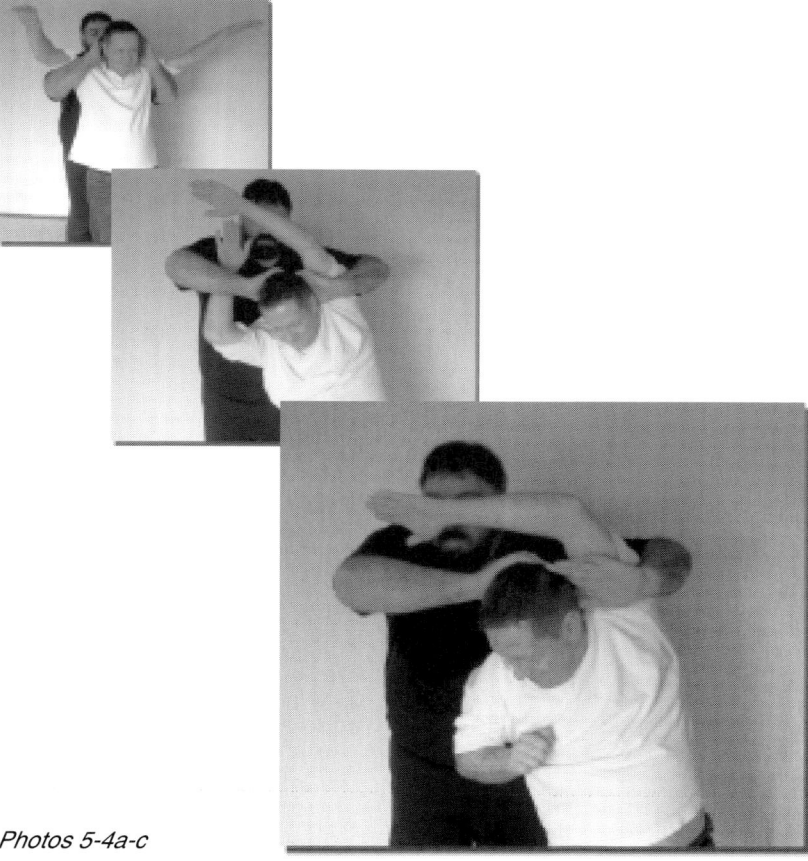

Photos 5-4a-c

Practice and practice some more. Eventually, you'll find techniques that work. May you develop an unorthodox style that confuses your opponent.

General Questions

If you really take on the task of becoming proficient at taking a grab, then you'll want to ask yourself a few general questions:

Are you being grabbed above or below your center of gravity?

Could you be thrown over from the position you're in by the person grabbing you?

Can you shift your weight to prevent such a throw?

Must you attend to the hold immediately – is it around the throat, cutting off blood, or oxygen?

What If Your Opponent Grabs With A Wrist Lock?

Yeah. Finally. Thank goodness. Remember, you're studying to be a wrist-lock expert. If you've practiced, the lock probably won't be anything too new.

You'll either already know the response – a good counter or reversal, or you'll be able to ad lib with an acceptable technique.

You want wrist locks to be your realm.

You're the expert. When someone tries a lock on you, you have to smile.

Why?

Because you know a variety of counters to that particular lock. Let's see ... hmmm ... which should I counter with?

What kind of pasta do I want tonight?

Definitely a feeling of confidence.

6
Patterns: The Secret of Learning to "Flow"

Learn your patterns the way I teach you, and you'll develop a whole new understanding of wrist locks.

You'll be able to find many more opportunities to use them; you'll flow into each position almost effortlessly; you'll deal with any resistance from your opponent automatically and efficiently.

Practice these patterns over and over. It might not be a bad idea to review the chapter on practicing. Practice these patterns to perfection. They need to be generalized so you can execute them successfully on a variety of people.

You need to be able to jump into any pattern from any point.

Most important, you will to need to explore. Start to alter the patterns you know. Add moves that you've learned from other sources. Explore what would happen if you rotated his hand or arm in the opposite direction. (Are you now close to a familiar lock?) Where's the nearest pressure point to a joint?

Eventually, you'll create your own patterns from scratch.

Each move will logically flow to the next. If your opponent resists your pressure, his force of resistance will flow right into your next movement. Either way, you'll trap your opponent in just a few moves.

In this chapter, you'll learn two excellent patterns. One pattern Dan Inosanto helped me learn after one of his seminars, and the other my teacher, Steve Golden, helped me learn during one of his classes. Both routines are very close, and I can't seem to remember which belonged to whom. Sorry, guys!

After learning the two patterns, you'll get specific advice on how to invent your own, how to generalize patterns so you can put locks on anyone, and how to incorporate lock patterns into a system with kicks and hits.

A few of the locks for these patterns are described in other parts of this book. They are described and diagramed again here, so you won't have to cross-reference while learning the pattern.

After you learn the pattern and experiment with your own variations, you should then intentionally cross-reference as much as possible. You get extra mileage out of each lock when you learn multiple uses.

It's very worthwhile to learn as much about each lock as possible. Pity the poor fool who only knows one way to get into a particular lock, and then never gets a chance to execute his practiced technique.

Wouldn't it be better to know so many locks and ways to get into the correct positions, that you automatically flow into a "proper" (if not "way cool,") technique that immediately puts you in control of the situation? I hope I've convinced you of this already in other sections of this book.

So, here we go.

You're about to learn some excellent wrist-lock combinations, but they'll be of no use to you, unless you do something with them.

After you really internalize each pattern, you have several options: You could review the sections in this book on reversals, both general directions and specific counters; then rehearse possible counters for each lock in the pattern. Have your partner practice the pattern on you. Pick different points in the pattern to execute a reversal or a counter. You should eventually be able to counter instantly every position in the pattern.

Of course, another thing you should be practicing is countering each lock in the pattern with a direct hit or kick. Remember, part of being a wrist-lock expert is knowing when NOT to use wrist locks.

Sometimes you'll need to counter with moves outside of your standard wrist-lock style.

Hits are faster, and a lot of times safer for you, even though they damage your opponent. So be it. So much for the gentle art. May the punch be with you! (Photos 6-1a-d)

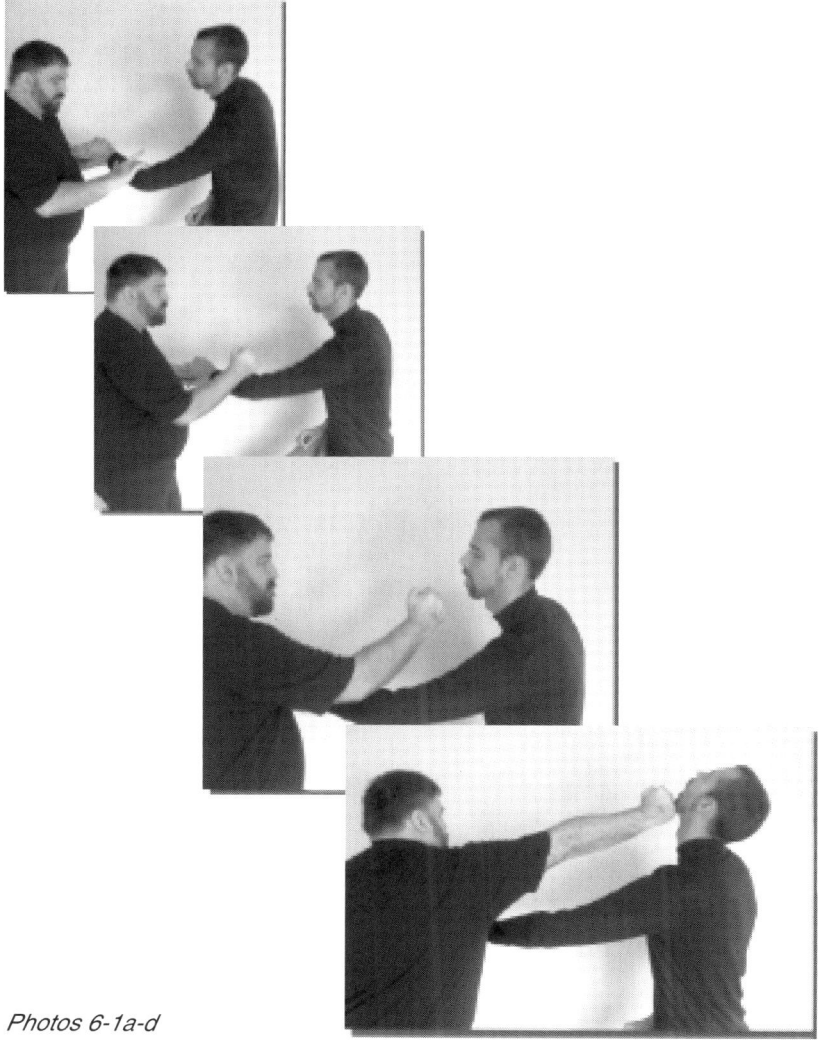

Photos 6-1a-d

Taking both types of counters one step further, both hits and other locks, can you build on your initial counter?

Can you take your opponent into a wrist lock after your initial counter-strike with either foot or hand, and can you flow with your opponent into another wrist lock after your initial wrist lock counter?

I'm trying to get you to the point that you are comfortable moving from one lock to another. No matter what someone puts on you, you counter.

You can initiate or receive; it doesn't matter.

You're comfortable "playing" with anyone. Keep at it. You will improve quickly. Keep trying to refine your technique. Work at precision.

Can you smoothly take your opponent close to *the point of no return* without his being aware of your intention, until it's too late?

Try to improve your speed at which you execute your technique, but don't move so fast that you get sloppy. Stay fluid. You want your technique to be smooth and precise. Don't rush your lock; increase your speed gradually.

Enough of all of this advice.

Let's jump right in and learn the two patterns. If I had to make a guess, I'd be inclined to say that I learned pattern number one from Danny Inosanto and pattern number two from Steve Golden.

Pattern #1:

Position #1

Grab your opponent's left hand with your right as in Photo 6-2a. (This is the same lock as the Basic Lock described on page 48.)

Bring your partner's hand up so that your thumb is on the back of the hand (photos 6-2b, c. Also, you are looking at the back of thehand and fingers.

Apply pressure down (photo 6-2d). This is the first position of the pattern; it's probably the easiest to get to.

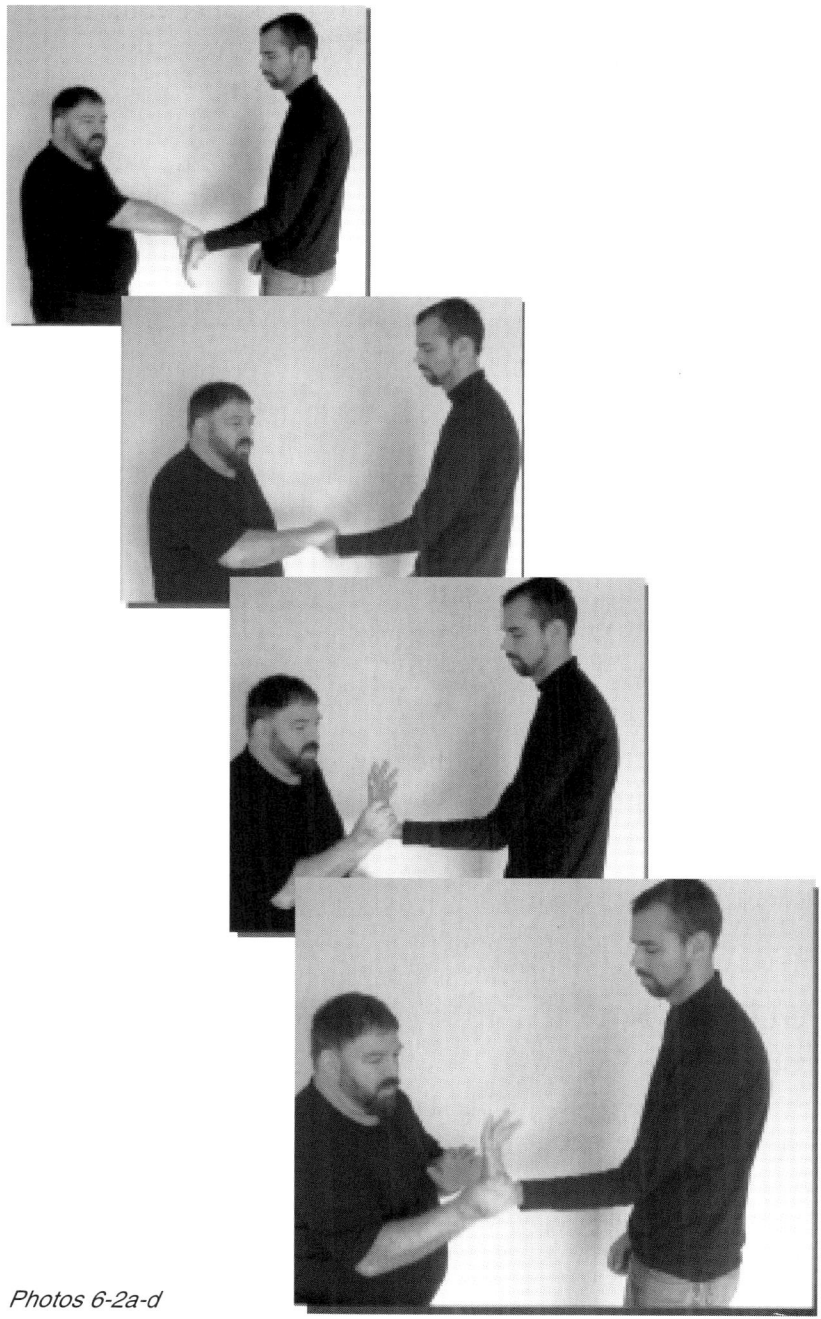

Photos 6-2a-d

Position #2

The second position is probably the hardest. Let's break down position two as much as possible. With pressure still on their wrist, rotate his hand counterclockwise in toward the center of his body AND grab the forearm with your other hand (photo 6-3a-d).

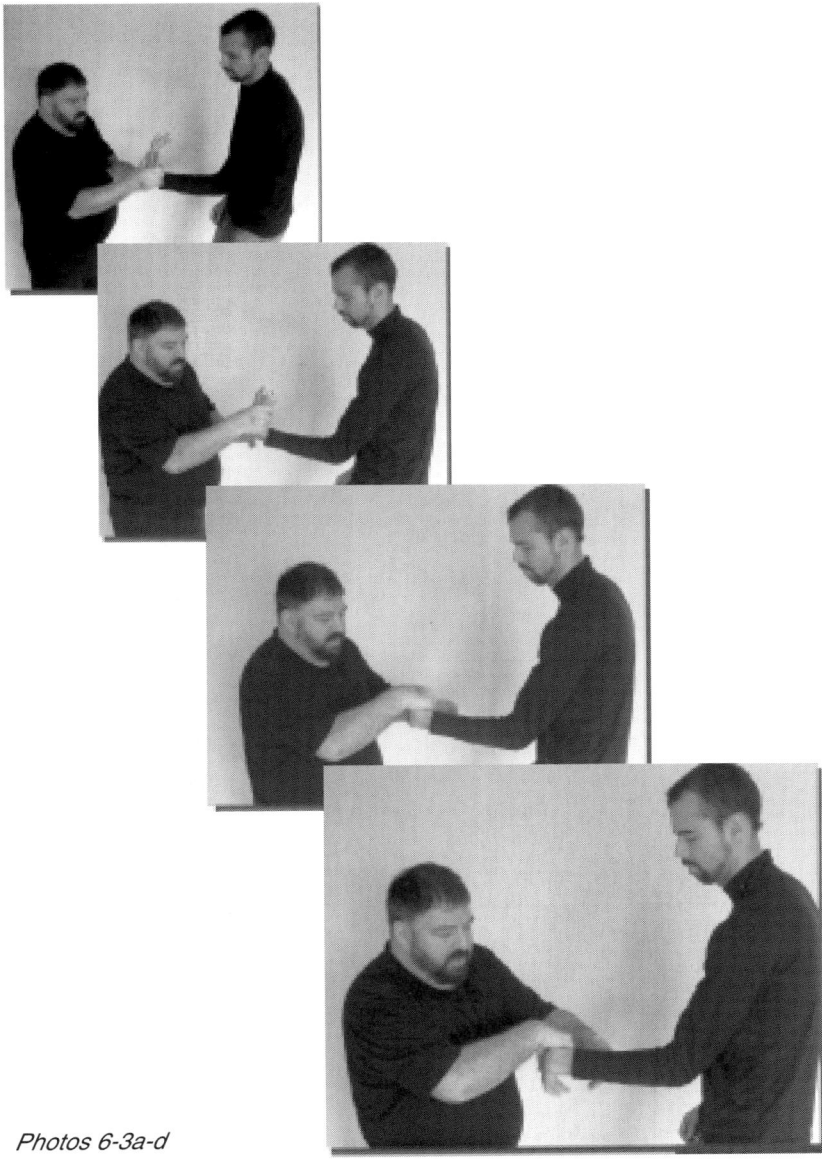

Photos 6-3a-d

Now this is where it gets a little tricky. Once you have gripped the forearm, continue rotating your partner's hand until the fingers of the hand are point to the outside (photos 6-3e, f).

The part that really takes practice is maintaining pressure on the wrist through the entire rotation.

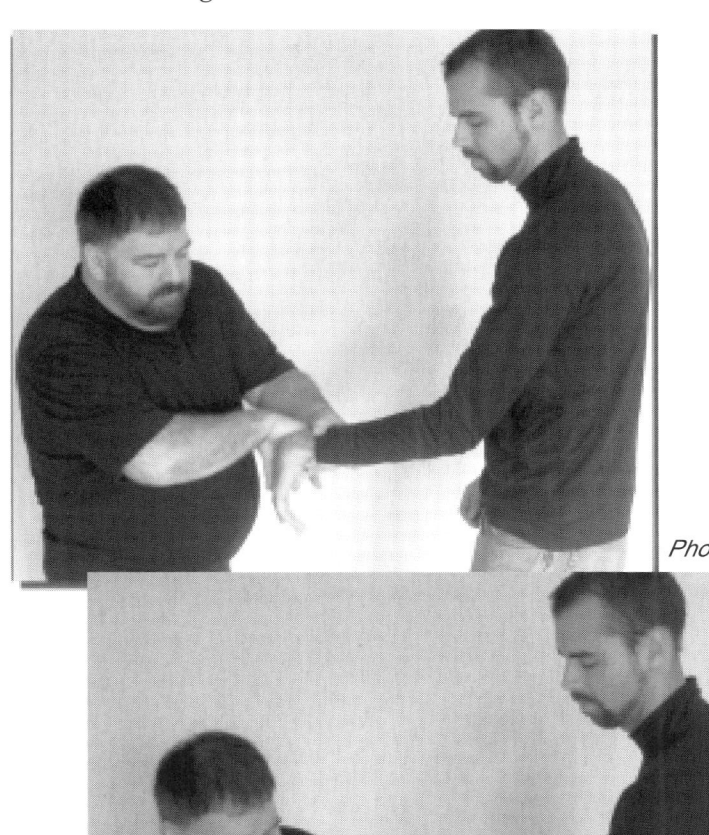

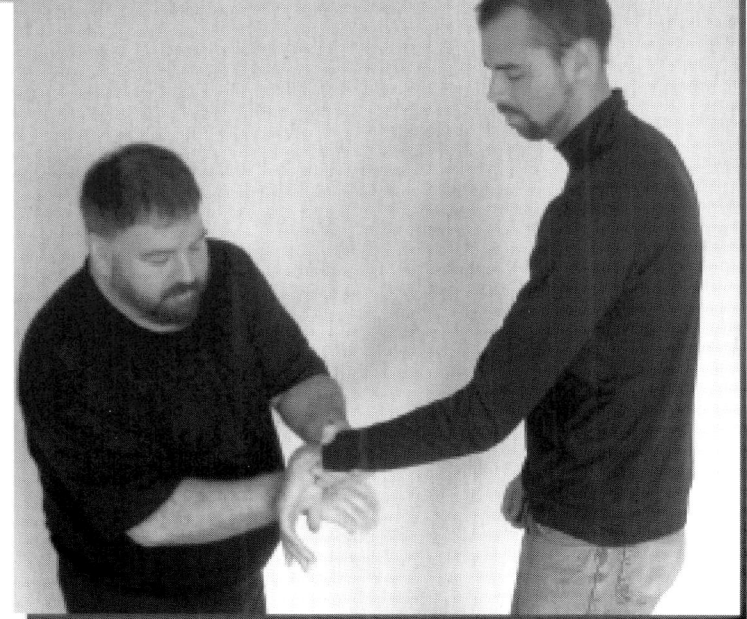

Photos 6-3e, f

Slide the bottom of your partner's hand along the inside of your forearm, keeping pressure on the back of his hand (photo 6-3g).

Continue sliding his hand until it wedges into the inside joint of your forearm and upper arm (photo 6-3h).

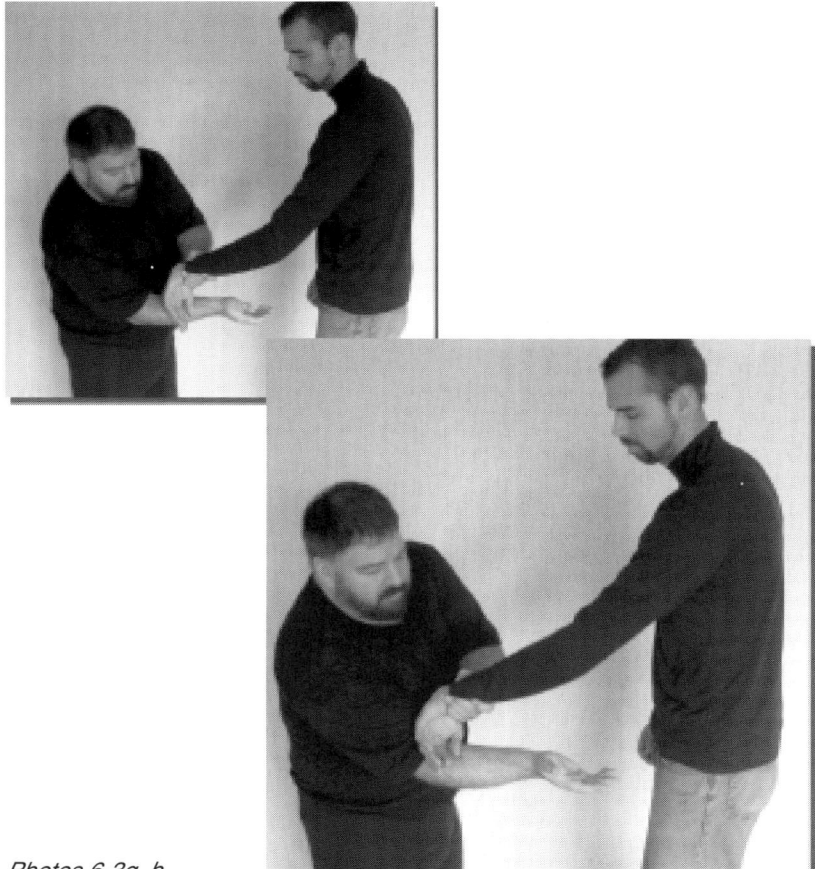

Photos 6-3g, h

Of course, all of this should occur in about a second, and remember to flow smoothly through (photos 6-3a-h).

If you made it through that second move, you're home free.

Whew. All the moves are easier from now on.

If you're having problems with this move, you have several options. You could try again later; sometimes a fresh outlook will do wonders. You could have a friend try to learn it, and then try to teach you; sometimes a different perspective will get you over a difficult hump. You could find a local martial artist who knows the move and ask to be taught.

You could write me for suggestions. No, giving up is not an option.

Let's go on to the third act in this sequence.

Position #3

The third lock is the Double Ninety-Degree Lock.

While maintaining pressure with your biceps agains the back of the hand and continuing to hold the wrist, use your free hand to reach up to the top of your partner's elbow (photo 6-4a, b)

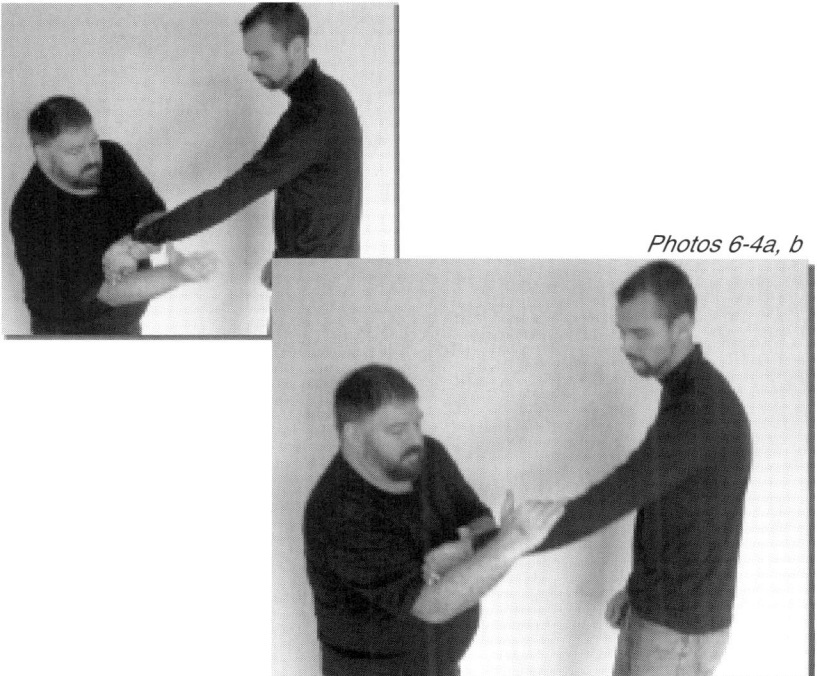

Photos 6-4a, b

Reaching the elbow with the free hand serves another purpose. Start to use your hand to bend the arm at the elbow joint. The lock gets its name, becuase you bend the elbow to a ninety-degree angle, and also the wrist stays bent at the same angle. Two bends equals double the control.

Now, reposition the hand holding the wrist to a thumb down grab. Your fingers will touch your partner's and your thumb your partner's thumb (photos 6-4c, d).

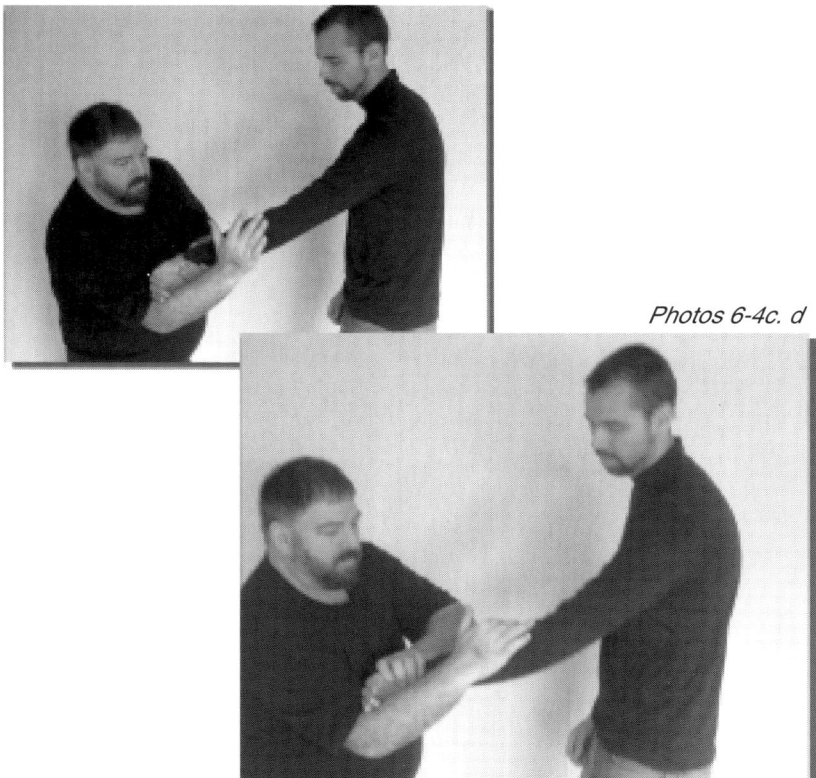

Photos 6-4c. d

Once you have the thumb regrabbed, torque your opponent's hand a little, by rotating the fingers in toward you, and your partner's thumb under and up.

If you have a bend in both the wrist and the elbow, and you have the hand torqued, then press on the top of the arm, at the elbow. Slowly lower the arm, keeping it parallel to the floor (photo 6-4e).

It's a great lock. Now, flow from it into ...

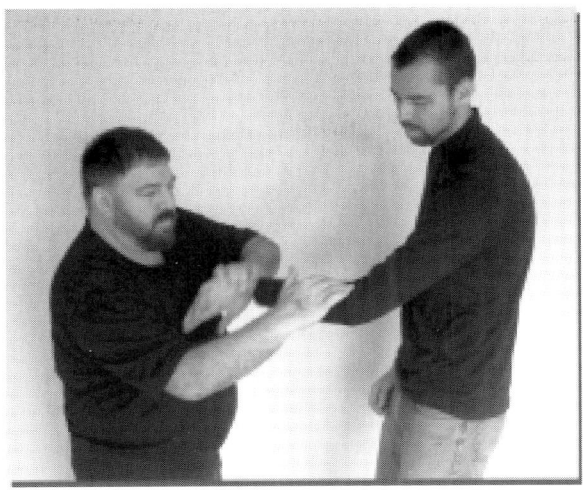

Photos 6-4e

Position #4

Flow into the fourth lock, after your partner has been lowered to a control position (photo 6-5a).

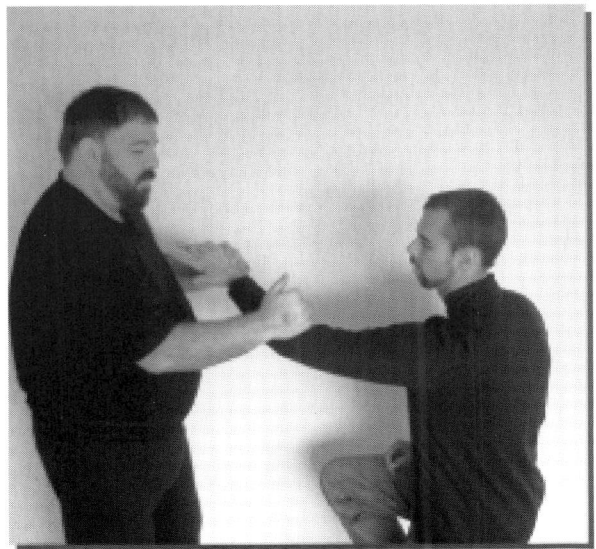

Photos 6-5a

Begin by pulling his arm out straight with the hand that is torquing your opponent's thumb. His hand should be palm up as in Photo 6-5b.

Pivot your body as necessary, so that you're standing behind his outstretched arm (photo 6-5c).

You are now ready to apply the fourth lock, which is an arm-bar. With your arm that is closer to his body, use your wrist to press on the edge of your opponent's triceps.

Apply pressure to control and lower your partner (photo 6-5d).

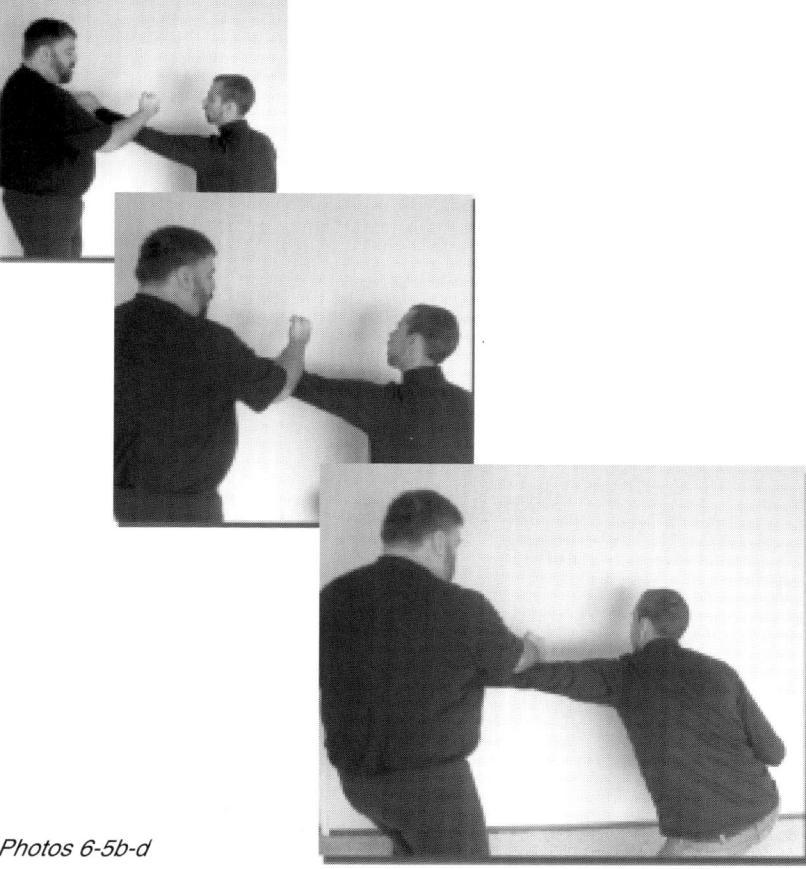

Photos 6-5b-d

For a more complete description of arm-bars, refer to Chapter 3, Feeling Where to Go. There are three variations, starting on page 37. There are also other variations on the Arm Bar throughout this book.

Position #5

From the arm bar, you are going to flow back into the Basic Lock.

Grab your opponent's outstretched hand with both of your thumbs applying pressure to the back of the hand (photos 6-6a, b).

Rotate the hand up as in Photo 6-6c. (For a **complete** description of the Basic Lock, refer to Chapter 4, pages 48-65).

Once you have rotated the hand back to the Basic Lock position, use your other hand to apply pressure down, toward the floor (photos 6-6d, e).

Photos 6-6a-e

Position #6

Continue pressure with only one hand (photo 6-7a); if you're holding his right hand, then continue pressure with your left, and if you have his left, then continue pressure with your right. As you put the pressure on his wrist, take a step to the side of your opponent's body.

Lift your free arm up through the "wing" of his arm (photo 6-7b), and hook your wrist over his (photo 6-7c). Pull down on his wrist for control. This hook is lock number six (photo 607d). Isn't it utterly "nifty-groovy ?" Lock number seven will be the final lock in this sequence.

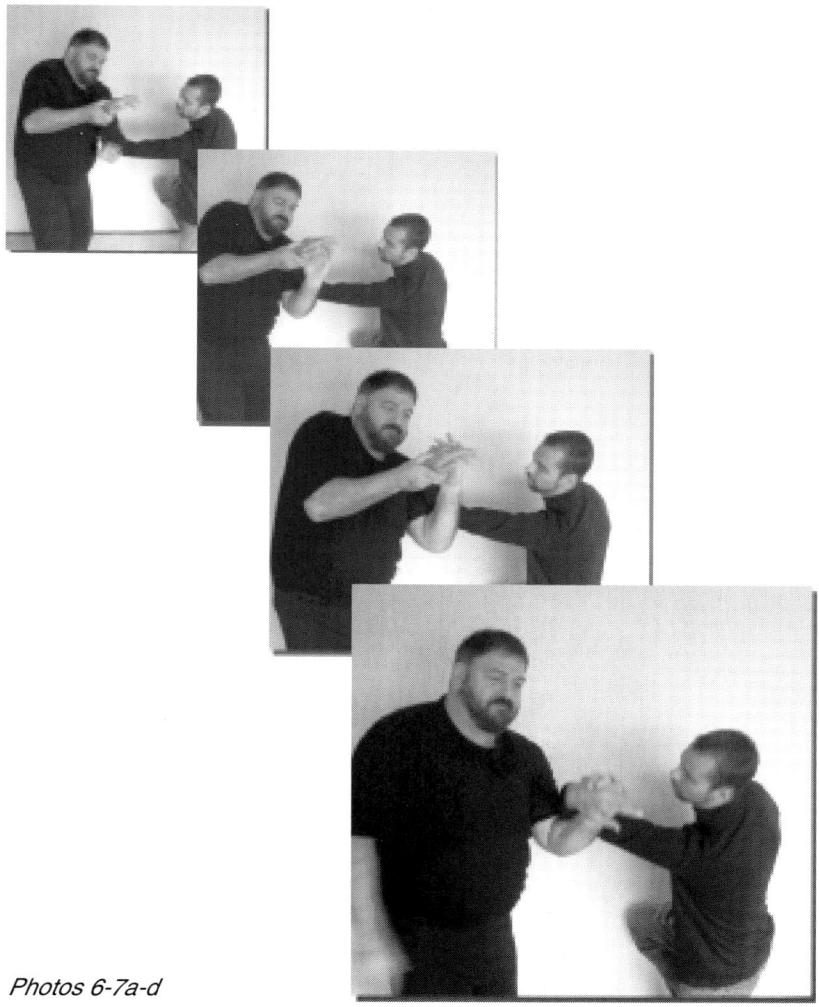

Photos 6-7a-d

Let's back up a few moves for a second. We started with the Basic Lock in move number five. Then you switched the hand which was applying pressure to your opponent's by going into a sixth position. (You're using your opponent's same hand all the way through this pattern.)

Now for the final lock, you're going to switch your hands yet again. Boy, are you learning to become versatile, or what!

Position #7

For lock number seven, you're using your free hand to transfer and then increase the pressure on your opponent's arm. (By now he should feel considerable pressure on his shoulder as well.)

In lock #6, you came up through the "wing" from below. Now, you'll use your other arm to come down through the "wing" from above.

While you still have him in position number six, raise your other arm above both your opponent's and your interlocked arms (photo 6-8a). Bring your arm down through the wing (photo 6-8b).

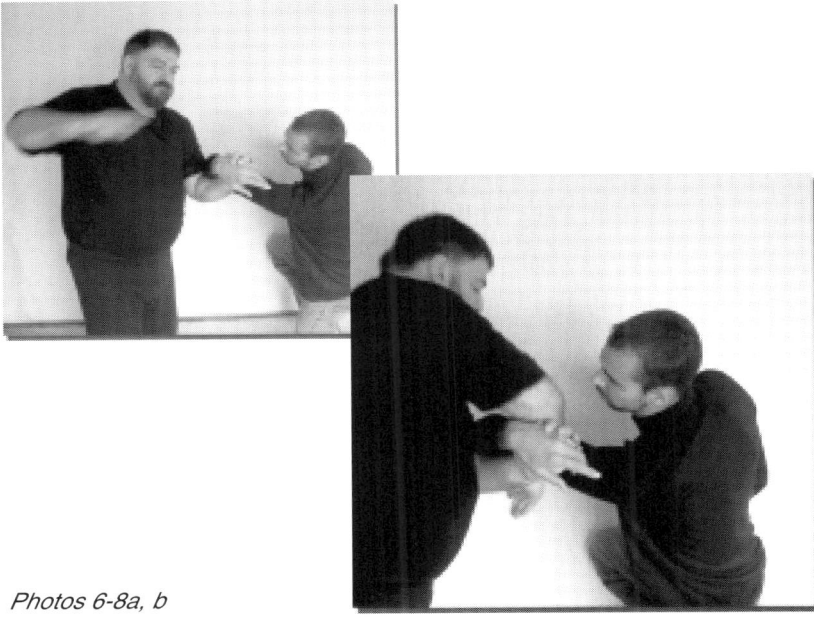

Photos 6-8a, b

Transfer and apply more pressure by replacing your arm that's coming down from above into the "crook" of the arm, where your other arm had the pressure; remove that arm as the pressure is replaced (photos 6-8c-e).

The pressure from lock #7 should go upward on a diagonal. It's almost as if you were punching toward the moon.

I know; what if the axis and azimuth are different where you live? I realize that the moon changes its position, thus changing your angle. Don't take me so literally!

As long as we're not taking the last part of my directions too literally, maybe I should also be careful with the word "punch." If you're just practicing, you don't want to actually punch. If you punched upward with full force, you could really mess up your partner's back. Be careful!

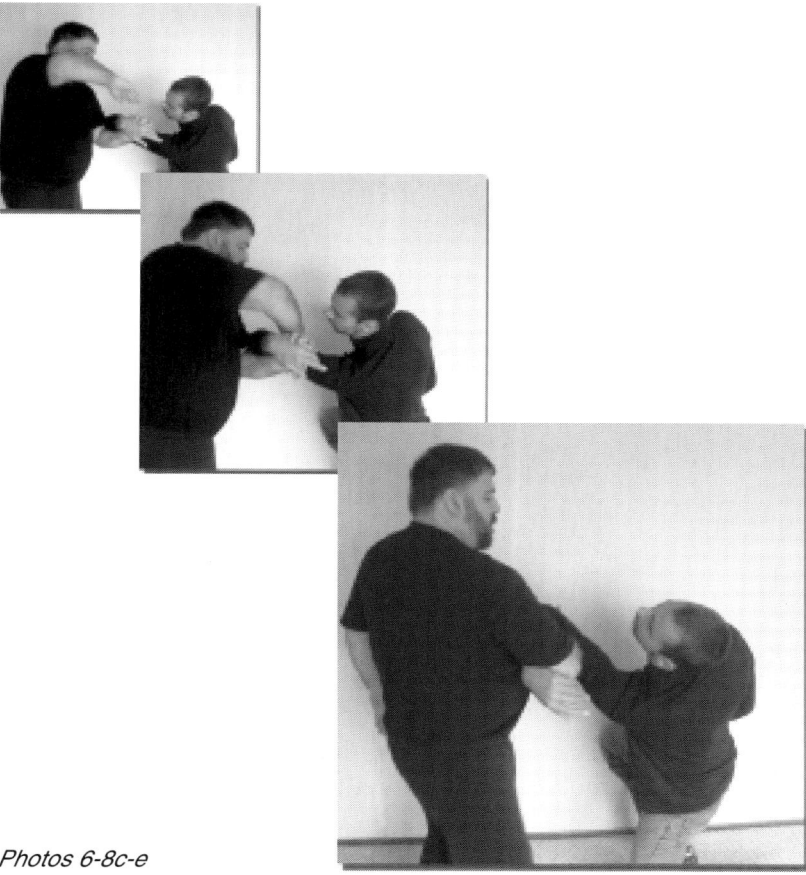

Photos 6-8c-e

Tips for Pattern Success

OK. You made it through the first pattern.

Now, I have some tips to speed your way to expert status. You know some of them already from other areas of the book; just consider them gentle reminders.

Tip #1

Have an agreed system of tapping out with your partner. You need to be able to tap your partner's leg or arm and vice versa to indicate pain.

Photo 6-9

Once you agree on a signal, don't use it too much. If your partner can withstand a little pain, yet let you know that you're close to his or her threshold, it can be a learning experience for you. You will learn to gauge your opponent's limits and use this knowledge to your advantage.

Tip #2

You can see whether or not you're having any effect on your opponent any time you're applying a technique. As you learn the threshold mentioned in Tip #1, you can learn to apply your technique with a short jerk (a staccato motion). You want to "punch" the technique with just enough oomph that it causes his whole body to respond with a short quick jerk. Look for a response to the *stimulus* you provide your partner.

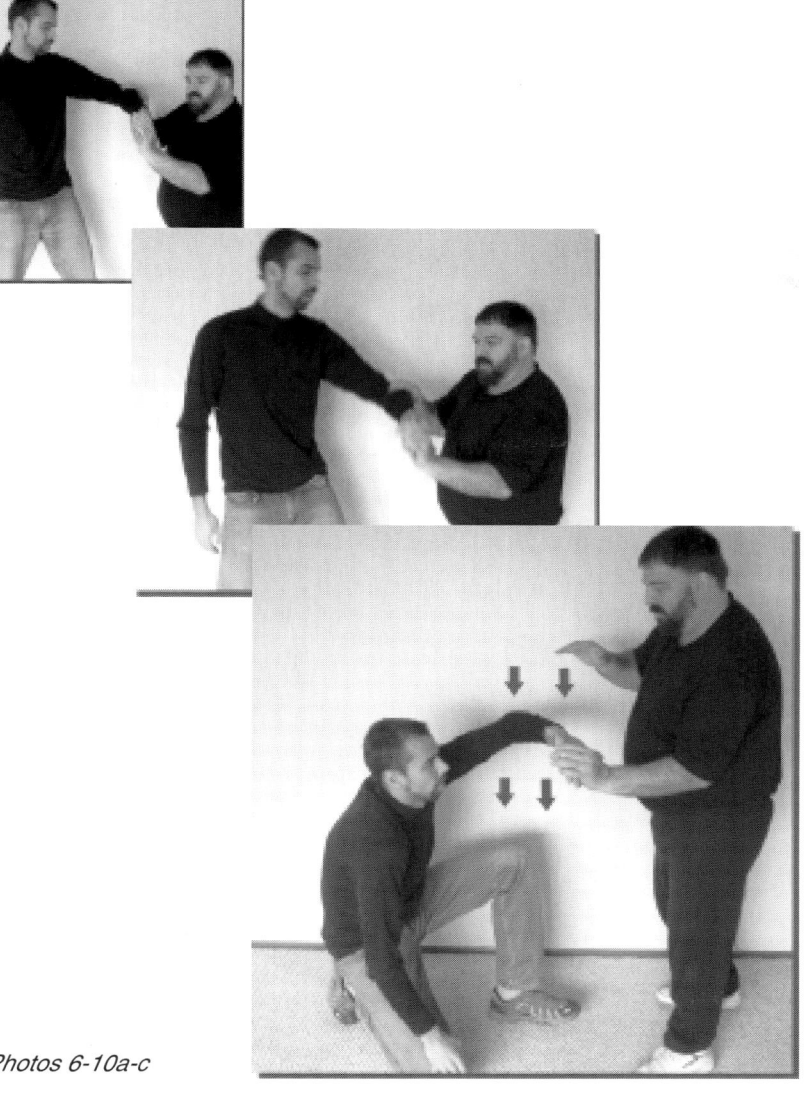

Photos 6-10a-c

You apply a short, quick motion, and the response is another short, quick motion (photos 6-10a-c). It should cause your opponent just a little pain. You're just looking for the reaction to see if your move worked. You're not trying to maim him permanently.

Tip #3

Change the pattern by adding moves.

Once you learn this pattern, you don't have to stick with it. Part of the beauty of becoming an expert is that you're going to branch off on your own.

You may reinvent the wheel a few times, but then again, you may come up with something completely different. One way to branch off is to add new moves into the pattern.

For example: go back to Position #3, when you had your opponent in an Double Ninety-Degree Lock. You pulled the arm out straight to get ready for an arm bar (photos 6-11a, b).

Well, what if you grabbed your opponent's pinky and third fingers of the outstretched hand (photo 6-11c)? Then you could bend them up toward the wrist. Presto! You've just changed the pattern. There are oodles of places to effect changes. You could even add to your changes and end up with changes on your changes. Wow!

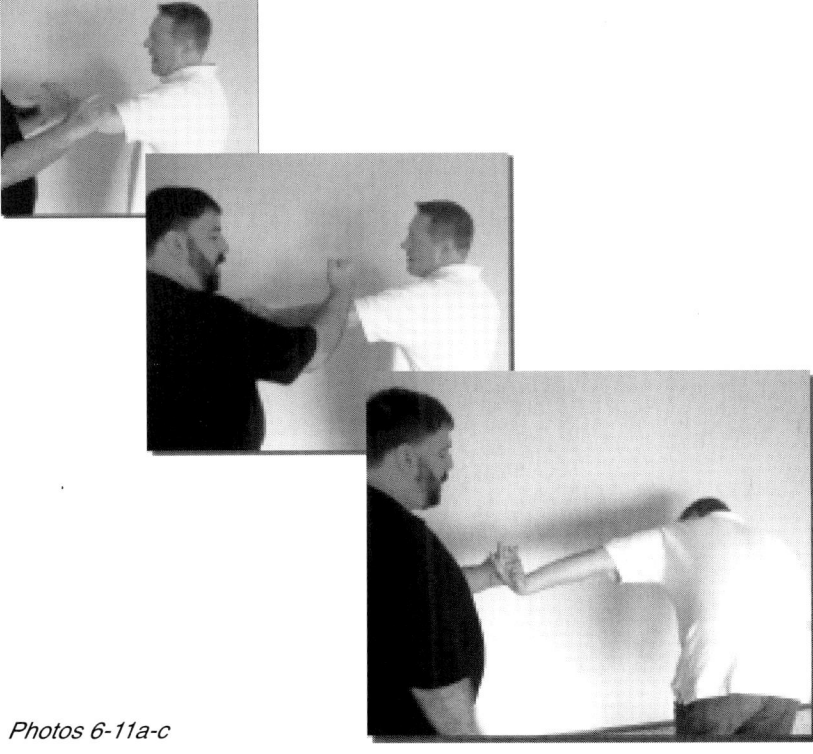

Photos 6-11a-c

Tip #4

Change the pattern by changing the order of the moves.

This becomes a lot easier as you add more moves to your pattern, but essentially, the idea is this: You pick two similar points in the pattern and exchange the sequences that follow each.

Look for the Basic Locks in the pattern.

There are at least two. After one Basic Lock you go into move #2, and after the other Basic Lock, you go into a wing lock.

If you were to perform move #2 in place of the wing lock, you would go right back into the beginning of the routine.

The routine wouldn't end, unless you changed the path to a different variation. Keep in mind, you can end the pattern on any move by applying enough pressure to take your opponent beyond *the point of no return*. By the way, you could choose to put a Wing Lock on in the beginning.

Remember, as you add moves you may start to see some repetition. This repetition isn't necessarily a bad thing.

Use these spots as places to interchange moves.

As you learn to interchange at will, you will come a long way toward learning to flow. You'll be an expert before you know it. Practice.

Tip #5

Don't just do the pattern for the pattern's sake.

In order to improve, you need to have purpose in your practice sessions. Remember, you're looking for ways to apply each technique within the pattern. You're looking for relationships in the different positions and the moves that follow. You're always looking for reversals, counters, and strikes.

Learn to be a smart fighter – know all the possible outcomes to a given technique.

Tip #6

Make sure your opponent can't kick at you while he is restrained in a hold.

Check your downward pressure on each hold (photo 6-12a). Sometimes the pressure won't be exactly downward; it will press into the joint. I'm referring to the holding pressure that you get with each position.

If your opponent is held firmly, he shouldn't be able to raise his leg. Any retaliation to your lock in the form of a kick should be impossible (photo 6-12b).

You're definitely going to need to experiment to find just the right pressure. Again, remember, most of the time, try to apply force downward.

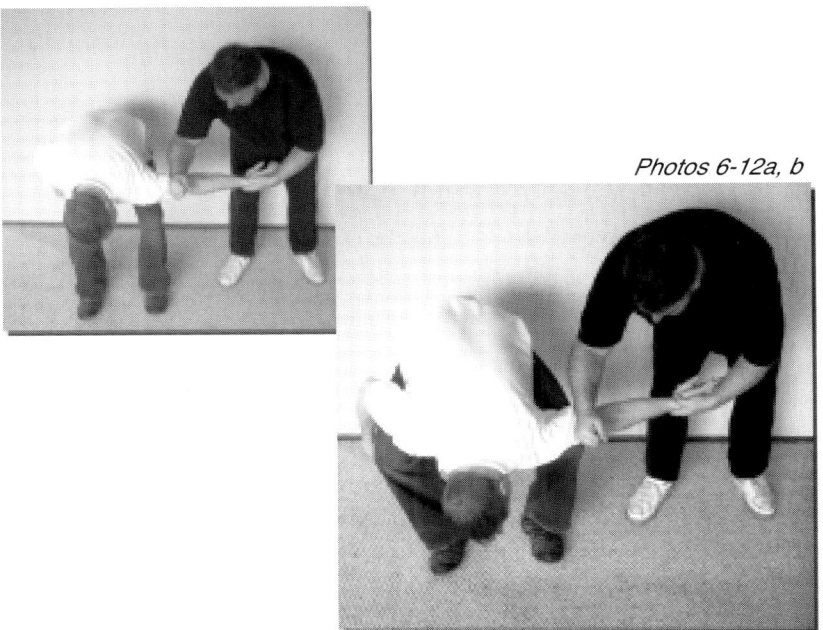

Photos 6-12a, b

Tip #7

Just as you have to be aware of your opponent's feet, you also have to pay attention to his free hand.

One solid punch from your opponent, and your wonderful lock is all over. The greatest error a wrist-lock artist can commit is to apply a wrist lock while in range of the opponent's *other* fist.

Let me rephrase that: **The most common errors that I see, over and over again, are martial artists applying a hold or doing a move to one side of their opponents' bodies while completely ignoring what's happening on the other side.**

This foolishness has even transformed itself into an art; some schools wait until you apply the hold and then go into a counter hold, without even acknowledging that they're in a danger zone. You could get picked off with a punch to your blind spot.

Let me illustrate: in Photo 6-13a, you're applying a lock to your opponent, but, because of distancing and positions, you are in a danger zone.

Photo 6-13b shows one possible undesirable outcome.

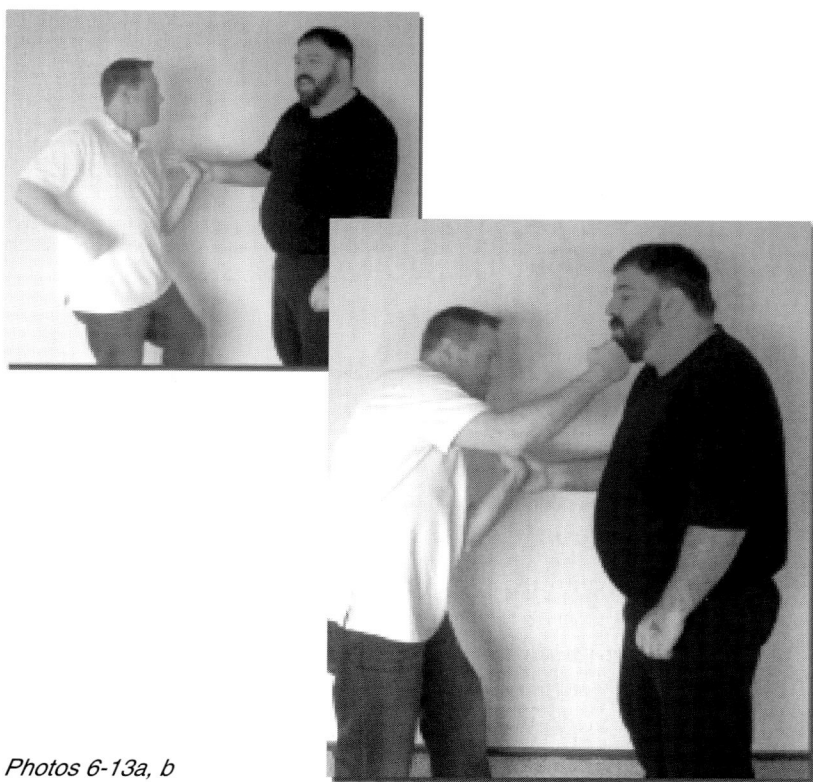

Photos 6-13a, b

By turning your body slightly and taking one small step backward, you take yourself completely out of range of the punch, while still able to apply the hold (photos 6-13c, d).

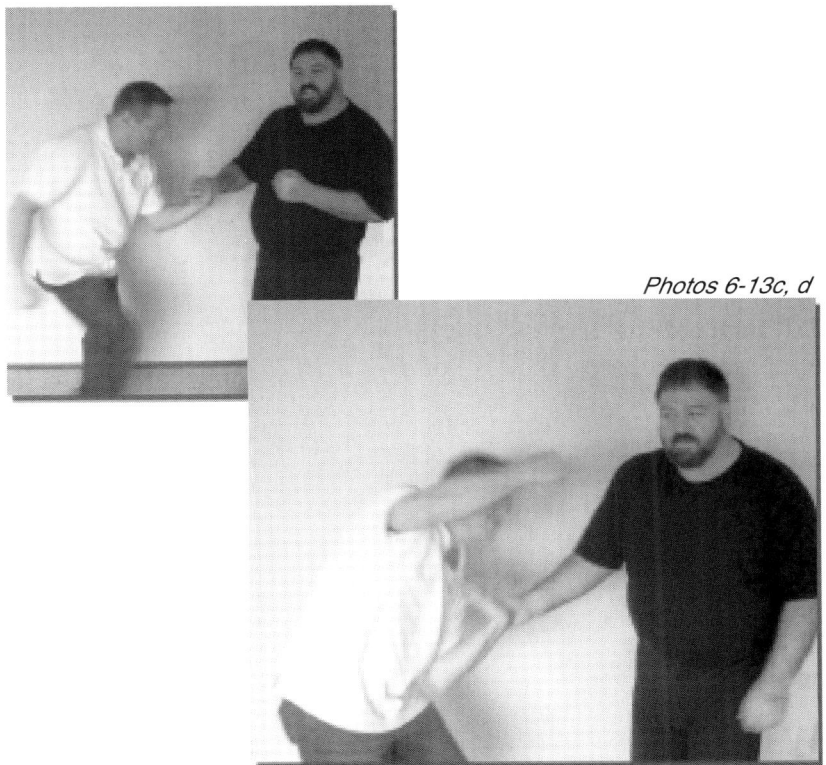

Photos 6-13c, d

If you feel that your opponent can still reach you, then take another step back extending your opponent's arm, as you maintain the lock.

Obviously, this is a very important point. In fact, **it's one of the most important points in the whole book.** Really!

So, why do I have it buried here under "lucky"number seven (it *is* one of my favorite numbers)? Well, call it one of my little *nuggets*. Sometimes, you have to go digging for gold. And to be frank, I won't be horribly upset if a few people miss a few points in this book. If you really want to become a wrist lock expert, you deserve these nuggets.

(P.S. Most golden bits of advice are not labeled; what is gold to one person, may be yesterday's news to someone else.)

I just want to make it hard for people looking for a few quick *magic* moves. Take the time to really learn *this stuff*; it really is worthwhile.

I can make you two promises: You won't regret having learned to be a wrist-lock expert (or a martial-arts expert), and some day your skill will come in handy.

Tip #8

Practice against *resisters*. These patterns are wonderful against willing opponents.

You get up there and grab the hand of some jovial person.

Your willing volunteer is completely relaxed. You apply technique after technique — hold after hold. You take this person through one of your more lengthy patterns. Life is good.

What do you do when you get a not-so-willing volunteer?

This person tenses as you try several wrist locks. You can't even get him close to the point of no return.

Nothing works.

A gray cloud has suddenly darkened your mortal existence.

Prepare for these difficult people (or real opponents) ahead of time. First, read the Resisters Section on pages 156-162. You should be practicing this way anyway.

Then, when you are working with your practice partner (a *willing* volunteer), have him or her tense at random points during your pattern.

Can you overcome this resistance by sheer force? Can you change the angle to salvage the lock?

Do you have to flow into a new lock?

Can you soften up your opponent by hitting?

For example, let's take the Arm Lock that has been discussed in other chapters. You start to grab your opponent's arm. You use your other hand to rotate his biceps toward you (photo 6-14a). Your other hand continues snaking up into a lock. —BUT— as you apply pressure to drop your opponent's shoulder, your opponent suddenly resists and stands up straight (photo 6-14b). What do you do?

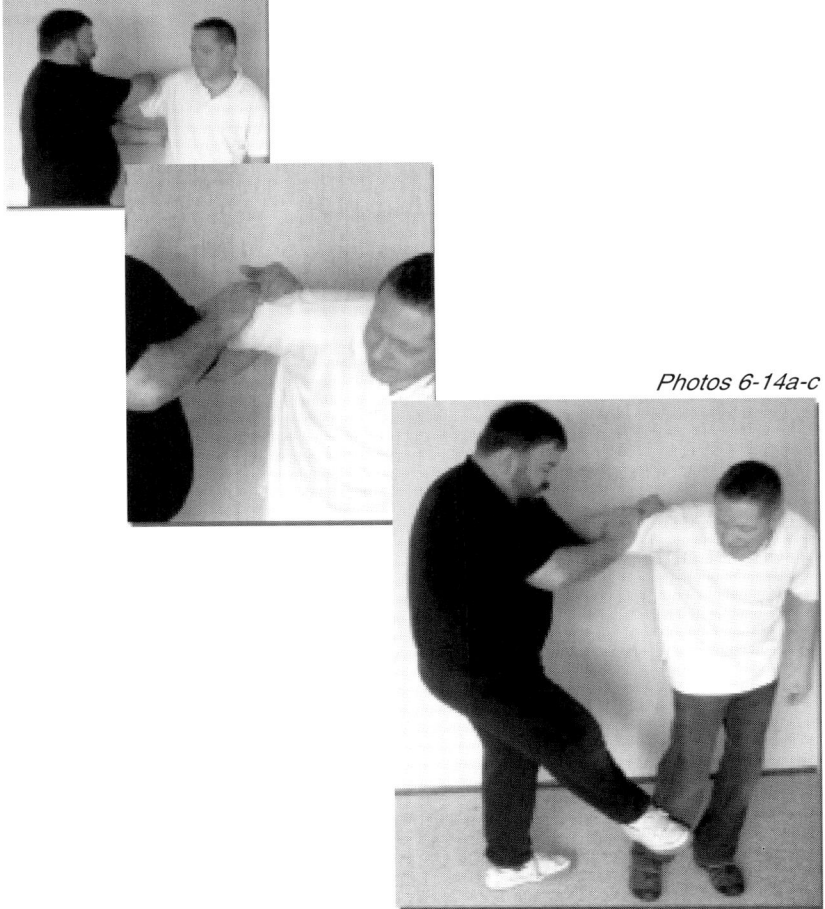

Photos 6-14a-c

I have found that a strike works wonders at times like these. There are all sorts of possibilities. I'll give you a few ideas and save my favorite response for last. Do give them a try.

First, you could try to loosen him up by kicking him in the shins (photo 6-14c), or maybe kick with continued pressure to the back of the leg on the calf.

Maybe he'd respond to a sharp punch to the stomach, or to the kidneys (photos 6-15a).

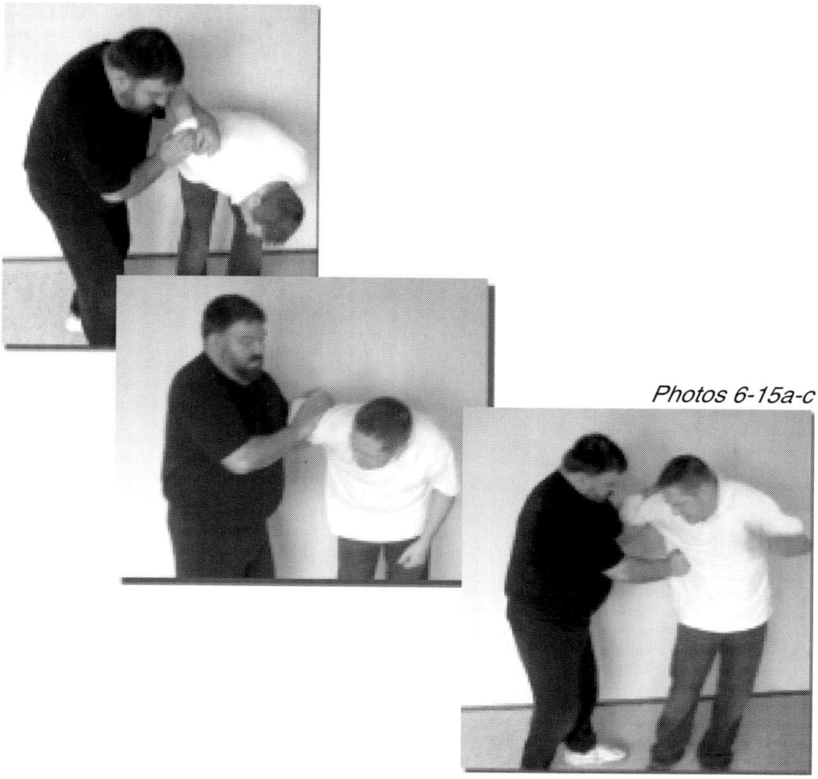

Photos 6-15a-c

You could grab his hair and pull for a control move (photo 6-15d). Even an ear grab might help.

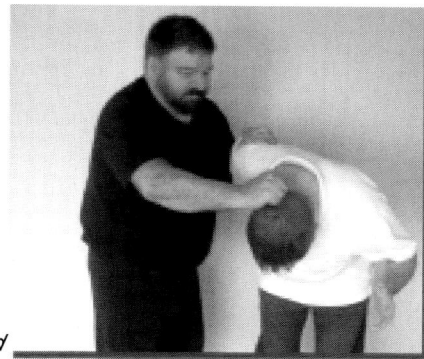

Photos 6-15d

My favorite technique, which allows me to reapply the same hold, is an elbow strike.

I slam my elbow into the middle of the scapula (photo 6-15e-g). This forces my opponent's shoulder down, which I need anyway. It gets the opponent closer to *the point of no return*. It causes pain, which is a distraction from the lock that's being applied. And it does *loosen 'em up*, which was my original goal.

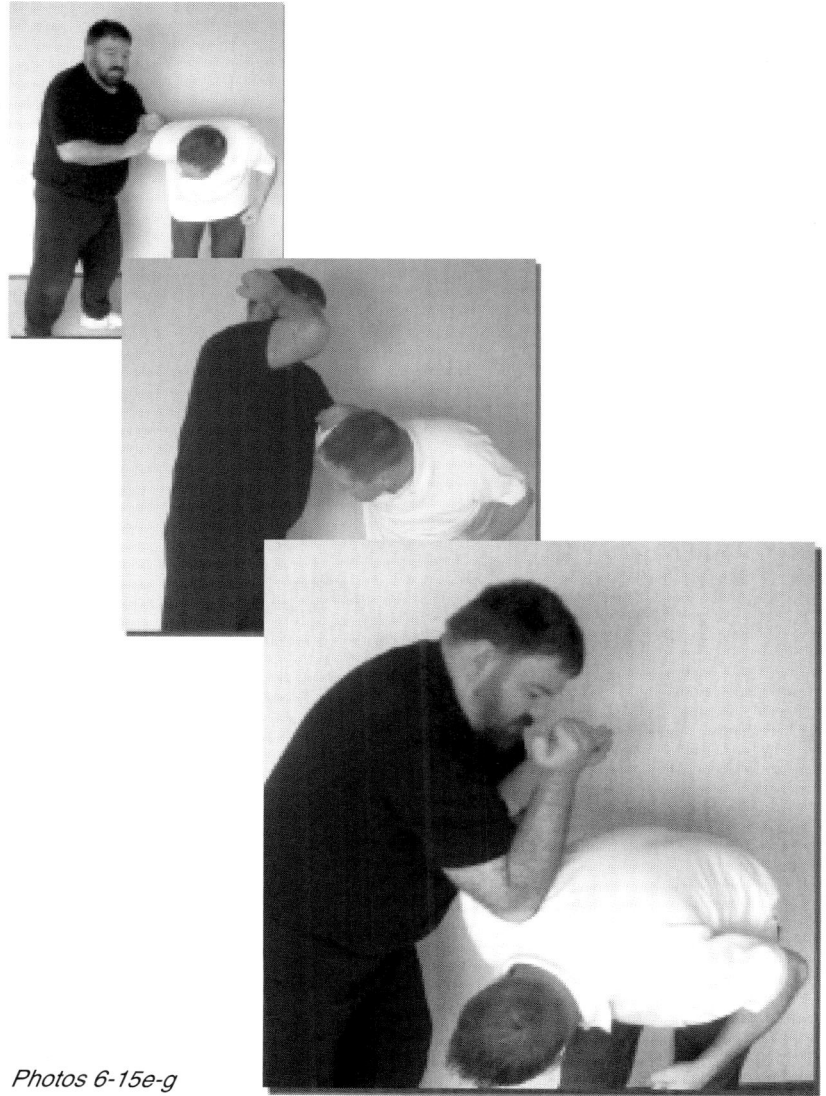

Photos 6-15e-g

Tip #9

Change the routine by substituting different locks for ones in the original pattern. In Tip #4, you rearrange the order of the locks.

This time, think *substitution*. You aren't adding new locks to the pattern, you're looking for places to turn or rotate the wrist or arm into a different direction in order to substitute a new lock for an old one.

You have to be creative.

To get you started changing the pattern, you should learn Pattern #2. It's very similar to Pattern #1; it's just that we go on a different *path* at times. Not so coincidentally, H...e...r...e... is Pattern #2:

Pattern #2

I think Steve Golden showed me Pattern #2. He taught it to me as a variation on what I had learned before. It starts out the same as Pattern #1, but then takes a sharp turn in a different direction with some very creative locks.

Position #1

We're going to start once again with the Basic Lock.

I am left handed, so normally, I am a little stronger locking with my left hand, but in the photos, I take the lock with my right hand, for the convenience of the *Righties* out there.

Grab your partner's hand with your thumb on the back of the hand as in Photo 6-16a. Rotate the hand into the Basic Lock (photo 6-16b).

Many beginners, out of eagerness to get to the next move, forget to apply proper pressure on the current technique.

Make sure you treat each lock as though it were *the* controlling move. (*Important nugget.*)

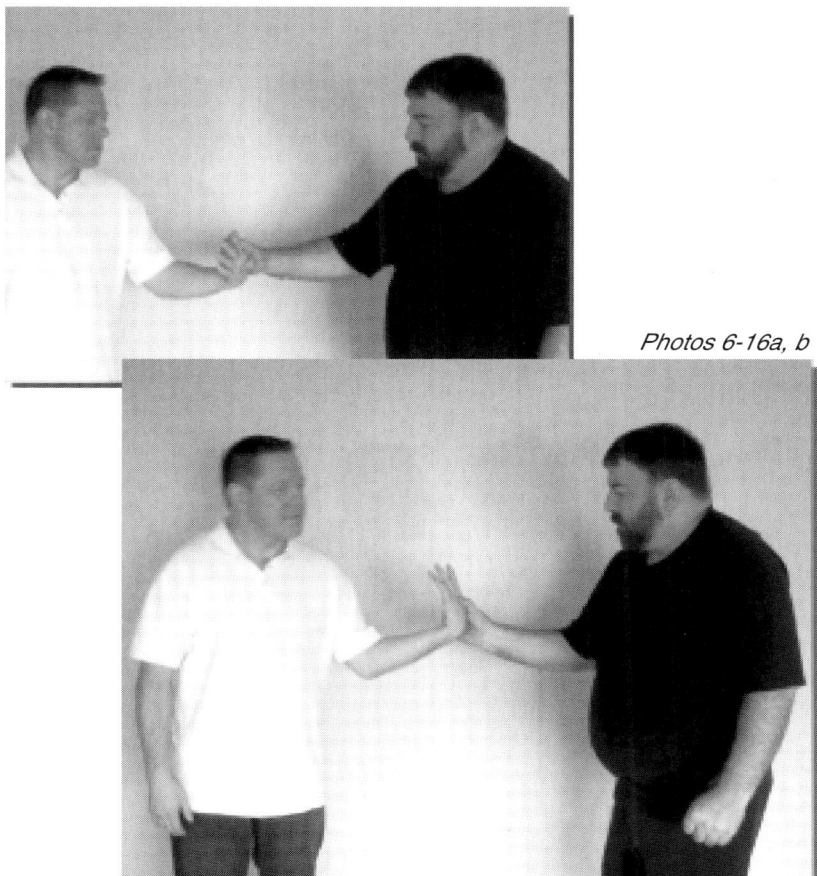

Photos 6-16a, b

Position #2

Do you remember the second position from Pattern #1?

I considered it to be the hardest – especially trying to describe it. Lucky me – I get another chance.

Maybe it will be easier to learn this time around.

Also, this time, I'll show you the sequence from a different camera angle. OK, let's continue....

As you rotate the wrist back in the opposite direction of the Basic Lock, keep pressure on his wrist (photos 6-17a, b).

While rotating the wrist, grab your partner's forearm with your other hand (photo 6-17c)).

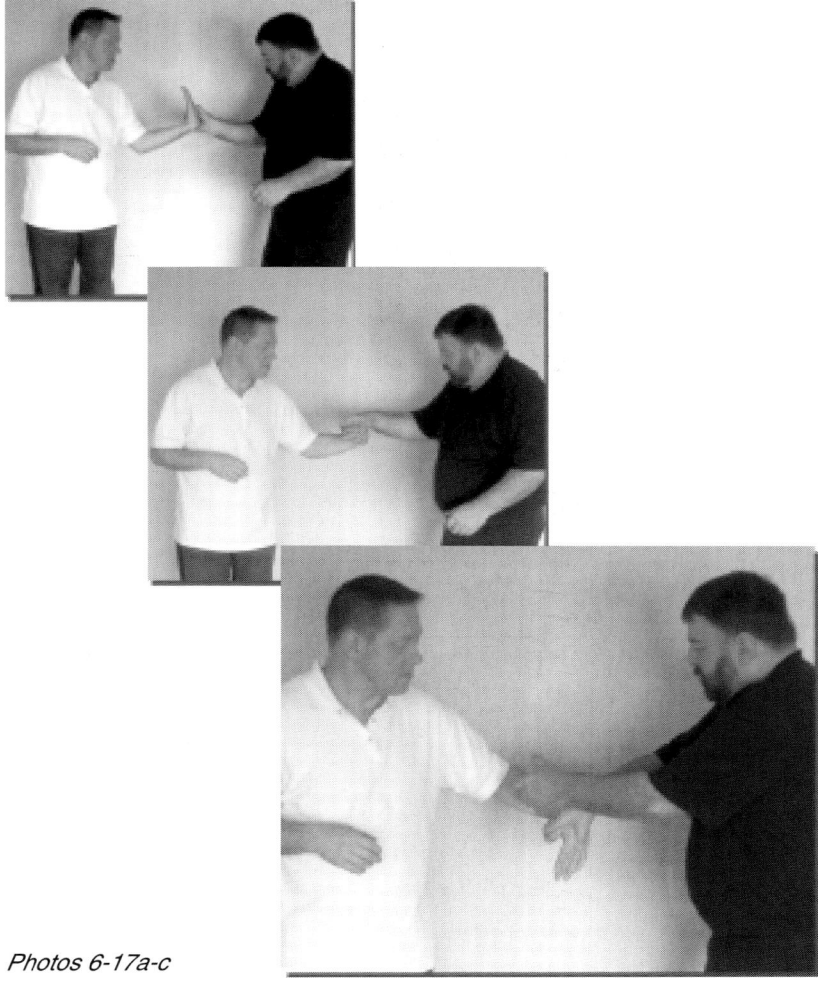

Photos 6-17a-c

Even while grabbing his forearm with your other hand, you should be able to keep the pressure (and control) with the hand applying pressure to the wrist.

While still grabbing the wrist, continue to rotate his hand counterclockwise in toward the center of his body and down (photo 6-17d).

Slide the bottom of your partner's hand along the inside of your forearm, keeping pressure on the back of his hand.

Continue sliding the hand until it wedges into the inside joint of your forearm (photo 6-17e). Remember, I am using lots of words and photos to describe a sequence that flows smoothly.

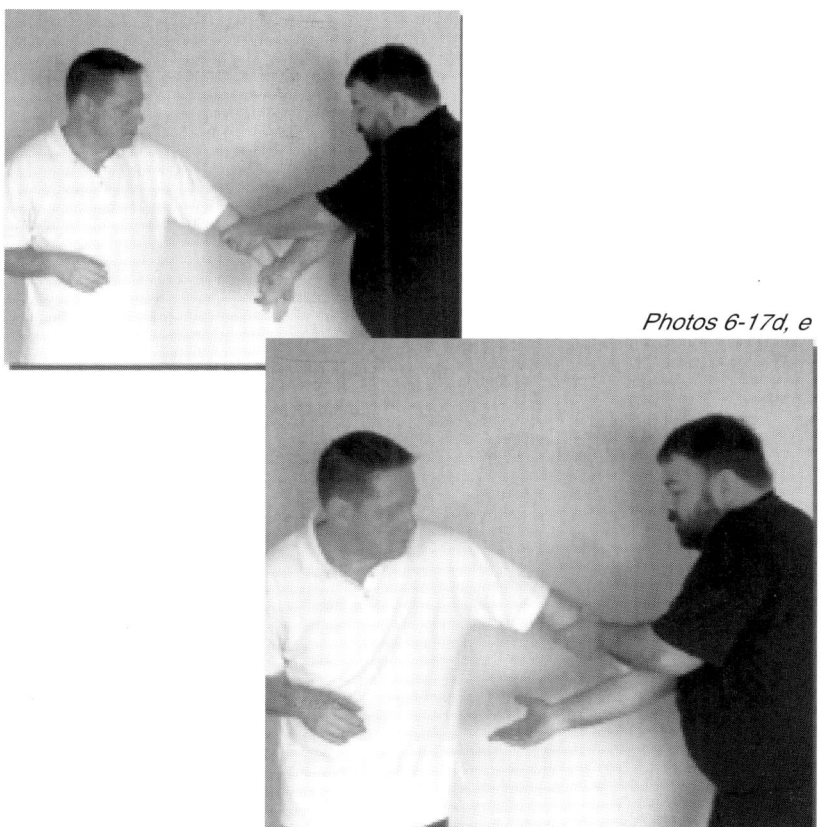

Photos 6-17d, e

Position #3

Now for the third position: you're going to end up standing side by side with your opponent.

Even though you just finished sliding the back of his hand up the arm to your biceps, you are now going to reverse the action and slide his hand down the arm, until you're applying pressure to the back of his hand with the palm of yours (photo 6-18a).

Keep pressure against the back of the hand at all times.

This is where you pivot around to the side. If you do it correctly, both your arm and your partner's should naturally move forward, in front and between both of your bodies (photo 6-18b). Remember to always have pressure against the back of his hand.

Shift his arm, so his elbow is pressed against the front of your body, someplace where a lot of pressure won't cause you pain (photo 6-18c).

When you have his elbow firmly against your body, press the back of his hand in toward your belly. You actually bend your opponent's fingers inward, toward the stomach.

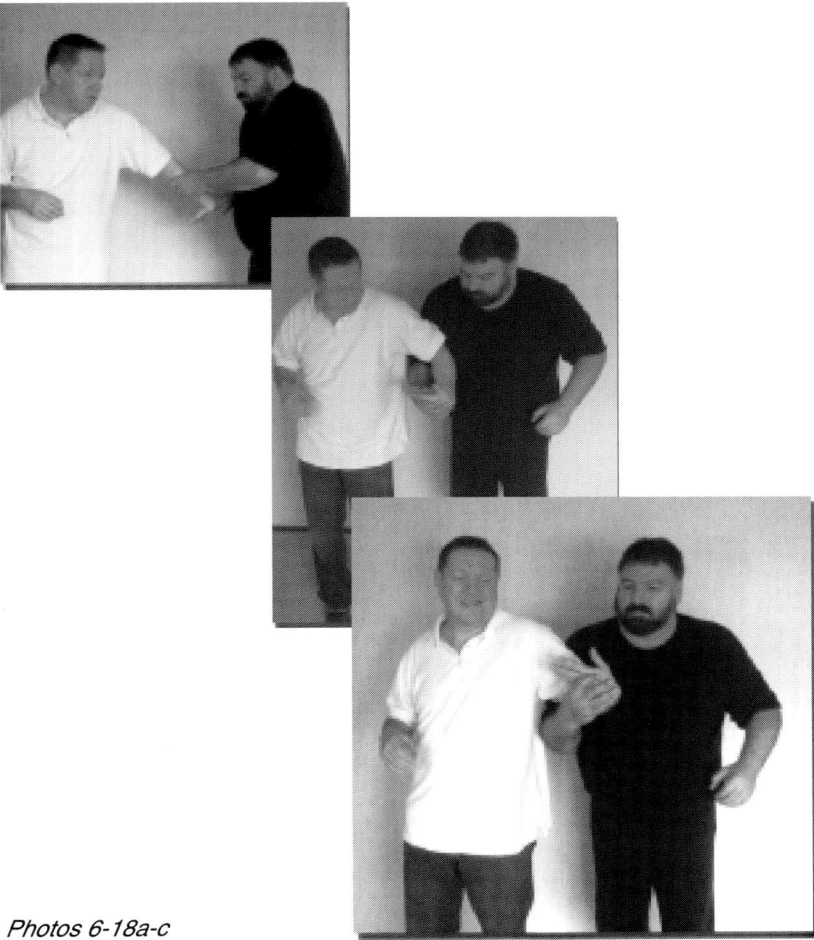

Photos 6-18a-c

Your lock is successful, if you have enough pressure applied to force your opponent to:

- try to tap out early.

- raise up on tiptoes – *discomfort* from the lock.

- utter a wimper of pain.

If you have problems getting your opponent up on tiptoes, try pointing your opponent's fingers down toward the ground. Causing more pain is usually nothing more than a little adjustment here and there.

And that is Position #3.

Position #4

Position #4 is both easy and gratifying.

In Position #3, maybe you were able to raise your opponent up on tiptoes, and maybe you had control, but you just couldn't quite take advantage of the "pain factor." For some reason, the minor adjustments aren't working.

You'll solve the problem, as you flow into Position #4.

Unless you are super short and your opponent is super tall or vice versa, you shouldn't have any problem with this one.

With your free hand, reach to your opponent's controlled wrist (photo 6-19a).

Photo 6-19a

Pull your opponent's arm out straight as you rotate his wrist, palm up, and at the same time straighten out and rotate your own, now free arm, palm up (photo 6-19b).

With your arm straightened and palm up, lift it into your opponent's straightened-out elbow (photo 6-19c). If you apply enough pressure upward, you should easily raise him off his heels.

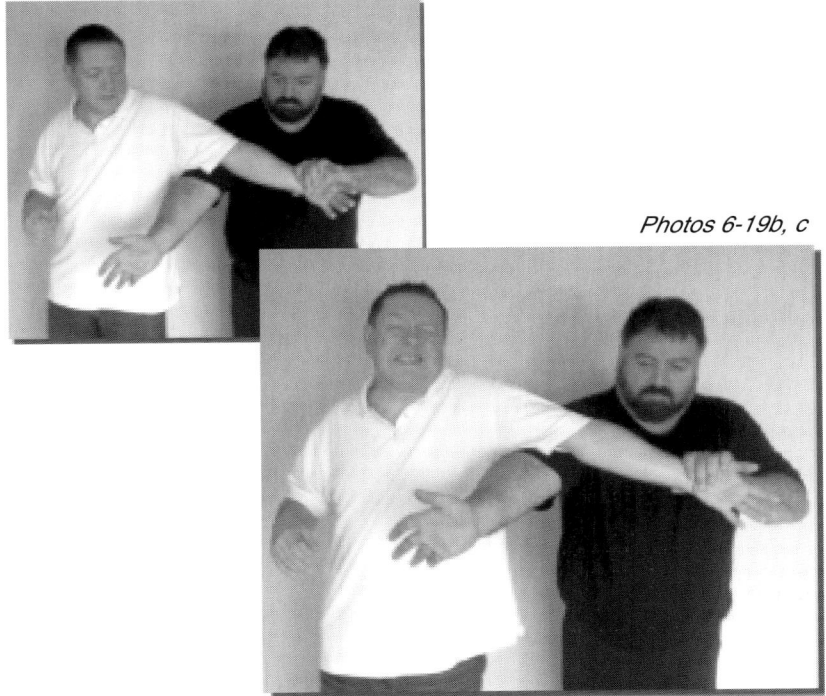

Photos 6-19b, c

If you're too short to apply sufficient pressure, you can get more leverage by lifting your opponent's arm onto your shoulder.

You then use your shoulder as a fulcrum. Careful, it's very easy to tweak your partner's arm. (On the other hand, you'll probably do all sorts of heavy-duty damage to a real opponent.)

Whether you use your arm or your shoulder, be sure to keep your opponent's arm very straight. If your opponent's arm bends, then he can get his own leverage to resist your lock. Not good!

Position #5

Position #5 is the ever-faithful arm bar. The question is how to get from Position #4 to the arm bar. Are you ready?

In the first edition of *Wrist Locks*, I had you rotate the wrist all the way forward to the other palm-up position first.

Now, I feel it's easier to teach with your arm pivoting to the arm-bar position, before you rotate your opponent's arm.

Start this position, by rotating your straightened arm to a palm-down position. As you do this, pivot the arm to an arm - bar on top of your opponent's arm (photos 6-20a, b).

Photos 6-20a, b

Once you have started the pivot of your arm, your controlling hand is going to rotate your opponent's arm forward, first to a palm-down position.

Then continue to rotate your partner's hand, until the palm is facing your stomach (photos 6-20c).

Maintain contact with your opponent's arm as you rotate your arm up and over. Really make sure you don't accidentally let off pressure at any time during this sequence. When there is a release of pressure, you are almost signaling your opponent to counter.

Push your wrist into the small of your opponent's triceps as you would for a normal arm bar (photo 6-20d).

You don't have to, but I feel that you should modify your grip on your opponent's wrist. Drop your thumb across your partner's hand and reposition your own hand, so that your thumb is on the other side of the opponent's hand (photo 6-20d).

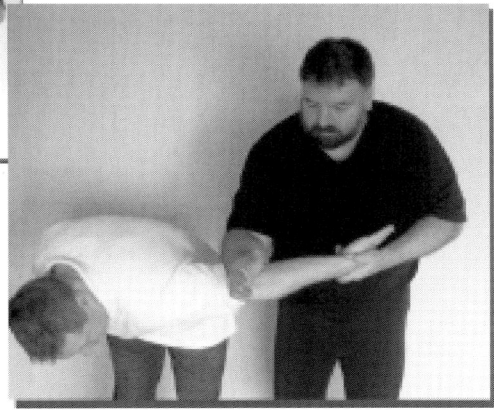

Photos 6-20c, d

Push on the back of the hand, with your opponent's fingers coming up and back toward the body. This allows you to apply controlling pain to two points of pressure at the same time. You can control with additional pressure to the triceps or to the wrist, **or to both.**

This is where the routine normally ends.

You put a good, solid arm bar on your opponent and that's it. But wait! I have two additional moves for you to add. I learned these in the Steve Golden class in a different context.

They just fit so well here, that I thought you'd appreciate them.

Bonus Position #6

In Bonus Position #6, take the hand that has your opponent by the wrist (either wrist-hold is fine), and bend it up over your arm (the one that's applying pressure to the triceps), as in Photo 6-21a.

Rotate the arm, so that it bends without breaking (photo 6-21b). After all, you should never abuse your practice dummy, I mean partner.

You have hit Position #6, when the arm is locked behind your opponent's back.

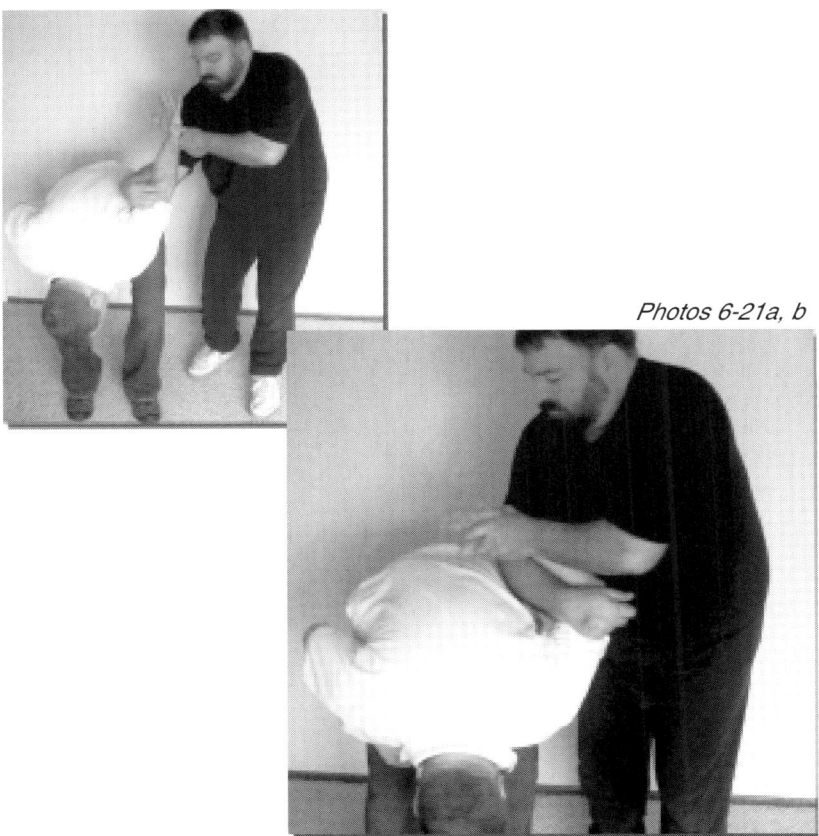

Photos 6-21a, b

Bonus Position #7

I tend not to use my free hand to apply pressure to the locked arm. Instead, I put an extra lock on my opponent's wrist. This one is definitely adding *icing on the cake.*

You need to grab your opponent's hand and/or fingers. This could be anything from a kickstart, to an upside-down handshake. Simply grabbing the fingers works, as well.

Then apply a wrist lock or a finger lock, while maintaining the arm lock (photos 6-22a, b).

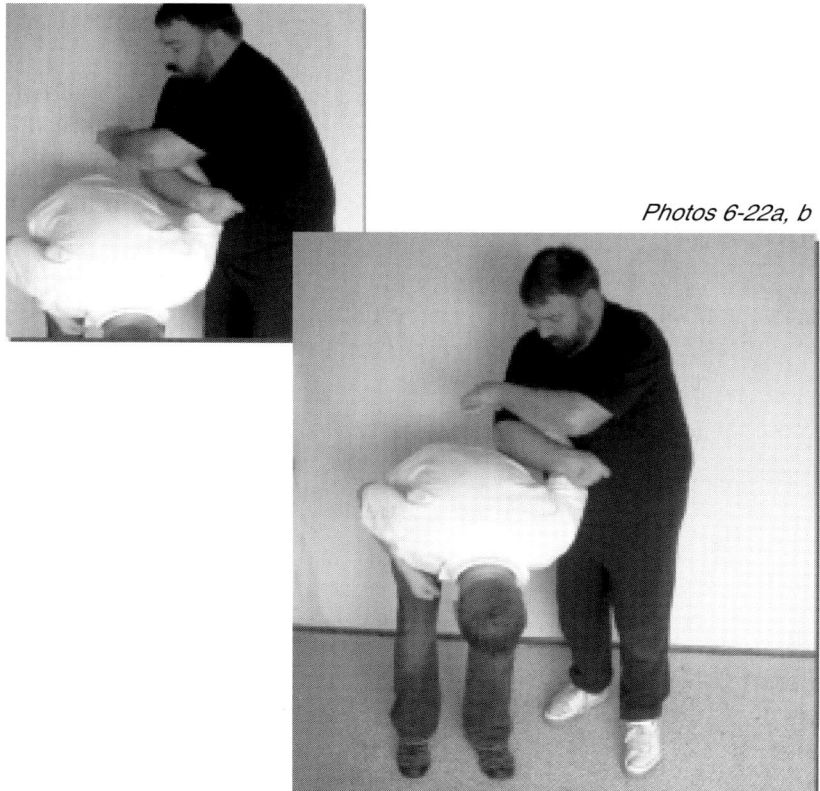

Photos 6-22a, b

This is the end of the pattern, but it doesn't have to be.

How many holds could you move into from this last one? Could you slip your arm out, while continuing the Upside-down-handshake Pinky Tweak?

If you were able to, you could then use it to bend his elbow to ninety degrees. If you still had the ... Pinky Tweak, this would open up all sorts of possibilities.

I don't want to ruin your experience of figuring this all out on your own. It will make you a much better martial artist; it's worth the effort.

A Little Advice

I want to emphasize that while patterns are the ultimate in strutting your stuff to people of other styles, they really are not the end all.

Pattern without application will get you nowhere. You always have to keep your goal in mind.

I know of martial art schools that teach stick fighting. In some of these schools, they only practice drills. Boy, do the drills look cool, but ... you guessed it. They can't apply the material.

They suck as fighters.

No practical application.

Don't be this way with wrist locks. Always keep in mind how you're going to use your techniques.

7
Generalizing to Different People and Situations

Let's assume that there is a particular lock or sequence in this book that catches your eye. You can't put a lock on yourself; so you get a partner.

The two of you practice your hearts out.

You wrist lock each other, until you have the particular lock down pat.

Then one day you try your wonder move on someone else and... it fails you miserably. Not only did it not work, it didn't even feel like "your move." What went wrong?

As you can probably guess from the title of this chapter, you failed to generalize your new technique.

You learned the move in the context of your partner's specific body and kinesthetic traits. Height, body type, muscle mass, flexibility, strength, coordination, and prior knowledge of wrist locks all affect the move's outcome.

If you have practiced this technique on only one person with one style of movements and reactions, then it's almost impossible to differentiate between the core technique and the excess movements that don't really contribute to the wrist lock.

Your moves won't work the way they are supposed to.

In fact, they may fail you when you need them the most. Don't gloss over this shorter chapter. It may mean the difference between success and failure.

If you don't generalize each and every move you learn, you won't master the core technique.

This phenomenon happens in other areas of life. Often a couple married for many years can dance divinely together, but turn into complete klutzes when paired with other partners.

Dog trainers know to drill their dog in a variety of environments; otherwise the dog may not be able generalize and perform under the pressure of a show.

Practicing is very important, but don't practice without generalizing.

> In martial-arts tournaments, the best fighters are those who have had experience fighting opponents from a number of systems. The fighters who only practice with opponents from their school aren't as prepared or effective.

In the field of magic, restaurant magicians are often "smoother" than their colleagues, because they get tons of practice in front of different people.

Magicians know the value of lots of practice. They also appreciate the value of a good dress rehearsal.

Watch good school teachers; they know how to generalize and reach students with very different personalities from different backgrounds. After years of presenting the same or similar lessons to various audiences, they get smooth and gain the competence to *go with the flow.*

Changes in the audience's behavior don't affect them. (Can you say the same for changes that your opponent makes in the middle of your wrist lock?)

An Experiment in Generalizing

If I still haven't convinced you of the importance of generalizing, try this little experiment.

Select two new wrist locks from Chapter 4, "A Dozen Super Techniques...."

Learn them both.

Pick one of the two locks, and only practice this lock with your partner. Practice the other lock on as many different people as are willing to lend you their wrist.

To make this experiment just a wee bit more scientific, you should practice both moves for about the same amount of time.

After about a month (or as long as you can hold out), get a volunteer, preferably somebody about your size.

Do both locks on this person.

Which lock was more effective? Which gave you more instant control?

You don't have to tell me the results – and definitely don't tell me the results if you still don't see the benefit of practicing on as many different body types as possible.

Categorize Your Opponents

Now for the main benefit of striving to generalize.

After you have practiced with *lots* (and I do mean LOTS) of people... you'll start to notice something.

Your practice partners will start fitting into certain groups. The way they react to your locks and their particular style of resistance will start to feel familiar.

You will react one way to "Super-flexible long limbs" and another to "Muscle-bound limited motion." You'll categorize people by strength, center of gravity, and even their thresholds of pain. You will adjust almost automatically, depending on all of the variables that your opponent brings into the exchange. The more you generalize, the easier it will be to recognize familiar responses.

You might come up with your own names, or maybe you'll just recognize each "feeling" without naming it. Your opponent won't know diddly about you, but you'll have a lot of useful information about your opponent.

You'll gain all of this information within the first couple of seconds of contact. Now if that isn't an advantage in a fight, I don't know what is!

So how do you generalize?

Doesn't it seem obvious? Practice with different people!

Finding Different Practice Partners

Admittedly, there is a bit more to it than that.

I have some specific advice. First, teaching students provides you with a lot of different bodies to practice on. (Don't abuse your students. Make it a positive learning experience for all.)

Again, try to make your students as good as possible with each particular movement. The better they are, the more challenging opponents they will be for you. It stretches your ability and forces you to get better.

If you belong to a martial-arts school that regularly has its students pair off, then make it a point to pick a different partner each time.

Don't always pick a smaller partner.

I was once at a martial-arts seminar also attended by an "amazonian" martial-arts group. Since I'm a fairly heavy male, I offered to work out with them, so they could get the feel of the techniques on someone who would be more likely to resemble an attacker.

All of them declined my offer.

They preferred to work among themselves. What kind of realism is achieved when a female weighing 105 lbs. attacks you?

I'm not a sexist. Really. I am a realist, and I'm sorry if I doubt that the average mugger will be a svelte female. They were deluding themselves.

Another opportunity for practice is when you *share* information with other martial artists.

This can be tricky.

There is a fine line between sharing a move that you haven't yet generalized and looking like an utter fool. So, you probably only want to try well-practiced moves on other martial artists, and be sure to emphasize that the purpose of the encounter is mutual instruction, not destruction.

You can make it more of a learning activity, if you preface the move with a statement like:

> *"I've got a new wrist lock that I'm learning. I don't have it down pat yet, but I do have the basics. If you'd like, I could show it to you. If you already know it, maybe you could help me perfect it. If not, maybe we could learn it together."*

So now you've got someone to work with; what's next? How do you start?

How to Generalize

When you generalize, analyze everything.

What differences do you notice between flexible and inflexible opponents? How about those who are so muscle bound that they can't touch their toes versus a weak bean pole? Can you feel the difference between a beginner and an expert?

> **Note:**
> In some styles, the "expert" is much easier to
> take than the novice; the experts have lost their
> creativity.
>
> They have become "technique-bound" to their
> style. Also, some experts don't resist the hold;
> they have learned to be good participants.
>
> These cooperative partners are great to have
> when you're just learning the move, but they're
> terrible for perfecting. You need someone to
> resist – someone who will lend some realism to
> your technique.

Have you started categorizing your opponents? Allow me to
introduce you to one of my favorites. Meet ...

The Resister

The resisters know enough to apply pressure or force in the opposite direction to the way you're directing their bodies (photos
7-1a, b).

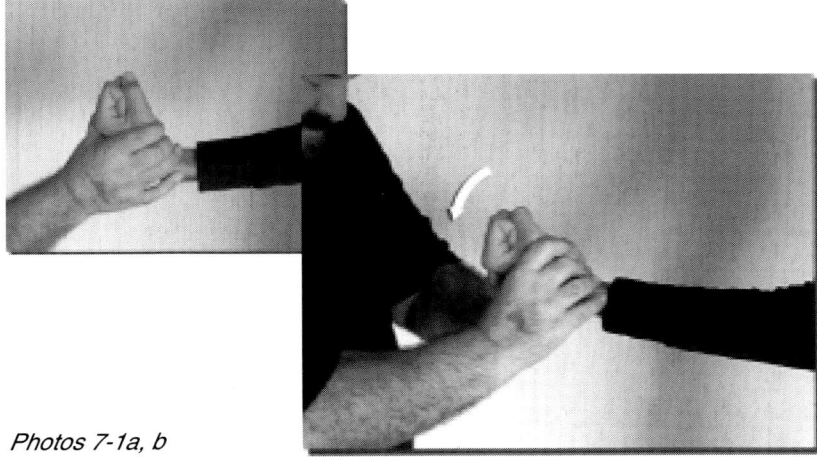

Photos 7-1a, b

They think that they're better than they actually are. Resisters tense a lot .

They'll try to out-muscle you every time .

So what do you do?

There are several different tactics:

If you're not committed to continuing with a wrist lock, you could always hit 'em!

You heard correctly.

If your opponent tenses up enough, think of the tense limb (probably the arm) as a solid column. Go around it and hit.

Hey, you may even end up loosening up your opponent enough to try the lock again.

A second tactic is to start to apply force in the opposite direction from where you really want to go; it's sort of like reverse psychology.

You start to move one way; he resists by going the opposite direction; you continue in his reversed direction, because that's the direction that you wanted to go in the first place. Sneaky, huh!

> If you're still confused refer to the Two-Hand Grab on pages 57-60. The tip on page 59 is an example of the technique.

You could also start to apply one lock on your opponent, and then flow into a completely different lock.

Going from one wrist lock to another is very effective and potentially more useful than just faking with an opposite-direction motion.

With the fake, you initiate the first move. When you allow the resistance to help you flow from one lock to the next, you are responding to a change in your plan.

See the difference?

Since you'll flow from one lock to another, all of your pattern practice will come into play.

Get started with this example:

Let's say that in your practice session (or a real altercation), you are in the middle of effecting an arm bar. You grab the wrist, straighten out the arm, and apply pressure with your right wrist to the edge of the triceps (photo 7-2a).

Photo 7-2a

~But~

Your opponent resists, by pulling away and bending his (or her) arm.

You already know that you could hit or kick and then try the same lock again.

Instead, let your opponent's resistance do the work for you.

Think back to your pattern practice. Which locks blend from or to the arm bar?

In the case of this example, your opponent's insistence on bending the locked arm is perfect for locks that ... require a bent arm.

The *Double-Ninety* Lock comes to mind (photos 7-2b-d).

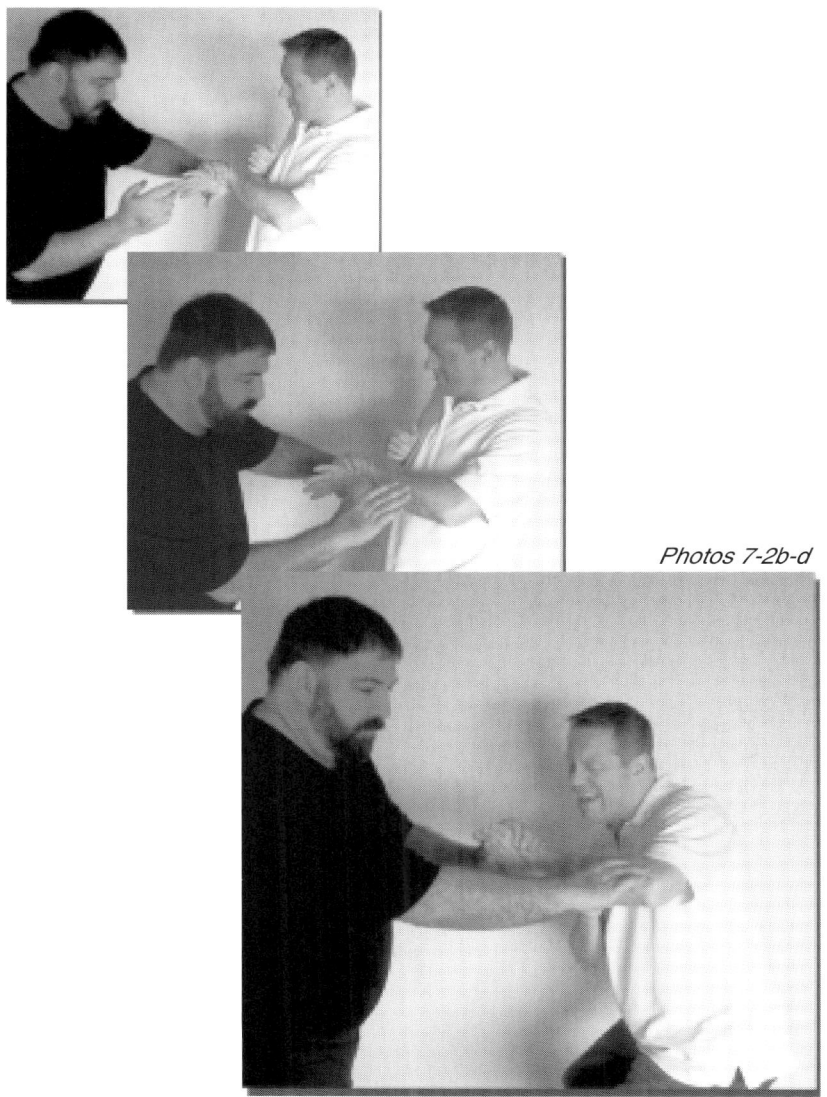

Photos 7-2b-d

You could even put the lock on your opponent's other hand.

Of course, this depends on where your opponent's hand is when you grab the initial hand.

Still, imagine the surprise when your opponent resists a lock to the right hand, only to find that you've just finished executing a different lock on the left hand (photos 7-3a-e).

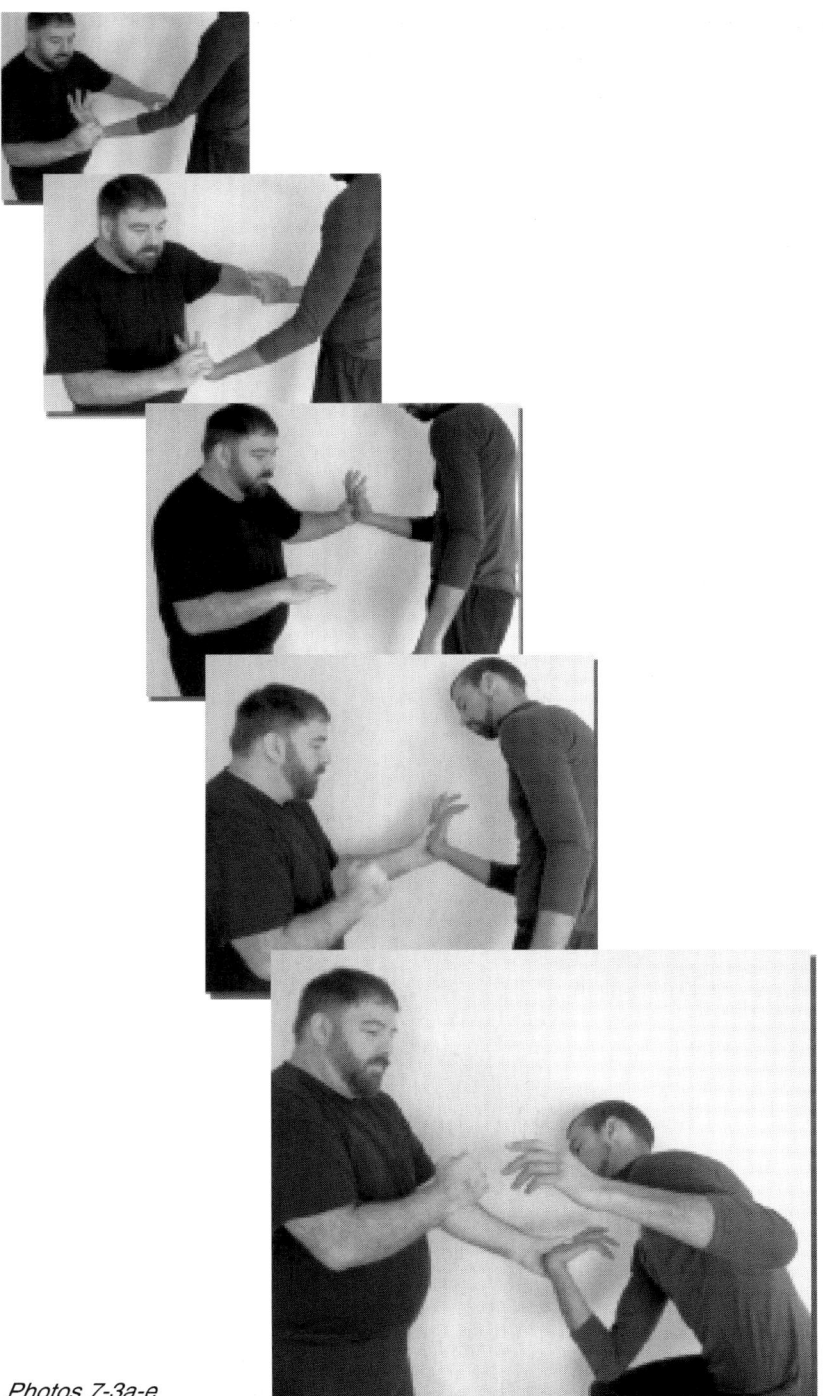

Photos 7-3a-e

A slightly riskier, but very satisfying alternative would be to overpower his resistance. It's not as tricky as it sounds, but it does take practice.

There are several ways to overpower a resister. To get you started and to really understand what I'm talking about, learn the Fist Circle Control. (Thanks to Simon Turner for helping me learn to resist resisters over a decade ago.)

You grab your opponent's hand for the Basic Lock. As you bend your opponent's wrist, you feel resistance (photo 7-4a). No matter how hard you try, the wrist straightens. If your opponent's hand was open before, now it's in a tight fist.

Logic would tell you to employ your other hand. Since you have decided to stick with this lock, grab with your other hand. Both of your thumbs should be on the back of your opponent's hand (photo 7-4b).

Now, try to bend your opponent's fist in and down, on a very tight circle (7-4c). Believe it or not, it is possible overpower the wrist. Experiment.

Photos 7-4a-c

Practice, until the Resister becomes your friend. This can become a great game.

At times, I have had resisters smile at me with overconfidence, as they resist my lock. Since I've already identified this person as a resister, I grin back at him as I make my lock work, or flow into an even better lock.

His smile turns into a look of amazement.   Boy, do I have fun!

Let's finish our "general" discussion on generalizing....

Generalize Your Way to Confidence

Generalizing also means learning contingencies.

You really want to be able to make a lock work on almost anybody, but if it doesn't, it shouldn't faze you.

Just flow into a different lock or hold that is equally as effective, or maybe you'll loosen up your opponent (our friend the Resister) with a punch or three, and then you'll try for a lock.

Work at generalizing.

The ability to generalize helps build confidence. You can lock almost anyone at will. On those few occasions where your lock doesn't work, you won't give it a second thought. You know exactly what to do instead.

If you really learn this aspect of wrist locking, you should know whether a certain lock is going to work on an opponent, even before you put it on.

This is not fantasy.

As long as you have had some prior contact with your opponent, you should know enough about his "type" to make your best locks work.

Remember

Generalizing is great for perfecting one particular move so that it works on the majority of people out there.

It is also a great way to categorize people, so you know how to change your technique according to your opponent's flexibility, speed, strength, or balance. This is definitely something that you want to perfect. Take my word for it.

Continue analyzing. Learn to recognize almost every body type. Keep at it until you really feel that "there's no one new under the sun." When everyone feels "familiar" to you, even when you've never worked with this person before, then you're "getting it."

> The few times you do encounter a new feeling, which won't happen very often, you will have enough experience and techniques under your belt, that they won't cause problems.

Depending on your level of experience, you might not respond with the best move possible, but it will be acceptable.

Then after the encounter, you hope that using this person and the new energy as your practice partner for an hour or two, will help you to start to get a feel for this new type of opponent.

You want to be able to further define your new category the next time you encounter the same feeling.

This is a path to becoming an expert.

Practice and always generalize. Remember, no surprises (I mean from your opponent to you; not the other way around).

8
Always React with the Best Lock Possible

If you take my advice and go beyond this book, which you're going to have to do to become a true expert, you will end up with a storehouse of locks.

Lots of novices ask me for advice on how to know which lock to do when. What if one reacts with the *wrong* lock?

This chapter contains advice on making sure that you don't make the wrong choice, when the time comes. Prepare a lot in advance, so that you can rely heavily on reaction and use a minimum of thought.

There are variables to consider when trying to determine the best possible response in any given situation. Each situation will be different, even though some of the responses will be the same.

It's important for *you* to go through this process of discovery. You have to teach yourself both *how* and *why* to respond to a particular attack.

So, let's deal with those variables and start asking ourselves some questions. The answers should shape your response.

Do you have a choice?

Your first question might be as simple as *do you have a choice?* Given your opponent's stimulus, or specific attack, do you even have a choice of techniques with which to respond?

If your opponent grabs across your body, say, right hand to right wrist, do you know more than one lock from that situation?

If you don't, then your choice of the best lock is easy. It's the one you know. It may sound facetious, but if you only know one response, it really does make the decision-making process rather simple.

Hey, either be happy with your one response that you do know, or take steps now to learn alternate techniques. (As a martial artist, shouldn't you always try to improve?)

If there are two possibilities

If you know exactly two responses, then you have to ask yourself which is better.

Questions to help you decide which move is more effective for the given situation:

- Which move is the quickest and most efficient?

- Does either move leave you a free hand with which to attack or exert even more control over your opponent?

- Can you apply a move and stay out of range of his other *weapons* (other fist, kicks from either leg, head butt, etc.).

- Are you personally much better at one of the moves?

- What follow-up responses are there for each move?

- What is your goal? (Not in life!) What outcome do you want at the end of this particular martial sequence?

• Do you want to end by controlling your opponent in a secure hold?

• Are you just trying to control your opponent enough to facilitate a more violent attack (hitting, kicking, and elbow strikes, to name a few)?

OK. Now, you've taken everything into consideration.

You're decisive. You've picked a move. Do you want to practice this one move in response to a specific attack?

You'd get great at it. And you've already decided it's the best.

I suggest that you continue to brush up on your other possibility. Don't completely remove it from your bag of techniques. You want an alternative. Besides, sometimes you just need to go in a different direction.

If you know more than two

If you happen to be fortunate enough to be able to call on three or more techniques, then you've got a slightly more complicated process to go through.

There are two ways that I suggest you consider.

The first method is a quick-and-dirty approach to choosing the best possibility. The second method is more lengthy, and whereas the first process can be executed either with pencil and paper or in your head, the second method definitely requires pencil and paper

Compare-and-Continue Decision Making

In the first method, you pick a technique, and keeping all of your previously asked pertinent questions in mind, you compare this move to any other possible technique for the specific situation.

After a little consideration, you judge one of these moves to be better.

One of the two moves will have "more going for it" than the other. It may leave you in a better tactical position. Or you may be able to execute the move a lot more efficiently. One move may leave you out of range of your opponent's *weapons*.

For whatever reason, one move comes out on top. So be it.

This is now your current best move for your hypothetical situation. Take this move and compare it to another of your possibilities. Ask all of the same questions of both moves.

Again, one move will come out on top. (If both ever come up equal, you either need to add more criteria to your decision-making process, or consider both as possibilities.) Whether it's the first move or the new move, you now have a *current best*.

You continue this process on down the line of your possibilities, until you've compared the current best to all remaining moves. The one that survives to the end is your best choice.

Do the process again with all of the remaining techniques, and you get your second-best choice.

Criteria Comparisons

The second decision-making technique requires pencil and paper.

List all of your possible techniques vertically, along the left side of the paper. Then list all of the criteria across the top (figure 8-1a, below).

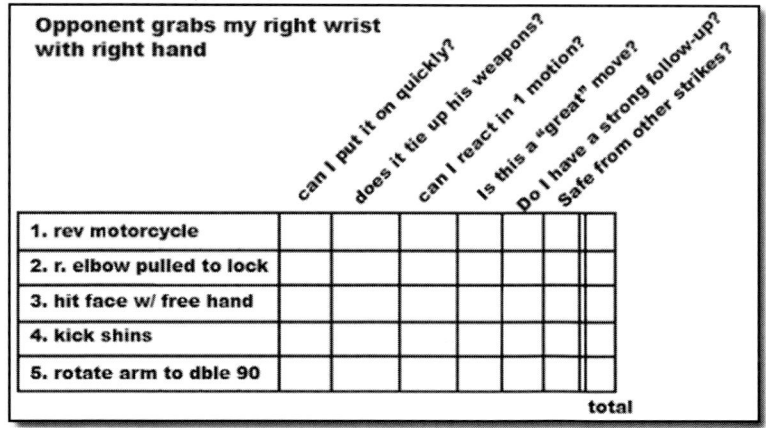

Assign a point value to each question.

For example, each question could be worth five points. You'll need to phrase each criterion so that a positive answer equals more points ("Can I accomplish the move quickly?" instead of "Does the move take too long?").

If one criterion is of paramount importance, you could make it worth more than five points. If it's twice as important, make it worth ten points; you decide its value.

All you have to do is ask each criterion question of each move; total the points on the right-hand side. The move with the most points wins. See Figure 8-1b, below.

Opponent grabs my right wrist with right hand	can I put it on quickly?	does it tie up his weapons?	can I react in 1 motion?	Is this a "great" move?	Do I have a strong follow-up?	Safe from other strikes?	total
1. rev motorcycle	5	3	3	5	3	5	24
2. r. elbow pulled to lock	1	4	2	4	1	1	13
3. hit face w/ free hand	5	1	5	5	3	5	24
4. kick shins	5	1	5	5	5	4	25
5. rotate arm to dble 90	1	3	2	1	2	3	12

In this case, given the moves that *I* do, my strongest choice would be *kicking the shins*. It only wins by one point; so *revving the motorcycle* or *hitting the face* are also good choices. Numbers two and five are definitely out – for now.

Caution

Don't become too predictable. If you go through this process with as many possible situations as you can come up with, and you choose your best choice for each possibility, you could be limiting yourself.

Only one solution to a given situation could leave you in a bind. Have many practiced ways out. Just because you're refining your system by pre-thinking possible outcomes, don't *only* rely on your "bests."

Oops!

If you happen to execute a technique, and it puts you in a worse situation, what do you do?

The easiest response is to hit or kick. I say easiest, because with an attack, you are countering immediately with an offensive response.

You don't wait by defending first.

There are worse responses than countering with an attack.

Other than immediately kicking or hitting, even before you assess the situation, you could "flow." Review Chapter 6.

When you find yourself in a less-than-desirable situation, is there another, safer move that you could flow to immediately?

Sometimes, the change of pressure to your new technique is confusing enough that your partner can't respond before you lock onto this secondary technique.

Remember, all of this analysis happens in the laboratory, so to speak, long before you'll ever actually have to react. You examine the technique now, and then practice it over and over correctly, in response to as many different variations as possible.

Then when the time comes, if it ever does, you'll respond with the given technique that you have practiced thousands of times.

It's a good feeling.

You analyze and practice as many different responses to as many different attacks as possible. You eliminate what is weak, keep what is strong. You emphasize the more-direct movements that leave you in a stronger, more controlling position.

This is how you go about the development of a system, or at least learning self-expression in the arts.

And what if you encounter an attack that is completely new to you?

You suddenly have to defend against something for which you haven't had thousands of practices.

If you have practiced a wide variety of techniques, then there will be *something* familiar about the attack. Maybe it's the way he's attacking. Maybe it's the position of his arms, or the way he's standing.

Anyway, a little assessment of the situation, combined with trust that your body will react correctly and even pick up on the familiarity in the technique, should take you a long way towards defending yourself. If you feel, I mean truly *feel* the technique that's either being executed on you, or that you're putting on someone else, you will learn to ad-lib.

Your impromptu responses will be as effective as your practiced techniques, because the former will be based on the latter. You will *feel* what needs to be done.

Now get out there and practice. Think about martial arts now, in case you don't have time to, later.

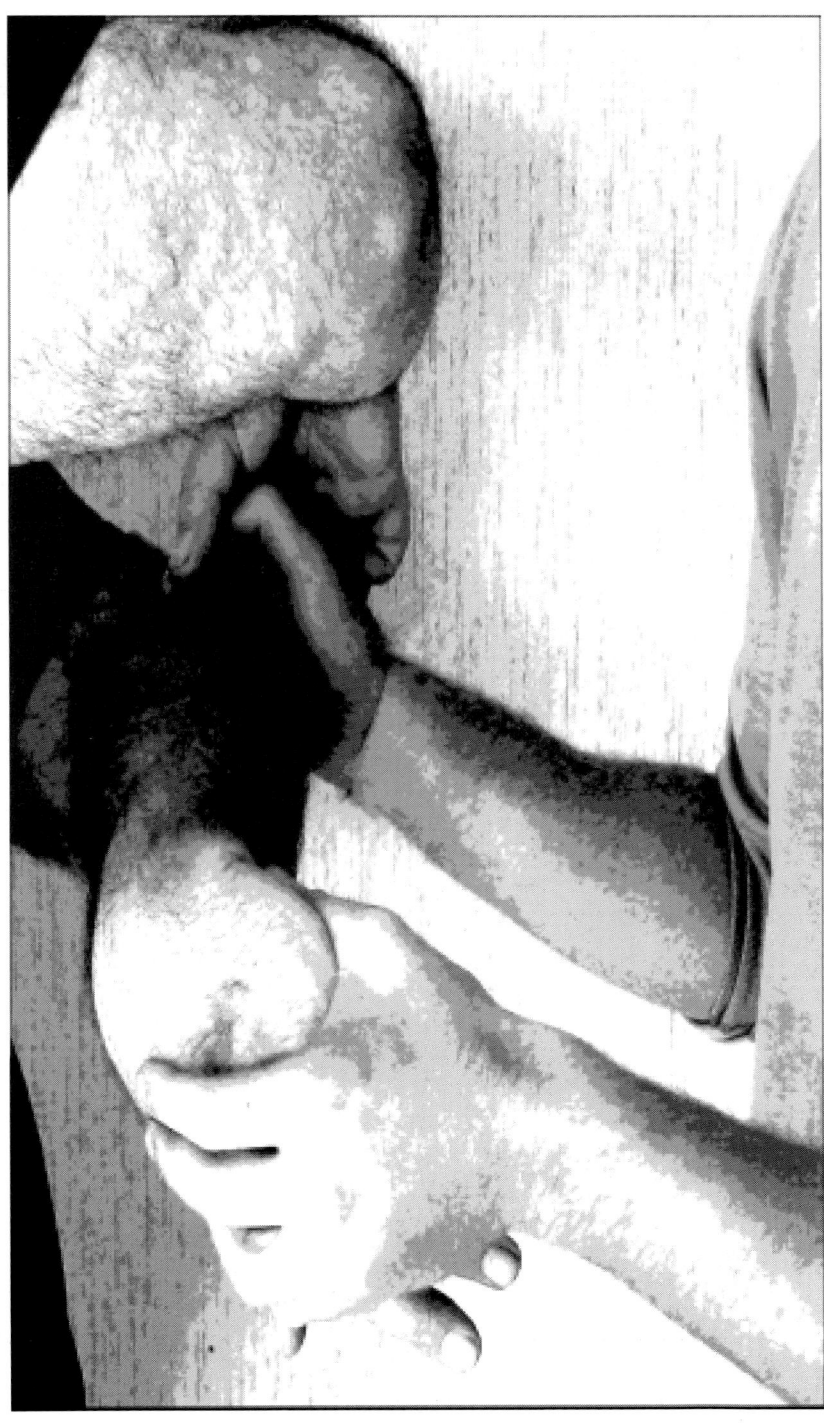

9
Mastering Counters
and Reversals

At the start of a **reversal**, an opponent has you in a lock. You execute a *maneuver,* so you end up with the **same lock**, or its mirror image, on your opponent.

A **counter** is like a reversal, except that you don't necessarily end up in the same lock.

Your maneuver, or series of techniques, releases you from your opponent's lock; you flow into an effective lock. For the purposes of this book, a *counter* will usually refer to ending up in a **different lock**.

A hit or a kick is definitely a counter, and in the real world I'd most assuredly use either or both.

Since this book deals with the realm of wrist locks, for our purposes, a counter will be a type of a lock – *most of the time.* (I do reserve the right to add some hits and kicks into the mix.)

A counter isn't necessarily better than a reversal. The desired result is the same. You start out trapped and end up trapping.

The only distinction I'd make between the two out in the real world is that your opponent might be better able to handle a reversal, because it's the same as the original move.

Your opponent already knows that exact move.

Teach Me to Fish

If you're not reading this book sequentially, would you at least make sure that you've read Chapter 3, "Feeling Where to Go," before you delve into this one? One reason you should is because it has counters and reversals for the standard arm bar. I have other reasons why you should read Chapter 3, but to figure those reasons out, you're going to have to bear with me through a small anecdote....

When I was a kid, my parents on special occasions (like a birthday) would ask me if I wanted this or that:

> "Keith, do you want a magician to perform at your birthday party?"

> *"No, thank you, I'd prefer to learn how to do magic myself."*

> "Keith, would you like this artist to do a portrait of you?"

> *"No, thank you, I want to take lessons and learn to draw."*

And so it went. (Yes, I have some skills that I have perfected over the years; I have mastered a few of them beyond the "Jack of all trades, master of none" syndrome.)

So what does all of this have to do with counters and reversals?

Stick with me just a bit longer. Or do you see where this is going?

Do you remember the old saying of **"Give me a fish, and I'll eat for today. Teach me to fish, and I'll eat for the rest of my life"**?

As a child, that phrase somehow stuck with me. I have always tried to learn to fish.

Finally – back to counters ...

Think of the chapter "Feeling Where to Go" as the *teach-me-to-fish* part.

Learn those principles, and you'll be able to flow out of locks that you've never felt before. You won't always rely on memorized techniques; you'll ad lib.

On the other hand, you have to be able to eat to survive, until you catch that first fish. Maybe the phrase should be *give me enough fish to survive, until I've learned to fish* .

The specific reversals contained in this chapter are your *fish*; they are your sustenance (and they may get you out of a bind or two). Still, don't rely only on them; you need to learn the art of *fishing* .

These moves are all workable.

I've given you a little more than half a dozen *fish*. They are all good counters or reversals. They aren't the only ones out there.

> Always keep searching for new, different, and better ways to counter. Once you've internalized the reversals in this chapter, you'll be inventing your own.
>
> Eventually, you'll know several counters for almost every lock that's put on you.

Those that you don't know won't be a problem either, because you will have thoroughly practiced how to feel where to go. You'll learn to go with the flow, or at least redirect it.

Let's flow right into the *meat* (or fish) of this chapter.

Reversing and Countering The Basic Lock

For complete details on effecting this lock, refer to pages 48-65.

Your opponent might have you in the Basic Lock, with thumb on the back of your hand (photos 9-1a, b).

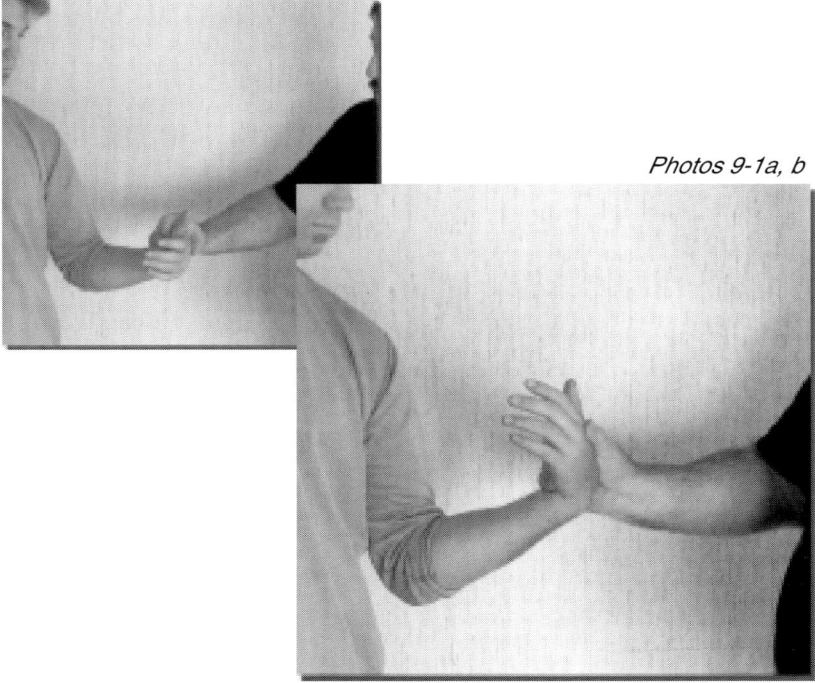

Photos 9-1a, b

It's also possible that your opponent has in you in a Basic Lock with a thumb control (photo 9-1c).

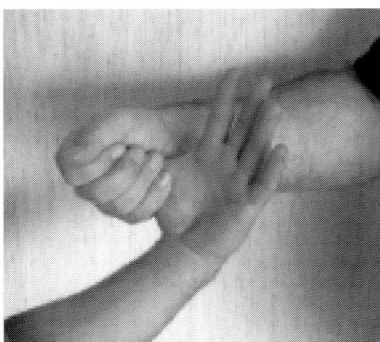

Photos 9-1c

There are lots of different counter and reversal variations, but *basically* (pardon the pun) you are trying to ease the pressure off the back of the hand, or off the thumb.

This release of pressure relieves the controlling pain felt at the wrist. I have several ways for you to release pressure, not the least of which is poking their eyes out. Oops! Did I write that?

The methods that I recommend for easing the pressure, other than punching and eye-poking, are to reach up and grab one of your opponent's hands and either apply the same pressure (another Basic Lock), or change it into a different lock (Double Ninety-Degree Lock).

Have your partner apply the Basic Lock either right hand to right hand or left to left (photo 9-2a).

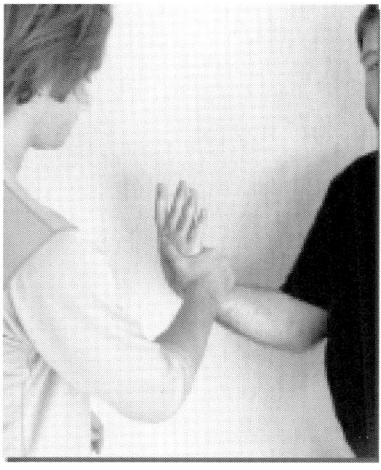

Photos 9-2a

Reach up with your free hand to the back of your opponent's hand (photos 9-2b, c, *below*).

 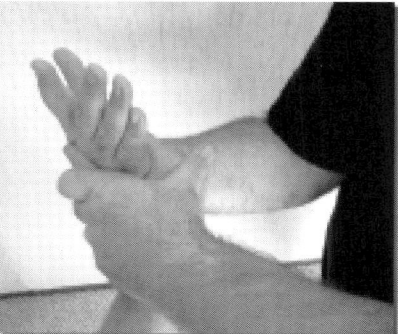

Now, peel off the wrist lock, by the fingers (photos 9-2d).

When you peel off your opponent's hand, make sure you pull with your thumb on the back of his (or her) hand, so you can apply your own Basic Lock. A true reversal (photo 9-2e).

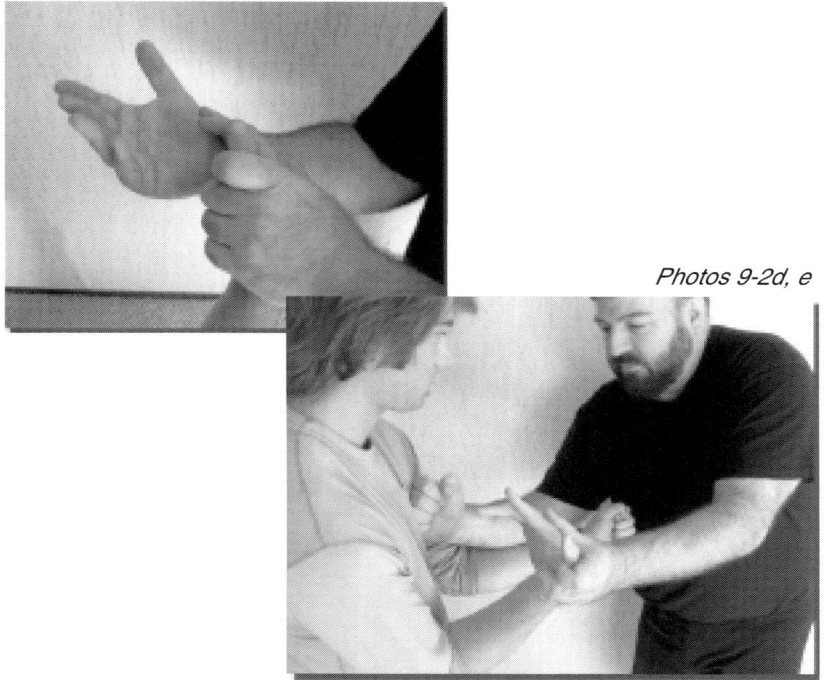

Photos 9-2d, e

If the pressure is being applied left to right or right to left (photo 9-3a), you're going to go into the *Double Ninety*.

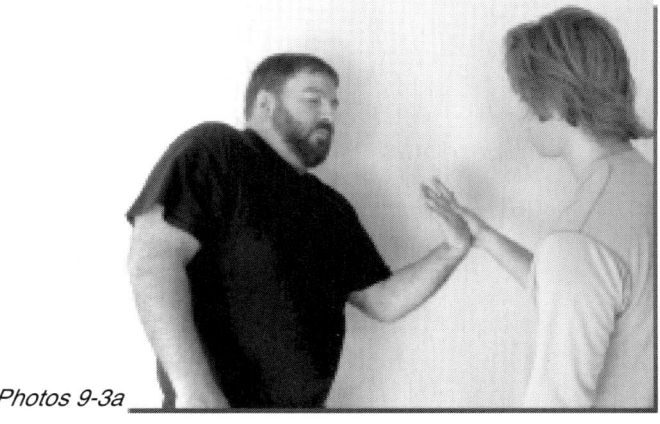

Photos 9-3a

Reach up over both your and your opponent's arms, and grab his hand as in Photos 9-3b-d.

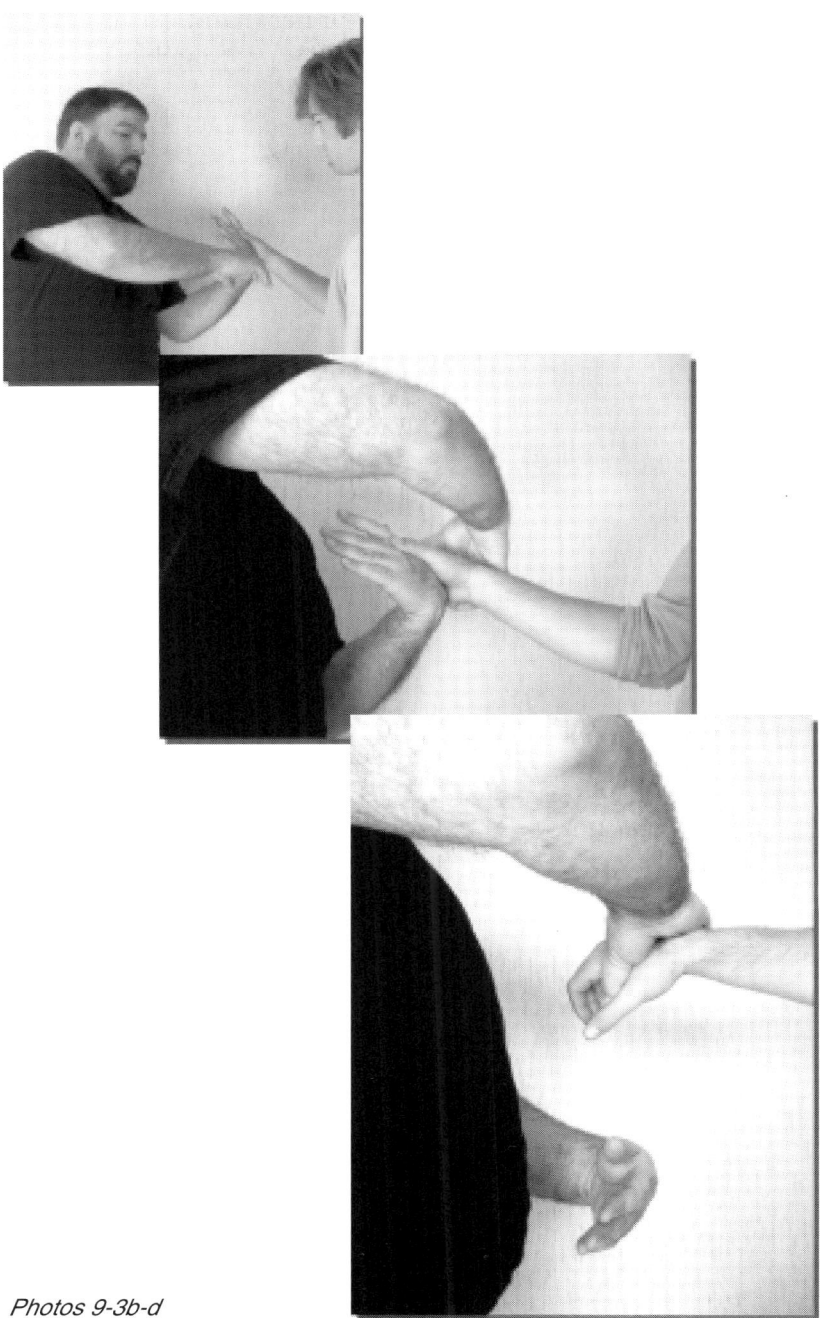

Photos 9-3b-d

Pull his wrist toward your body (photo 9-3e), and use your other hand to pull the elbow into the ninety-degree position (photo 9-3f).

From this point on, you just continue with the traditional *Double Ninety*.

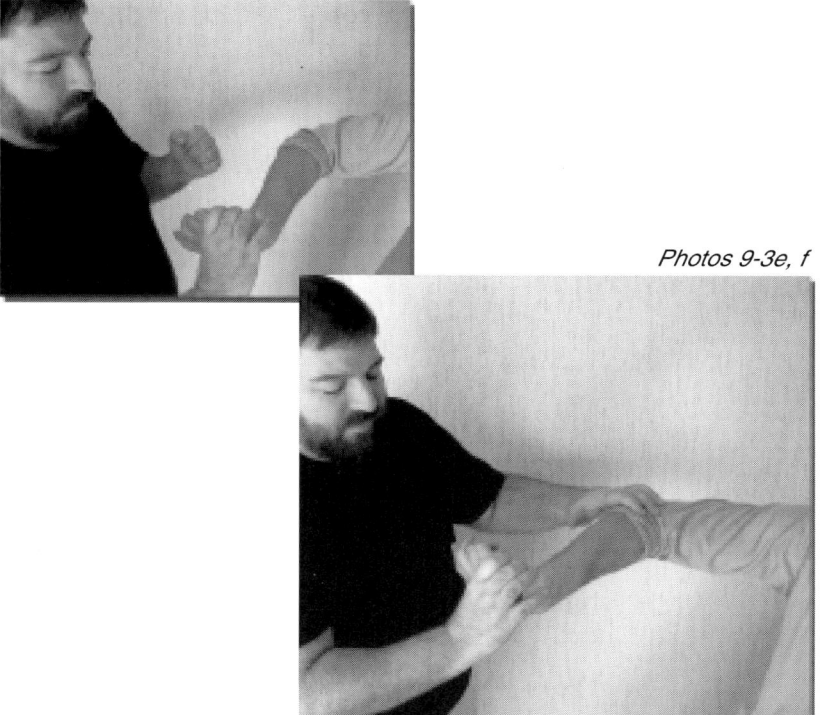

Photos 9-3e, f

What if both hands are effecting the Basic Lock on you? Which hand do you grab?

As to which hand to grab, you'll have to adapt to each situation. Which hand is applying pressure? Which hand can you get to most easily? By grabbing one hand, are you putting yourself in range of a weapon (fist or foot)?

Because of angle variations and differences in hand positions, my advice is to figure the shortest distance between your hand that is going to effect the reverse, and the opponent's hand that you're attacking.

It may or may not be the hand applying pressure. Try to grab the hand with your hand in the position in which you want it on the lock.

It's OK to rotate your opponent's hand and arm; you just don't want to do a lot of adjusting of your own hand positions.

After you rotate the hand into the correct position, you apply the lock as usual. You may want to go immediately into a follow-up, since this is the same hold your opponent started with.

Maybe the person opposite you won't recognize a follow-up from one of the patterns (Chapt. 6). Try positions #6 and #7 from the first pattern. By going into one or both of these positions, you're immediately taking your opponent into (hopefully) unfamiliar territory.

Let's move on to another reversal....

Double-Ninety-Degree Lock Reversal

You'll find the original description of this lock on pages 79-80. We end up in Photo 9-4a, which will be our starting point.

Photos 9-4a

Before we do the actual reversal, did you notice an obvious counter? If you didn't immediately see that you could do the reversal from the basic lock (although for this lock it becomes a counter, instead of a reversal), don't fret. You'll start to see more possibilities as you learn more moves; it takes practice.

Even if you didn't immediately pick out the counter, you can still turn this into an exercise of experimentation. (See Chapter 11 for more on inventing your own moves.)

Let's play around with this counter for a minute of two. Then we'll move on to the actual reversal.

The basic grab for the *counter* starts in Photo 9-4b. See if you can take it the rest of the way into The Basic Lock (photo 9-4c).

It shouldn't be too hard. Can you do it efficiently?

Take time to figure this one out; you never know when you're going to need to instantly release pressure from this lock.

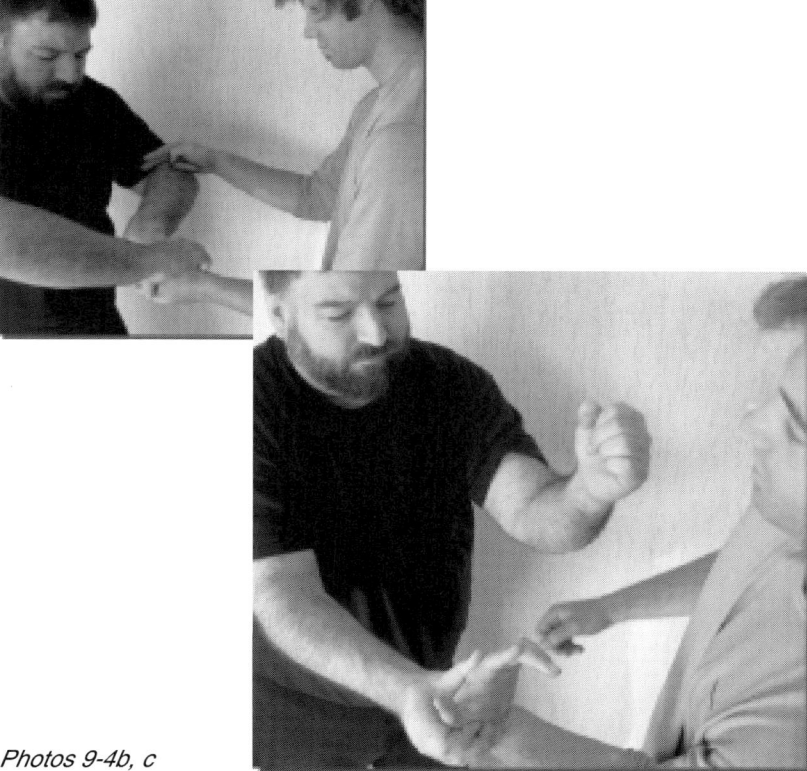

Photos 9-4b, c

Now, onto the real reversal. Starting again from Photo 9-4a, reach up with your free hand and grab the hand that is putting pressure on your elbow (photos 9-5a, b).

Grab this hand with your thumb down. Now just as you did with the counter of the last lock, you pull this hand toward your own body, bending his wrist to a ninety-degree angle (photo 9-5c).

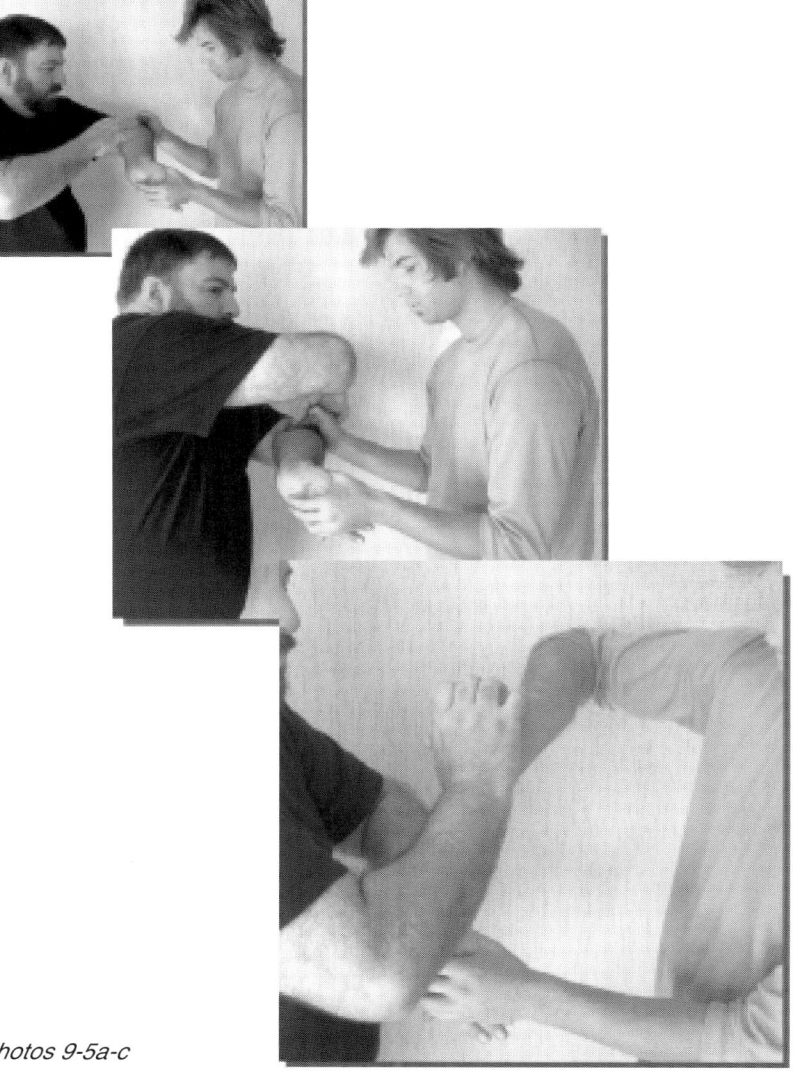

Photos 9-5a-c

As you find the correct angles for your *Double Ninety-Degree Lock*, twist up with the hand holding the wrist (photo 9-5d).

Use your other hand to pull his elbow to the other ninety-degree angle (photo 9-5e).

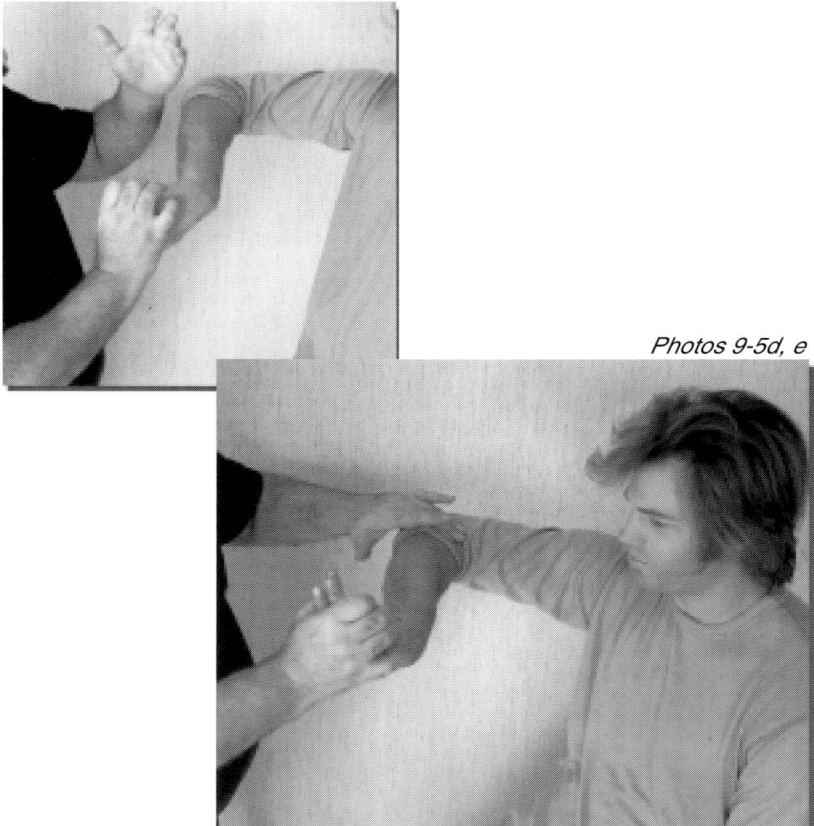

Photos 9-5d, e

If you need to review the original *Double Ninety*, refer to page 79. Don't sacrifice the lock to the reversal.

In other words, don't spend all your time perfecting the escape part of the reversal just to go into a crappy, unpracticed wrist lock.

Make sure you do justice to the *Double Ninety*.

Countering the Chicken Wing

Let me preface this reversal by saying that I don't usually counter this lock passively.

I take more of an attitude of offense. I'll begin with a passive response. Next we'll add just a *little* strike. Finally, I'll show you one of my typical responses to this lock, even though it is in no way, shape, or form *a lock*.

The Chicken Wing is Idea #3, in Chapter 6. The *point of no return* is very critical on this move. It comes early. When the move is being placed on you, your shoulder drops from the force of the lock, and it quickly becomes impossible to effect a counter (photo 9-6a).

Photos 9-6a

Reach your locked hand over toward your opponent's shoulder and pull the arm down. At the same time, you pull an *over-the-top* move with the locked arm (photo 9-6b).

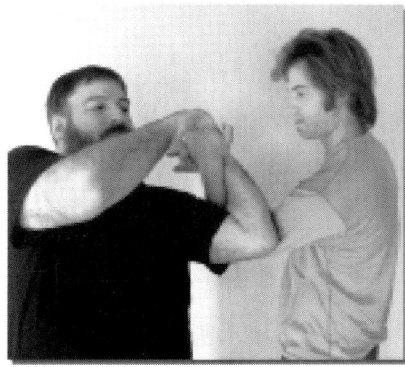

Photos 9-6b

Raise your elbow and go downward with your fist, as though you're arm-wrestling (photos 9-6c, d). Grabbing your own fist with your free hand definitely helps your possibly poor body position. Use the weight of both your arms to pull his shoulder down (photo 9-6e).

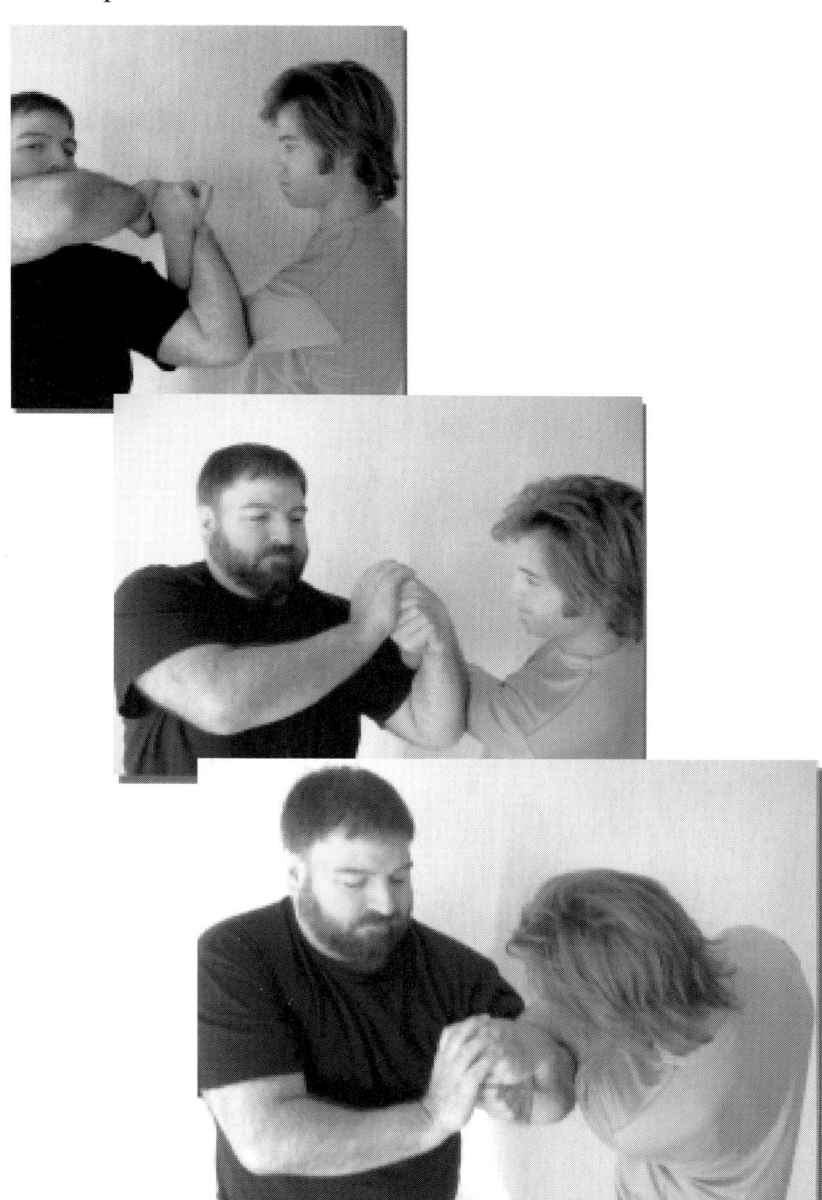

Photos 9-6c-e

Now, it's time to get a bit rougher. To be frank, I often think about hits to soften up my competition before applying an actual lock.

As you pull down for a reversal, slam your elbow between the shoulder and the shoulder blade. This forces your opponent down, which is exactly what you were trying to do with the lock in the first place.

A lot of times, I end up using some sort of strike to the shoulder to help me get out of the original pressure of the Wing.

Remember, I'll do whatever it takes to avoid getting pushed to the point of no return.

Be careful.

Now, that you've reversed (or at least started the motion), your opponent can grab his own fist, to help himself along. Just the way you grabbed your fist to help you pull downward, he can use his free hand to help pull upward.

If you're only interested in wrist locks, you could skip this next counter. It's a strike counter, rather than a lock.

I think you should give this move a try; always keep those *horizons broadening* .

I have several responses to a Wing. One of the better ones from my Twin Dragons days is a whip-strike to your opponent's head....

Note: My wife, Kate, gives a good demonstration of this whip strike in **The Punch eCourse**.

She shows how a small, petite woman can generate a lot of power. And she does this from a seated postion, while her attacker grabs from behind.

The instant you feel a Wing being applied, you bring your free hand up, as in Photos 9-7a abnd b. Whip your fist around your own head, allowing the punch to destroy anything in its path—namely, your opponent's head (photos 9-7c-e).

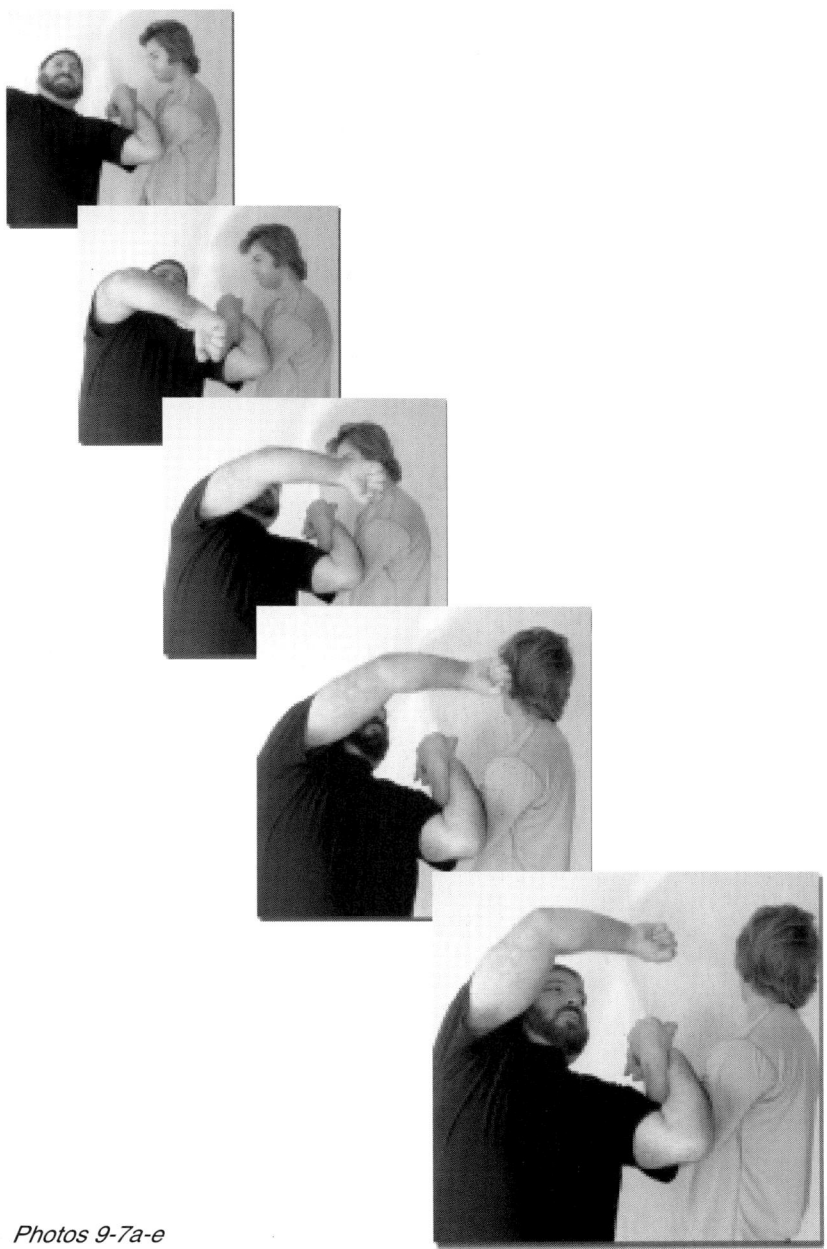

Photos 9-7a-e

Be ready with an immediate follow-up technique, as soon as you get any sort of release from your whip-strike.

The whip-strike is only the first move in your counterattack (photo 9-7f).

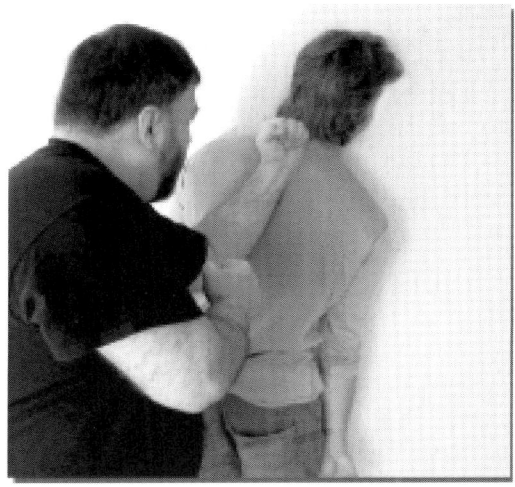

Photos 9-7f

Taking the *Lift* out of an Arm Lift

This is a variation on the arm bar.

In fact, it's the last response to the classic arm bar found at the end of "Feeling Where to Go" (Chapter 3). You are on your toes, as a result of your opponent's lifting his arm into yours (photo 9-8a).

Photos 9-8a

You need to get rid of the opponent's arm that's causing you pain. Push the arm down and away from you at your opponent's wrist. Grab the wrist or lower forearm, as you push the locking arm away (photos 9-8b-d).

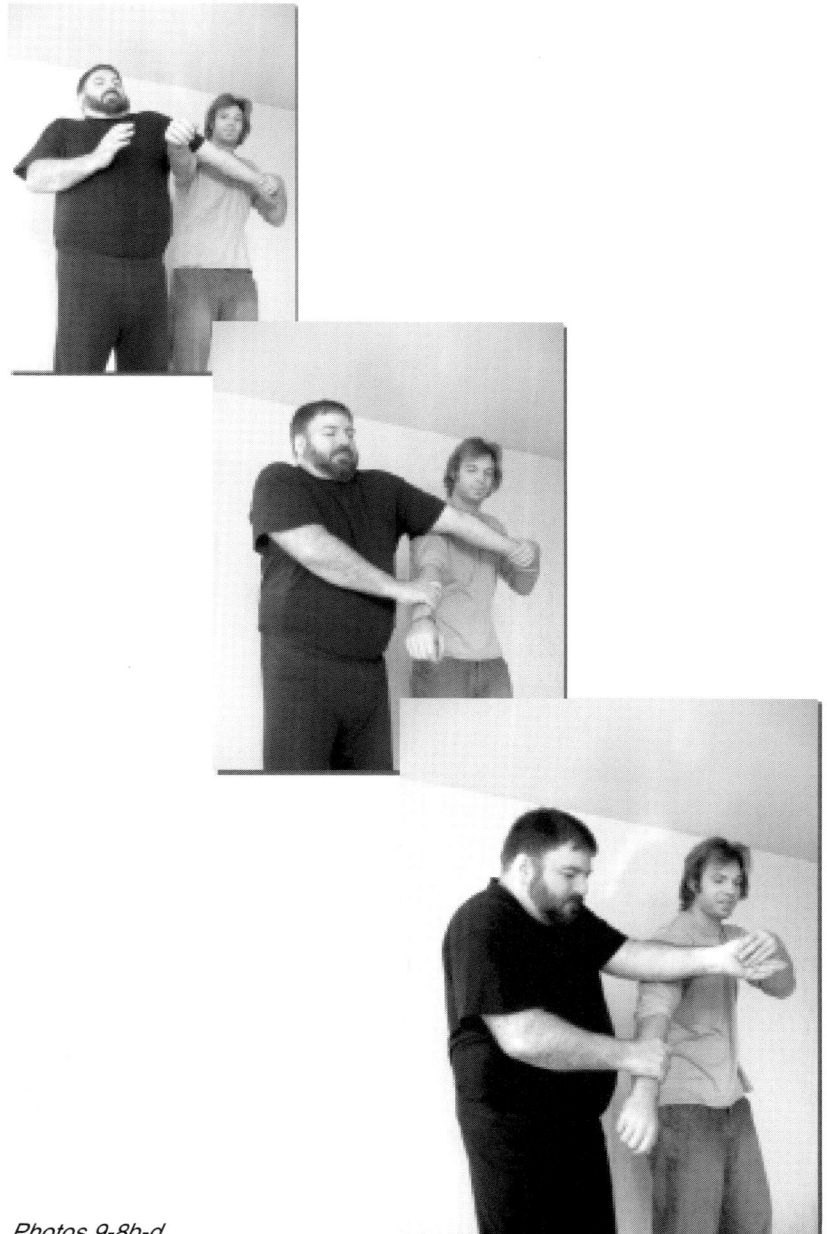

Photos 9-8b-d

Rotate your partner's wrist, palm up, so you can apply an arm bar as a counter (photos 9-8e-h). I couldn't resist a kick to the face at the end of the sequence.

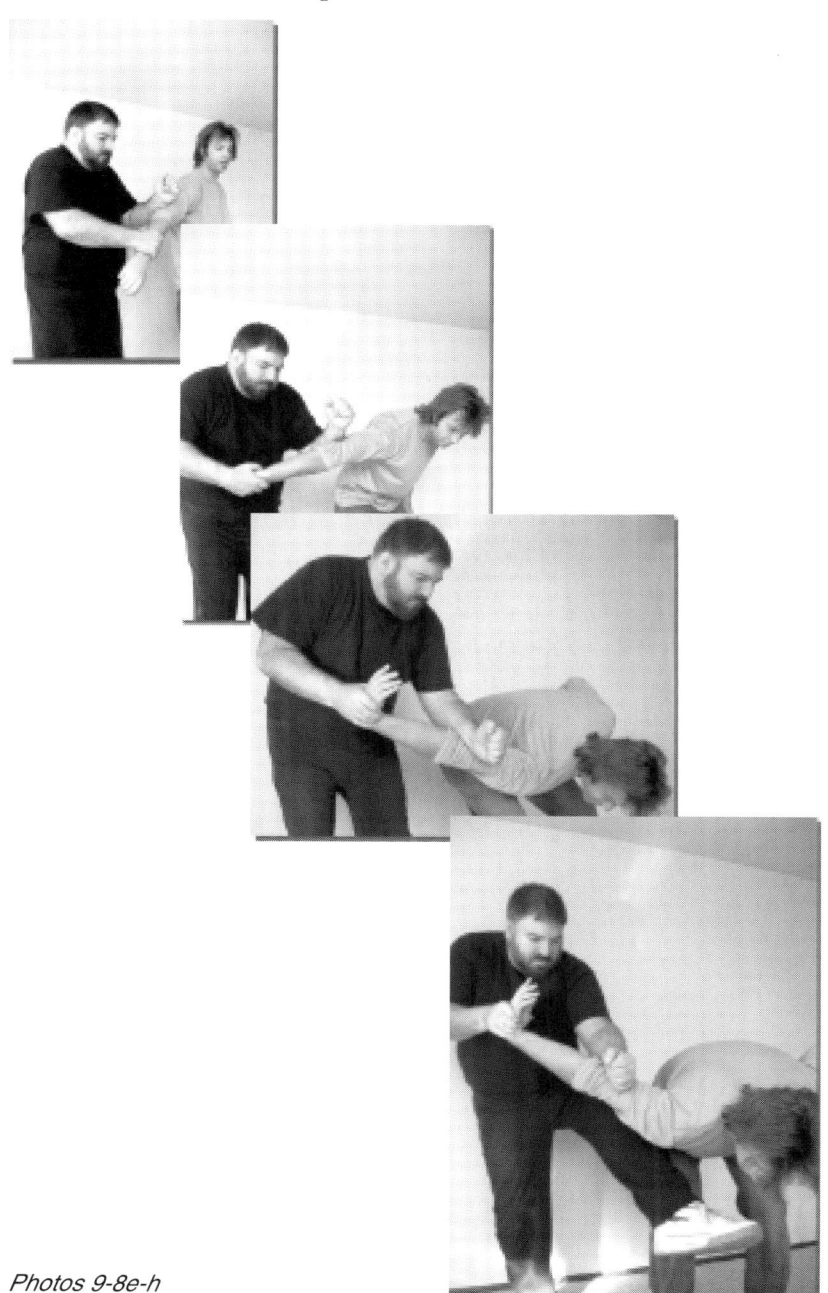

Photos 9-8e-h

Can You Get to a Reversal?:

Going into an arm bar, requires you to place your free hand on top of the opponent's arm, so that you can apply pressure downward from above on the triceps.

Can you figure out how to rotate your forearm downward, and the opponent's palm upward to go into a true reversal?

Reversing the Kickstart

Reversing the Kickstart (found on pages 56 and 59) is simplicity itself.

Since you started the position from an upside-down hand-shake, you and your opponent are basically mirror images of each other, except he has a "vertical-position advantage" (photo 9-9a).

You can easily remedy this situation.

Photos 9-9a

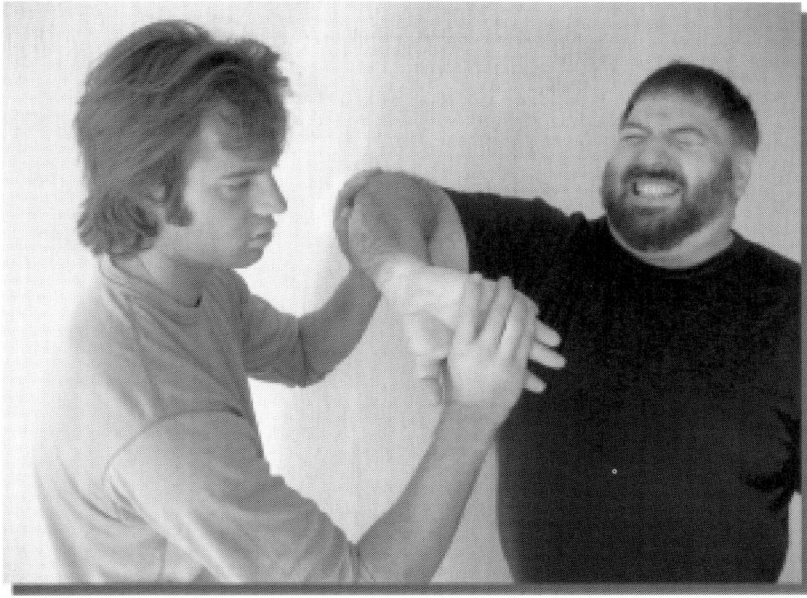

Start to bend your opponent's wrist (photo 9-9b). Start to lift your partner's elbow up (photo 9-9c), and drop yours down as you kickstart the little finger. Press down at the elbow for control, and ... follow with a solid punch, if the situation warrants (photos 9-9b-f). *Careful with your practice partner.*

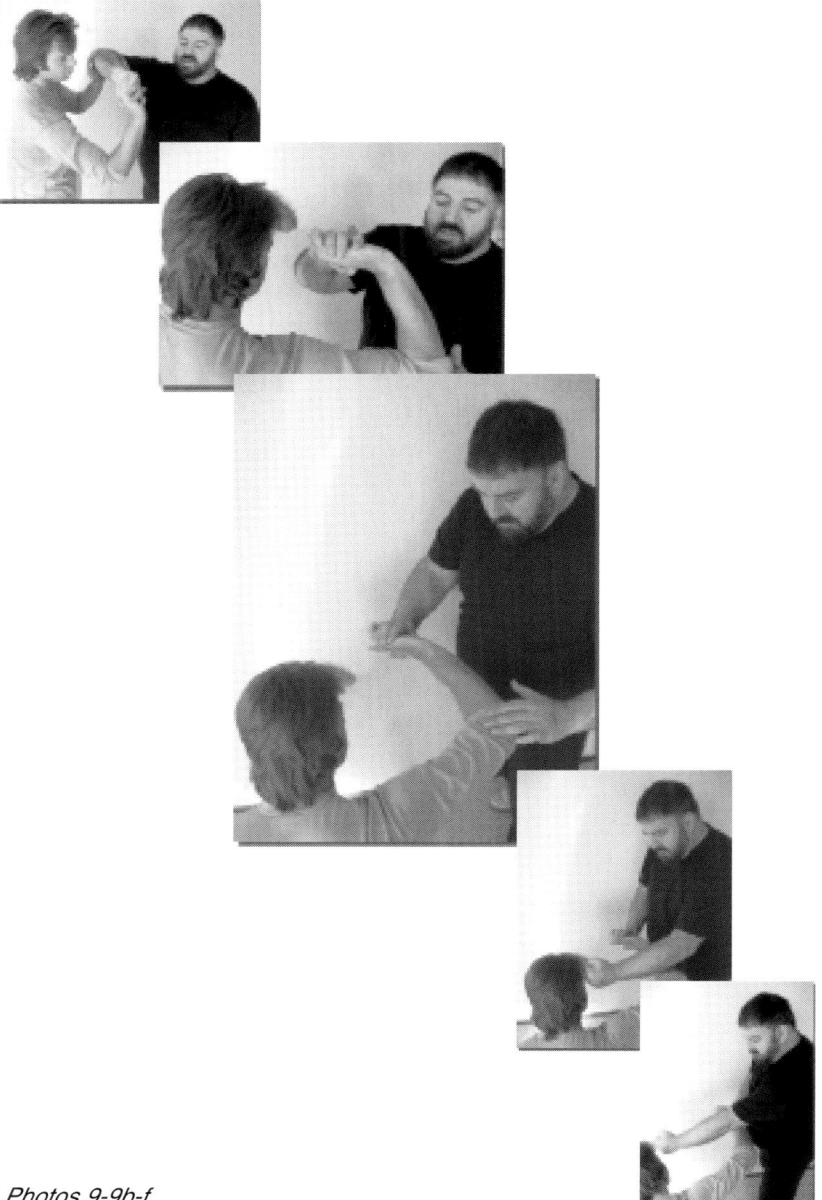

Photos 9-9b-f

Kickstart Problems

While shooting photos for this book, some of my students were having difficulties causing pain with a good pinky tweak (photo 9-10a). This problem occurred mostly during reversals.

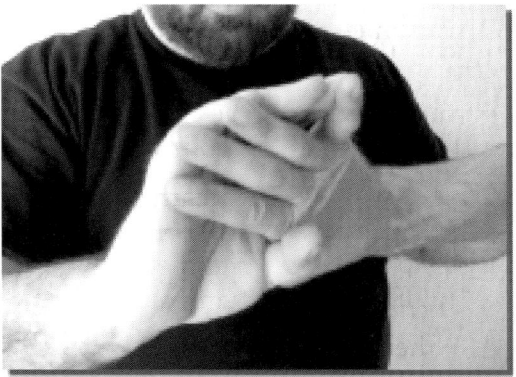

Photos 9-10a

Instead of pushing the opponent's little finger out with yours, roll your fingers over the top of the little finger. Then crush the little finger into the third finger (photos 9-10b-e), as you effect the rest of the lock.

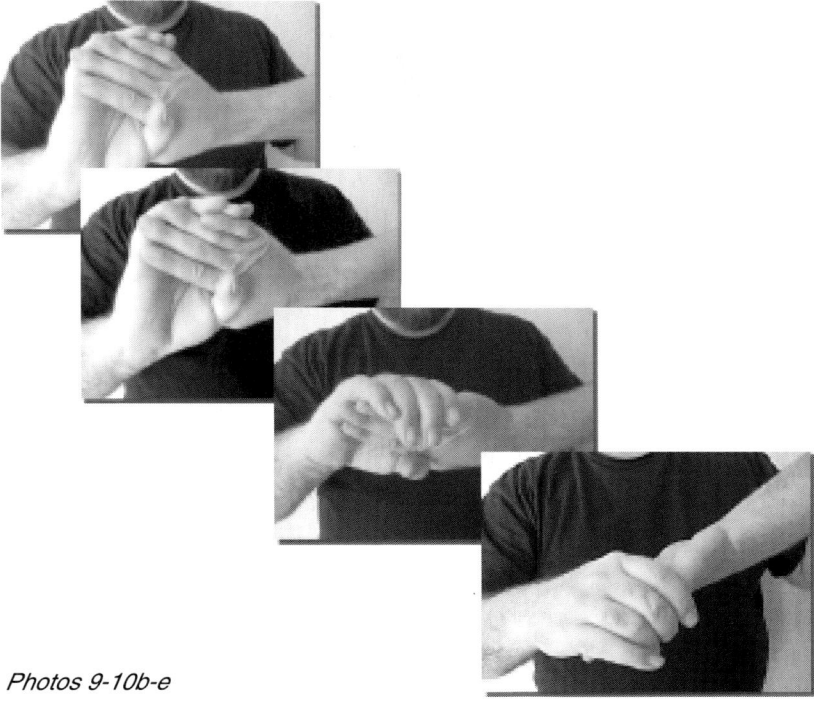

Photos 9-10b-e

The Rev Reversal

Revving the Motorcycle is the twelfth move of the "Dozen Super Techniques to Stimulate Thought" (page 95).

Obviously, to perform this reversal, or any of the others for that matter, you have to have someone who can perform the move on you.

You need to teach your partner how to rev the cycle. Make sure he can actually put painful pressure on your wrist.

I'm a firm believer that the best way to really learn something is to teach it (See Chapter 13). So, teach your partner well. After all, you want to be able to reverse it on someone who can execute the technique as well, if not better than you can.

Grab your partner's wrist, either right hand to right hand or left hand to left hand (photo 9-11a).

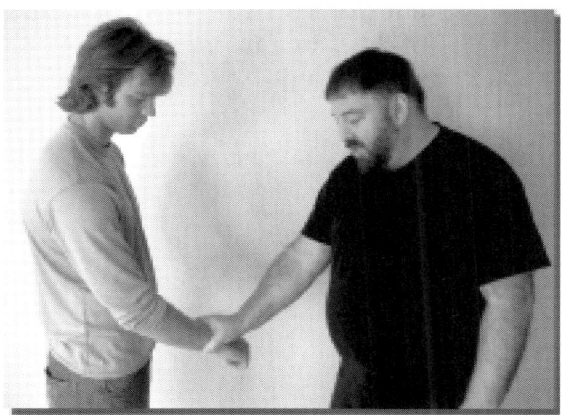

Photo 9-11a

Now, your partner puts the move on you.

First your partner clamps your fingers solidly to the wrist (photo 9-11b), then continues with the other hand, reaching up and and around to grab your wrist (9-11c-e).

Next, you feel the torque or the revving of the motorcycle (photo 9-11f).

And finally, your partner begins to lower your arm, parallel to the floor. A nice, clean Revving The Motorcycle (photo 9-11g).

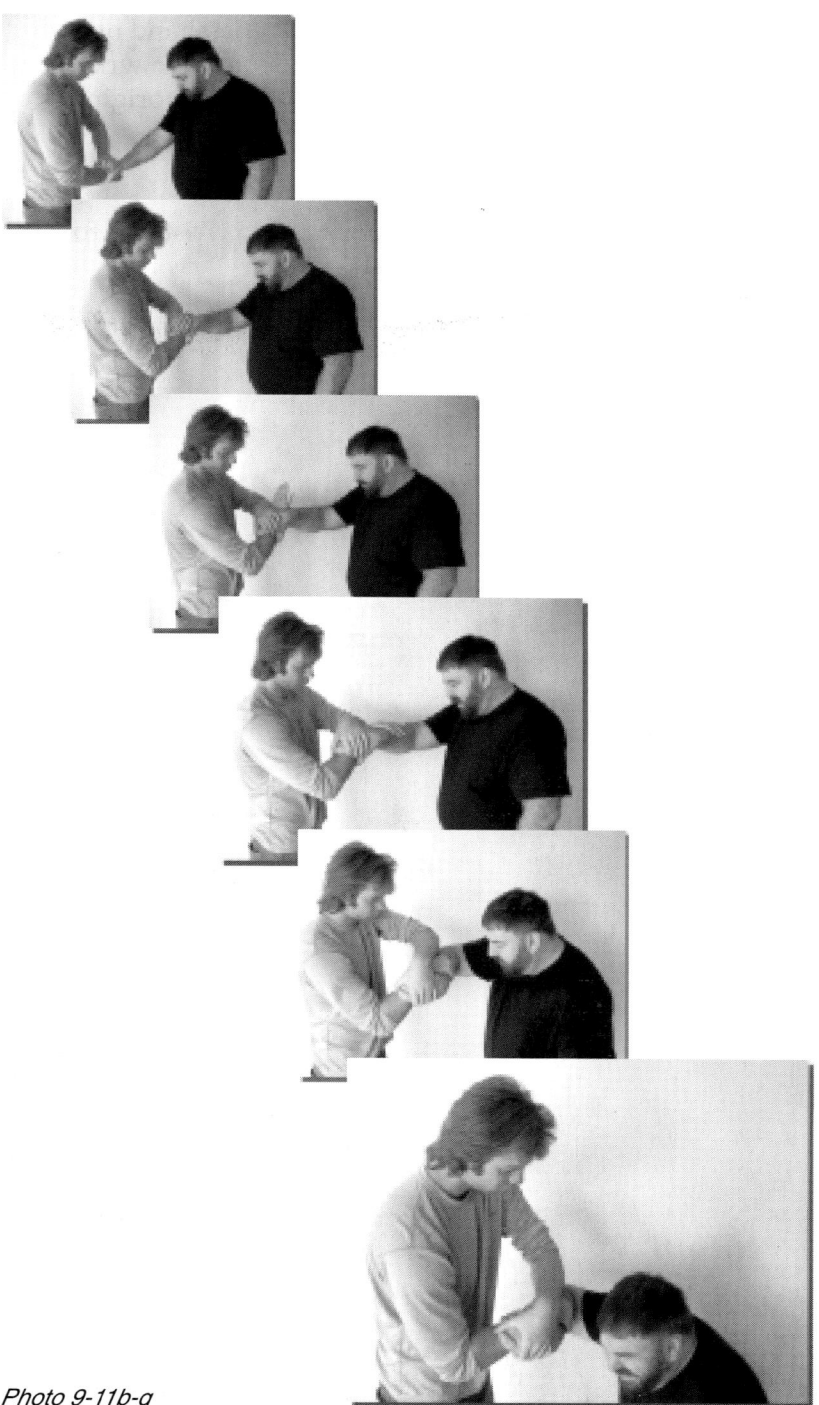

Photo 9-11b-g

Your response is that you first clamp your open hand onto your opponent's fingers, holding them to your own wrist (photo 9-11h). This is just like the beginning of the original move.

Next, you drop your elbow.

While still holding the fingers, you rotate the wrist and forearm, or *rev the cycle* as in Photo 9-11i).

Then lower your partner's arm to the floor as if performing the original move (photo 9-11j). And that's the reversal.

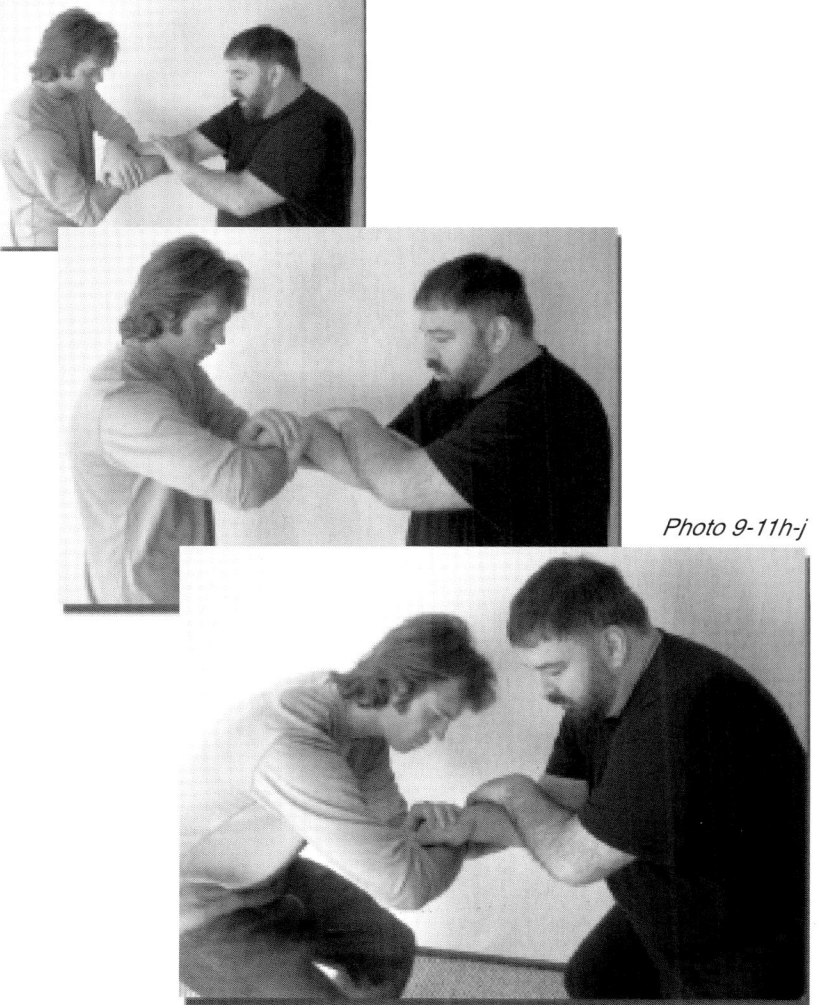

Photo 9-11h-j

You see that this quickly becomes a game of the person who gets his elbow the lowest wins (photo 9-11k). Good luck!

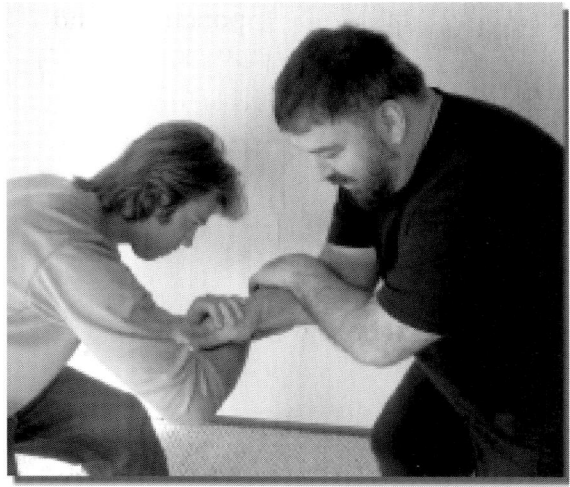

Photo 9-11k

Are You Comfortable With Reversals Yet?

Are you beginning to get a feeling of how to release pressure and then look for a graspable limb to apply your own lock?

Do you think you could take a random lock from anywhere and slowly work through a functional counter?

As usual, if you're feeling a little apprehensive about experimenting, you should practice Chapter 11 (Experimenting) and definitely Chapter 6 (Patterns).

There are a lot of benefits to be had from patterns (just remember Bruce Lee's constant reminders about getting stuck in the *classical mess*).

Spend a lot of time figuring out how to counter every move of any given pattern. You should be able to spot a pattern being executed on you at any point, reverse, and go into a pattern of your own, until your partner reverses it, applies his own, which you'll take. And so on, and so on. This is real flowing.

Of course, you also want to be able to shut this whole thing down instantly, on any given move.

You should be able to smoothly take your opponent beyond the point of no return, and lock him into an inescapable hold.

Playing with flowing for an exchange of ideas is fun, but if you mean business, you put these locks on with full force and speed – no playing around!

Becoming an Expert at Counters and Reversals

Getting to expert status in reversals is going to take a little work. Practice everything in this chapter. Look to other styles for *their* reversals and counters. Are they *doable*? Some are awful.

Do they even have any counters?

A lot of systems don't include wrist locks, let alone counters. Sometimes you put a lock on an opponent from a different style, and ... that's it.

Your opponent has no clue that a counter even exists.

Well, that won't be it for you. You won't be left clueless. Because of the research you will undertake in your quest for reversals, you'll instinctively know exactly what to do.

Of course, you'll be nice and teach reversals to your partners. It will help them, and it will continually force you to improve.

A Game We Play

A lot of times when my students and I are working out of my garage, I set limitations on our response choices. Sometimes I say feet only. Other times I might require them to defend themselves using a stick in their weaker hand. One game that we almost always play is to try to end any sequence with a wrist lock. That's right, you may hit and kick as many times as you want, as long as your last move restrains your opponent's motion.

On certain days, I add the following rule: All ending locks must be countered with a reversal or a counter. No exceptions.

This is a bit of a brain/body-teaser for my students. Sometimes they come up with clever responses. Other times ... let's just say ... back to the drawing board.

Hey, you can't win them all.

Another restriction that I sometimes place, is to have them play the game as though the first hits counted.

If you got "slammed" in your right arm in the first part of the sequence, then you are obligated to limit your use of that limb when trying to complete a counter to the wrist lock.

10

Using Pressure Points to Enhance Your Locks

This chapter won't make you an expert on pressure points, but it will give you some wonderful add-on moves. These are finesses that you need to reach your goal to be a wrist lock expert.

In this chapter, we're concerned only with pressure that will aid your locks. You'll learn some good principles that you can use alongside a variety of locks.

A bonus is that these are lesser-known moves. They are VERY effective.

Nose Control

Not all pressure points seem like those from the traditional spy movie where the arm is barely touched, and the victim cries out in pain.

Sometimes pressure against a protuberance (or the underside of a protuberance), such as a nose, can be a wonderful controlling technique.

Readers from many styles will be reading this book. I don't want to impose my style of fighting, just my wrist locks, on you.

Still, I'd like to give you an example of one way we might take a punch. If your style blocks first, then slow down the incoming hit any way that you'd like.

In this example, face your opponent with unmatched leads (right to left). As your opponent punches in, start to move your forward hand before anything else.

Respond with your punch. Ever-so-slightly after the punch starts, you take a small step to the outside, and also raise your rear hand into a check position (photos 10-1a-c).

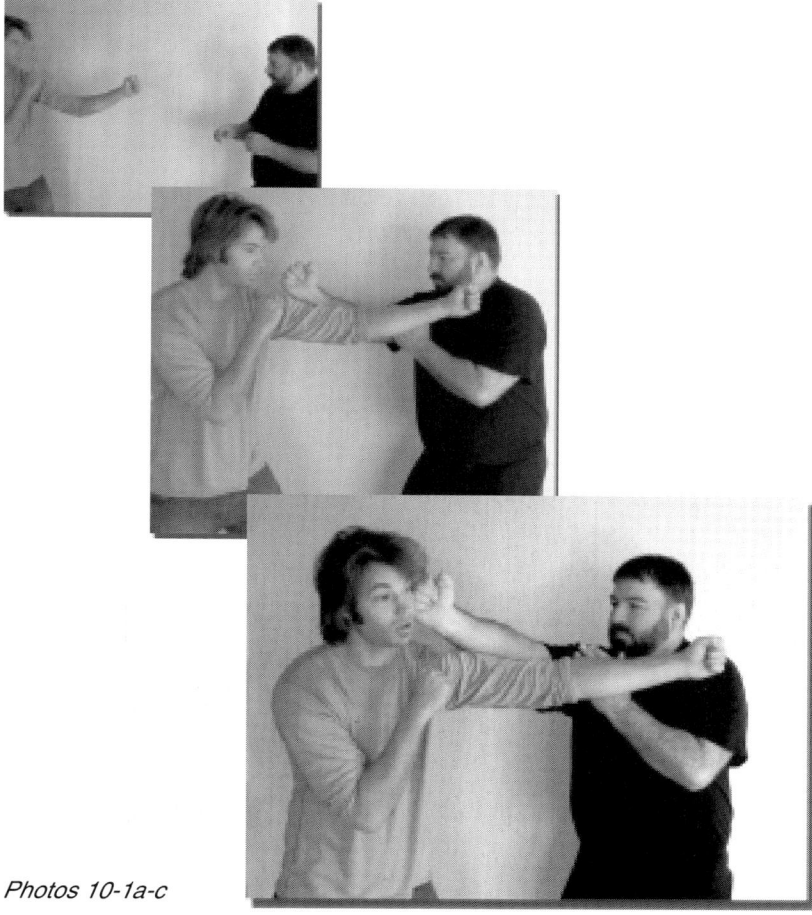

Photos 10-1a-c

Remember, if you have a different way of taking a punch, that's fine. Just make sure to end in a check position to the outside of your opponent.

At this point you have options: You could strike, you could apply a lock, or you could control him by his nose (or all three, if your style is eclectic).

Now, your check hand and your punching hand change roles. Your check hand starts to move toward your opponent's face, and at the same time, your punch hand drops to check the arm (photo 10-1d, e).

Moving the hand that's doing the hitting first, follows the philosophy of Bruce Lee. In my opinion, this is an immediate way to tell how faithful someone is being to the Bruce-Lee ideal. And it's an efficient way to respond, too.

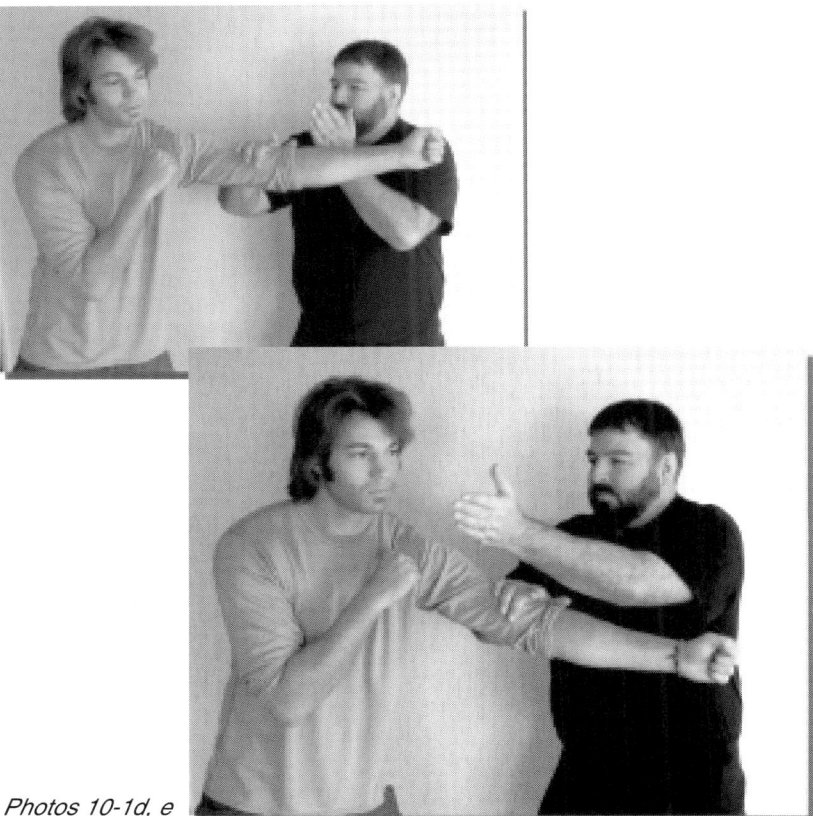

Photos 10-1d, e

Your forefinger makes contact with the underside of your opponent's nose.

Now, you are going to do two motions, one right after the other. First, straighten your arm, twisting your opponent's head to the side. Then in the middle of that motion, push against the underside of your opponent's nose, and direct your push down toward the floor (photos 10-1f-i).

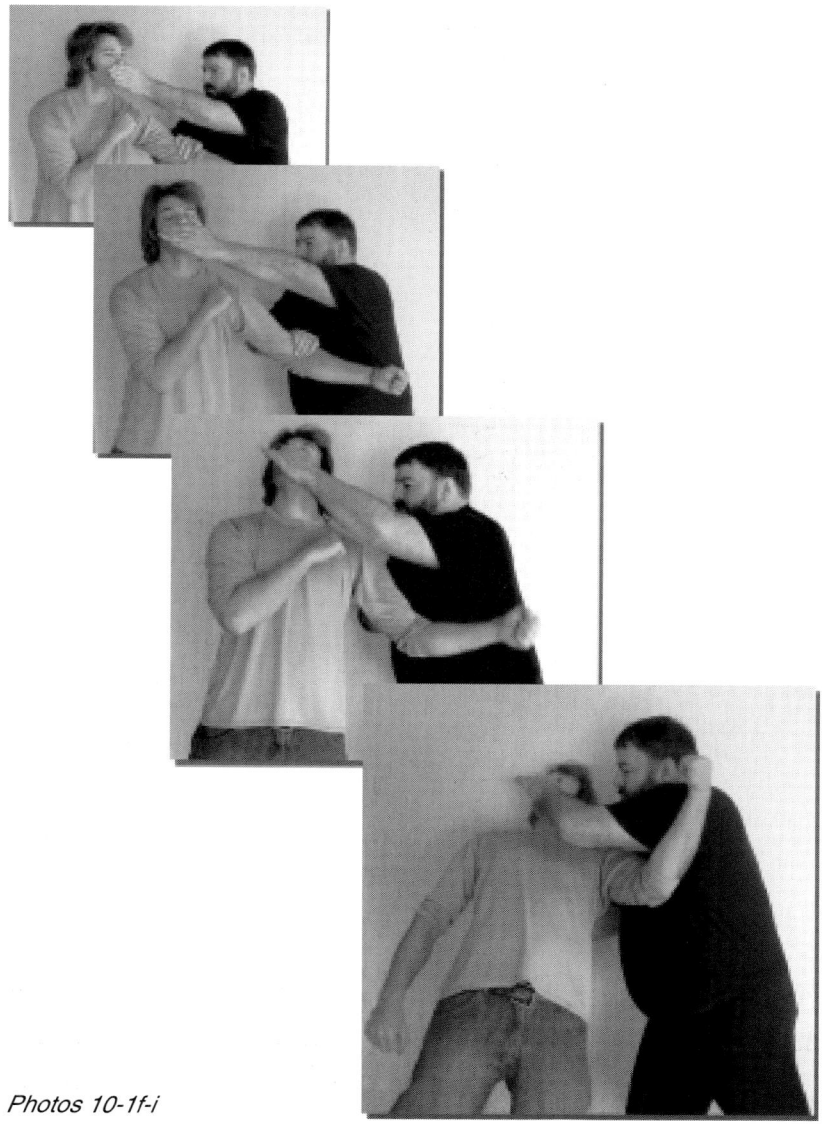

Photos 10-1f-i

Note: Be careful. This one drops your opponent quickly. In the photo, I catch and support my practice partner, with my free hand.

In real life, that hand would control the arm closest to me.

If you get the motion right, your opponent will drop quickly, unable to resist.

The perfect nose control turns the head to the side, and then pushes it down. You'll feel the point, where your partner can't resist. At that point, turn your pressure down toward the floor (photos 10-2a-c).

Photos 10-2a-c

Let me show you what your hand does to his head. So that you get a better idea, I'll take the head out of the picture.

In the first motion, you twist the head to the side. As your opponent's head whips around, you see the palm of your hand.

At about that time, the ability to resist should vanish. So, you rock the head back and straight down (photos 10-3a, b).

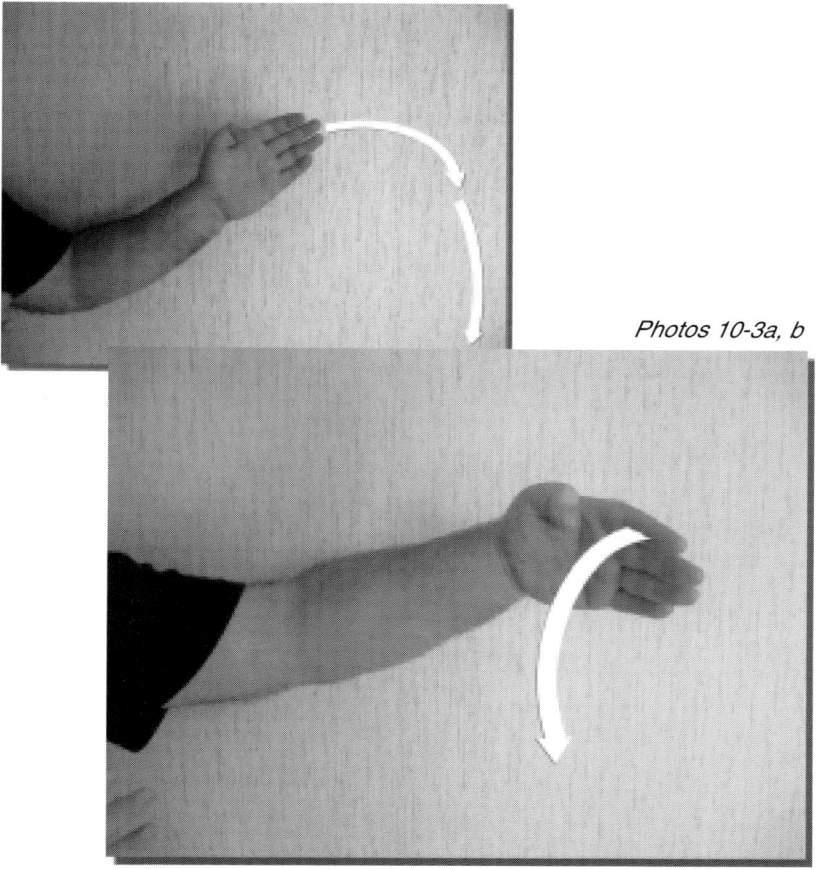

Photos 10-3a, b

You can use this move as a control by itself, or as a lead into another move, like an arm lock.

See what other moves you can get to from the position with your opponent's head bent back.

Knuckle Rubs

This move has a lot of uses.

You can get people to lift their hands, or remove them, any time you want.

For example, if someone has you in a bear hug (grabbing you around the waist from behind), if you can rub the back of one of the hands holding you, you can usually force a release.

Form your hand into a fist, with the knuckle of your middle finger jutting out. Take this knuckle and insert it into a spot between two bones on the back of your opponent's hand.

As you push down with a lot of force, rub your knuckle back and forth vigorously in the same area. You should be able to cause pain. Grind your knuckle into the back of your opponent's hand (photos 10-4a-c).

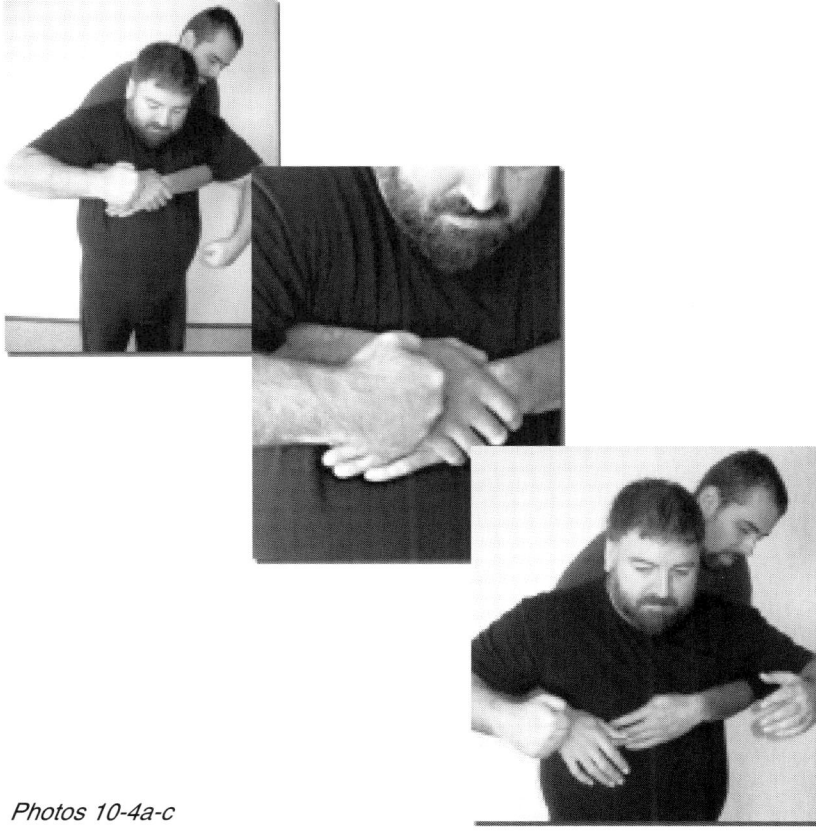

Photos 10-4a-c

Brainstorm a little. See what situations could use a little knuckle-rubbing. Could you produce the same effect on any other parts of the body?

For example, the feet have a bone structure similar to that of the hand, but I bet you could find other places to cause pain.

Pascal's Law Refined

In the first edition of Wrist Locks, I suggested that pressing on the inside of a joint might produce pain.

Since then, I have revised Pascal's Law. I think you should try to find pain centers above any joint of the body.

As long as you're checking above the joint, pressing on the outside of the joint is now fair game, too.

Try above the knee, on the side (photos 10-5a, b).

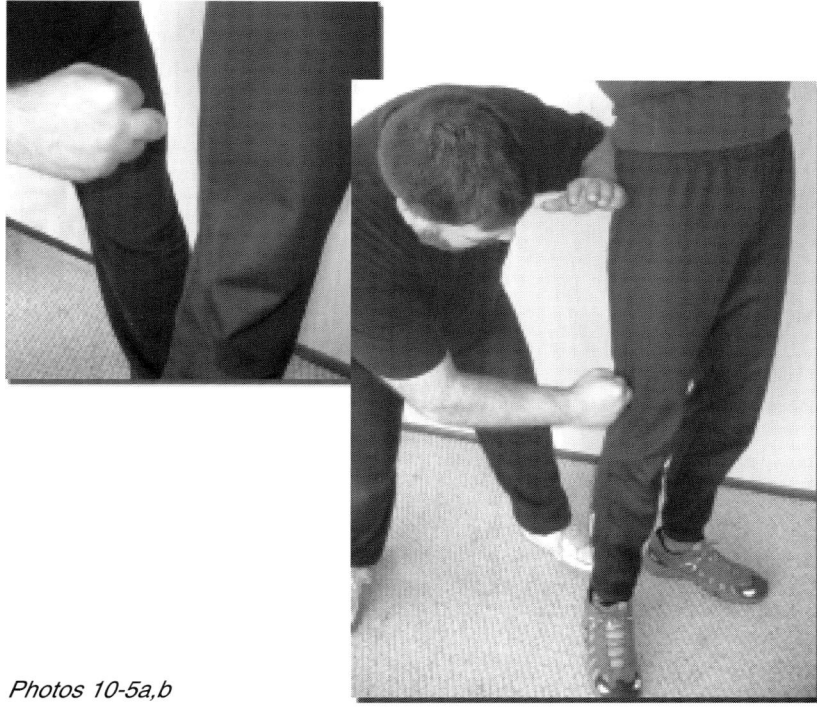

Photos 10-5a,b

I know you like the Pheonix Eye (middle knuckle raised) from the knuckle rubs, but you could also grab. If you have a strong grip, you can cause pain just by digging your thumb into a pressure point (photo 10-5c).

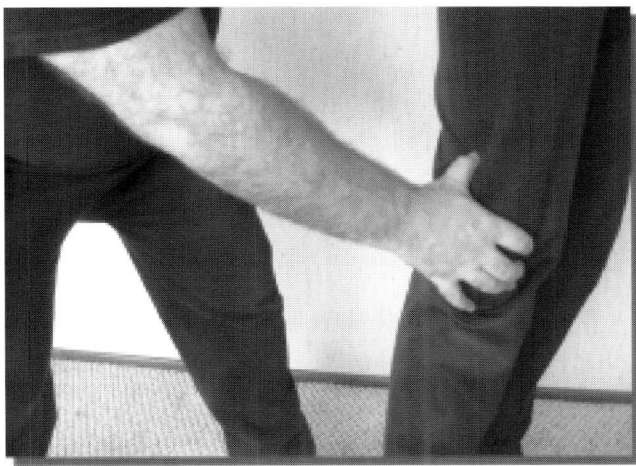

Photos 10-5c

And speaking of a good grab, you get double the pain when you grab pressure points above the elbow. With some experimentation, you should be able to cause pain on both the inside and outside of the arm (photo 10-6a).

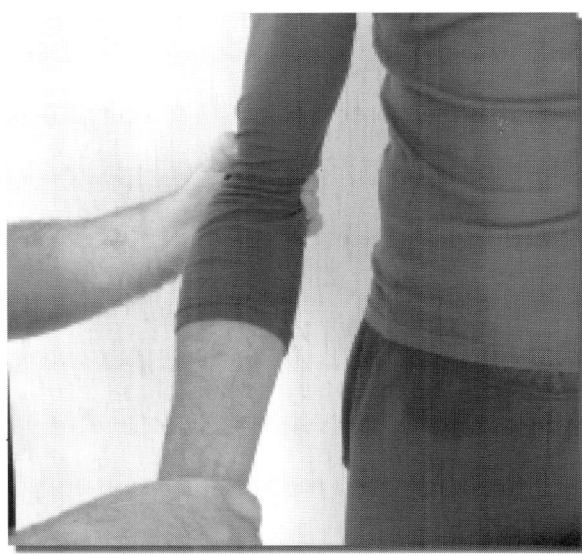

Photos 10-6a

With a good squeeze, you can even find sensitive pressure spots behind finger joints (10-6b).

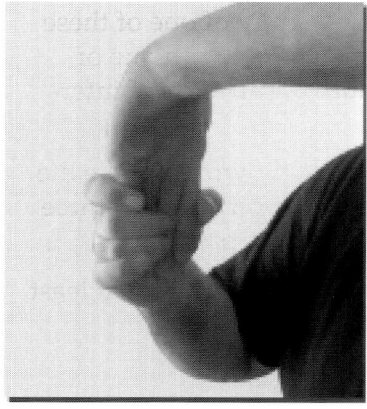

Photos 10-6b

Are you interested in an esoteric pressure point? You won't be able to effect this one on everyone. Still, it's gratifying when it works.

Roll the edge of your straightened forefinger into the veins about an inch above the inside of the wrist (photos 10-6c, d).

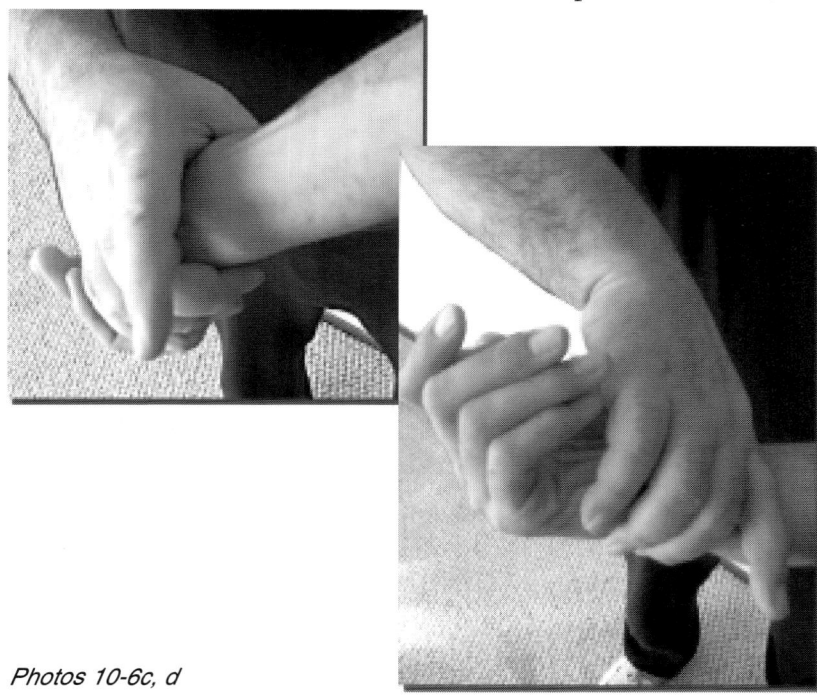

Photos 10-6c, d

Look to use these pressure points while you're putting a lock on your opponent.

If your free hand happens to be in the vicinity of one of these tender areas, you might want to try digging in with one of your fingers or thumbs. You'll probably get all sorts of interesting reactions.

Don't forget that the shoulder is a joint. That would make the armpit the fleshy underside of the joint. The armpit has three different nerves that can cause a great deal of pain.

Just shove a thumb up there, and you'll probably find at least one.

Hair Pulling

My teacher, Steve Golden, taught me with actual painful lessons, that you can control with a hair grab (photo 10-7).

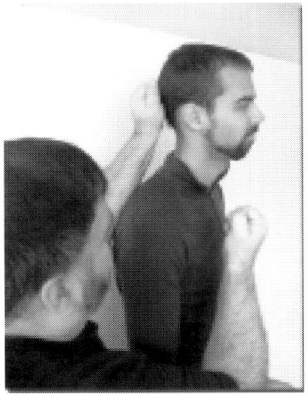

Photos 10-7

As long as you can grab some hair, it will work on people with short hair.

Also, hair pulls are always more painful if you pull against the grain. Grab the hair on the back of someone's head; pull downward. Now, pull up. Up hurts more, right?

I have also learned the hard way that beards and moustaches are fair game. You can often pull and twist in the direction you want your opponent to go, and his head will follow.

Are Pressure Point Charts Useless?

In the last edition of *Wrist Locks*, I didn't print a pressure-point chart.

I gave advice about not expecting too much from your pressure points.

That advice still stands. Use them as an aid to your locks. They add extra control, or cause a bit more pain. Sometimes, they do carry the whole show, but it's always better if they aren't the only techniques you're employing.

I still don't put a lot of faith in pressure-point charts for inducing pain. A little experimentation and the guidelines from this chapter should be enough to get you started, if pressure points are new to you.

Instead of a small chart, in this new edition, I have included a photograph of Mike, one of my students, with arrows pointing to a bunch of key spots, where you can cause pain with a strike or poke (photo 10-8a).

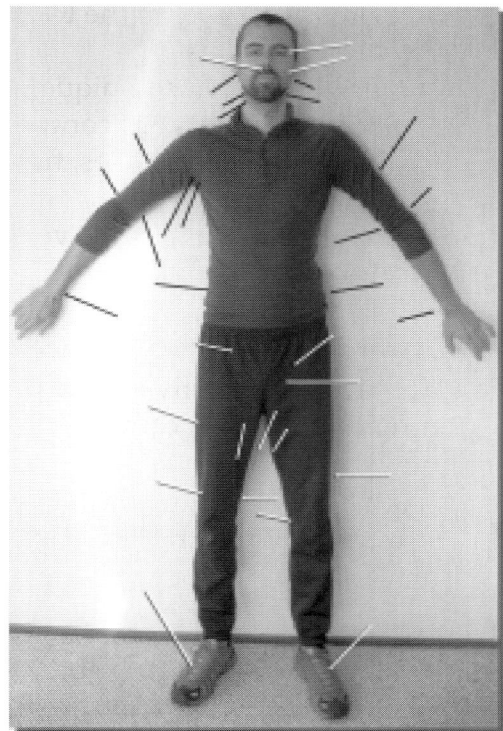

Photo 10-8a

Here are some of the pressure points that I seem to use the most:

- Right behind the ear is a little indentation called the Mastoid Process. Pressure hurts.

- There are three painful pressure points in the armpit.

- You've already seen a pressure point behind the inside (and outside) of the elbow. Actually, there are two points within an inch of each other on the inside.

- Check out the fleshy part under your jaw. Hooking a thumb there could cause a lot of pain.

- And as long as we're hooking thumbs, what about in the mouth. You go in and up along the side. Stay out of the way of the teeth.

  This is an effective technique, but do you really want to take the risk of contracting something? Explore other alternatives, first.

- Last, but not least... create your own pressure points.

  Never forget the handy pinch. It's dirty, but it's effective. Any fleshy part of the body can be turned into a pain center.

  Pinch and twist hard. You'll get it. The inner thigh, inner part of the arm, neck, etc....

Before we end our discussion of pressure points, I have two warnings. Please don't skip over these....

Two Important Warnings

First Warning

No Carotid Holds. These are holds that put pressure on the carotid artery and cut off blood pressure to the brain. They're risky.

These "sleeper holds" are good for knocking someone out, but there's always a chance that he won't wake up.

I don't want that responsibility or liability.

If you're interested, they're listed in many places. Even the high- school wrestlers seem to find out about them with the greatest of ease.

Yes, I'm good at them. No, I don't teach them. No, I probably wouldn't need to do one, even in a *pinch* (pardon the pun). There's so much else out there. You'll have to make your own decision.

Second Warning

Some people get overzealous about pressure points. They've seen too many movies.

I won't tell you that everything out there is ca-ca, because there are a lot of good books in print that contain pressure points. I'm just not sure I'd rely on a quick little nerve hit to cause your opponent to drop dead 24 hours later (Dim Mak).

Look, I don't want to feel it to believe it. So, if such a move is not pure fantasy, I really don't want to have much to do with it.

Also, If it's not fantasy, I'm not sure how much good it would do me. I don't want anyone to "drop dead" on my account.

And if by some strange twist of fate, I had to abandon my moral standard and cause a death, I don't think I'd want it to happen 24 hours later. I'd probably need immediate results.

Just be careful with what you find. There is crap, useful knowledge, and dangerous material (carotid arteries, etc.). Embark on nerve and pressure-point studies with caution.

11
How to Experiment and Invent Your Own

With what I'm about to say, I don't mean to dissuade you from experimenting , even before you've read this chapter.

Some of you will go on to read this chapter anyway; good for you. You creative types will have a lot of fun coming up with new moves. Even if you "reinvent the wheel," and come up with a move that has already been invented, working it all out to get to the correct move is very good for you.

You learn during the act of creation. Sometimes the process is more important than the move.

After the above preamble, now let me tell you – *you could skip this chapter*. You don't have to go the creative route to become a wrist-lock expert.

Some of you doubt your creativity, and don't want to take time to explore the creative right side of your brain, although those of you pursuing the martial-arts path will eventually need to get in touch with both sides of your brain.

Your definition of expertise might not include the ability to overcome the majority of those who try to put a lock on you. Maybe just collecting a variety of locks into your repertoire is your goal. Your definition of expert status may include the ability to effectively teach the art of wrist locking to others.

Even if your goal is to be able to strut your stuff in the wrist-lock arena, you still don't have to invent your own.

I have found that I most easily win in a wrist-lock situation when I pull a move out of my "bag of tricks," that my opponent has never seen or felt.

Only a few people truly know how to feel where to go. You will need to work on this skill as you move closer to expert status. Most, other than those from a system similar to mine, are dumbfounded by my unfamiliar techniques.

So how do you know to apply a wrist lock that is "unfamiliar" to your opponent, if it's not one you invented?

You don't *know*; you make quick, educated guesses. First, instead of (or along with) inventing your own variations, you learn a ton of locks from a variety of styles. Then you basically avoid *giving* your opponent what he (or she) wants.

If your opponent's moves indicate expertise in Aikido, then maybe you dumbfound this opponent with a lock or two from the Chinese styles. If your opponent tries to apply a Ju Jitsu hold, why don't you respond with a technique from one of the Filipino arts?

Since you're a versatile expert, you have this choice; many others are limited by their specific styles.

There are lots of telltale signs that provide clues as to what style you're up against: large body-pivots in Aikido, the hiking-up of the pants before a kick in some of our Korean arts, the closed roundhouse of some of the JKD off-shoots, the shuffling footwork of a boxer, and so on.

Plus, don't forget the actual techniques themselves.

Each style has a few locks that are specific to that particular style. Learn to recognize them, and you'll be able to deduce a lot about the rest of this person's fighting style.

You should also spend time learning the locks that are common to several styles. After all, sometimes switching to a different style doesn't help, if your opponent is familiar with it from his (or her) own style. Your opponent may know the move anyway, from some other source. You can never tell.

That's why you're spending time learning counters, reversals, and patterns – You want to be able to automatically flow into something else, even when you encounter the unexpected.

I've spent all this time describing alternatives to experimentation and invention. Maybe I should spend a little time actually teaching you how to experiment, since that's what this chapter is about.

OK, so you want to invent your own moves. How does one get started?

First, develop your core knowledge. Know some locks. Actually, know a variety of locks. The more, the better.

Another Point of View:
Some would say that you can't be truly creative if you know someone else's moves. Those few have their point of view, and I have mine.

I think that the more familiar you are with a number of positions and pressures, the easier it will be to stretch your imagination. You have less of a distance to stretch, because you already have some *meat* to what you're doing.

And while the process of reinventing the wheel is beneficial, you don't want to spend all of your time just getting to the point that it took complete systems hundreds of years to invent.

Benefit from old knowledge; don't get stuck in a mold from it; just glean what you can.

Learn lots of moves from different disciplines.

In fact, in my three stages of becoming a lock inventor, the first stage *is* learning a bunch of moves, just so you have that *substance*.

In the second stage, you combine your moves and change angles and positions to create your own locks. In the third stage, you figure out how to apply all of these locks and holds to real-life situations.

First Stage

For Step #1 toward the goal of invention you should start out by learning the locks in this book.

They are effective. Learn others too; be well-rounded.

When you are familiar with a variety of locks (maybe you already are), I would advise you to learn the patterns in Chapter 6. Embedded in that chapter are some tips and principles which are important to inventing your own. After all, one of your goals might be to invent new patterns.

For example, there is commentary on looking for counters, countering with direct hits and/or other locks, building on initial counters, adding moves onto other moves, changing the order of positions, maintaining continuous pressure, substituting different techniques, guarding against kicks, and lots of other principles that you should keep in mind while inventing your own "stuff."

You should feel very comfortable blending from one move to another after going through Chapter 6.

If, for some reason, you still feel as though you need some reinforcement, try Chapter 9 (Reversals).

Second Stage

Now, you should be ready to start experimenting. You have the tools. Now, let's get creative. The first step was to get some tools to work with; you need some basic ingredients. The second stage is taking your ingredients and recombining or changing them to invent your own.

Pick a joint, any joint ... finger joint, wrist, or elbow.

Grab the appendage of your partner that is attached to that joint (arm, hand, finger). Try bending the appendage in different directions. Your partner should be relaxed, in "cooperative mode." When bending the appendage, where do you encounter resistance?

Can you apply pressure in one direction or another to cause pain?

What happens when you change the direction of your hand-hold?

Can you make these holds workable?

If you feel frustrated, you might want to back up a step and acquire even more moves first. Try going to books (like this one) or videos for some new positions to start from.

Now go forward to the experimenting stage again. How can you change these new positions to suit your needs? How can you blend them with positions you already know?

Try changing the angles on the locks from other sources. If the holds from other sources put you in unsafe positions, change the distancing so you're not in range of a stray fist.

You also may have to change the pressure to protect yourself from your opponent's feet. Just because you have to change a few angles doesn't mean that a lock isn't useful. Modification of this type is what will turn you into an outstanding wrist-lock artist.

Can you combine moves from your books and videos?

In other arts, some people believe that there is nothing new under the sun. The way to achieve originality is by the recombination of that which already exists.

One way to combine is to add pressure to a different joint, while maintaining pressure on the original lock.

For example, when you have an arm bar, you modify it by adding a finger lock.

Third Stage

The last stage of experimentation should be to apply these locks to possible real-life situations.

You definitely need to memorize and internalize some of the points in the next chapter. The advice on when to and when not to use wrist locks will apply to your creations as well.

You don't want to try to perform a lock at an inappropriate time. For example, attempting to transform a punch straight into a wrist lock is very risky.

A punch is dynamic; most opponents won't oblige you by leaving their fists in one spot. You're trying to grab something coming at you and, just as important, something is being withdrawn at an almost blinding speed.

So, you're either going to have to slow that punch down, or you'll have to perform your lock from a more static attack, like a grab. After all, if you can't get control of an arm or wrist, how are you going to perform your lock?

Take my word for it: slow attacks are better.

Attack this stage of invention in one of two ways. One day, use one method of invention, and the next, switch to the other.

Eventually, you'll settle on the method you feel is personally the most productive.

The first way to invent is to start with the stimulus, and try to pick the proper response from your arsenal of techniques. The second way to invent is to back out from the response, and see if you can find a stimulus, like an attack, which would necessitate your specific response.

In the first way, you begin with a single attack, like a specific punch. Don't be too general and just say "Let's practice a wrist lock for a punch." Decide; will it be a right-handed or left-handed punch? Is the fist vertical or horizontal? Is it coming from above or below? What is the intended target? If the punch is following a direct line to your body, what is the angle of attack?

All of these questions are important in determining a counter-attack, and all make you think of that general "punch" as a much more specific technique.

So, now that you can get more specific, you're ready to take a punch, right?

Wrong!

Remember, I advised against taking an attack that is coming in with a lot of speed with a straight wrist lock? Have you forgotten so soon?

Maybe you should start with a grab. It's more static, remember?

Just like the punch, the grab needs to be considered in a specific manner as well – Single or two hands? Palm up or down? Grabbing cloth or skin?

You should also consider what part of your body is being restrained, and if a certain part of your body is more exposed to danger (your eyes being close to his fingers, for example).

After your opponent grabs you, start looking for different positions that you could get to.

What locks can you effect by grabbing the hand that's holding you?

What are the different ways that you could grab that hand?

Do you need to have it release its grip before you flow into a counter?

Can you use misdirection and grab the hand that's not holding you? All of the attention and focus is being placed on the hand restraining you; why not use this to your advantage?

You pay attention to the restraining hand as well, as you secretly grab the other hand into a smooth wrist lock.

Could you perform a lock without grabbing either hand?

Maybe your opponent's arm is in the perfect position for an arm bar. Don't try to force a wrist lock, if there is some other restraining or striking technique that "fits." Go with the flow!

Let Me Get You Started

If you are feeling a little lost at this point, don't despair!

You should eventually just jump right in and start experimenting, but if you're feeling just a bit hesitant at this point, that's OK. I have an example here to get your feet wet, or at least slightly moist with the wrist-locking experimentation experience.

Go ahead and have your partner grab you. The grab should be with one hand to your clothing, at about chest level (photo 11-1a).

Now let's start thinking creatively. I would start my experimentation process by working on the grab hand.

If I just wanted him to let go, I could rub in between his tarsals with the middle knuckle of my middle finger (photo 11-1b).

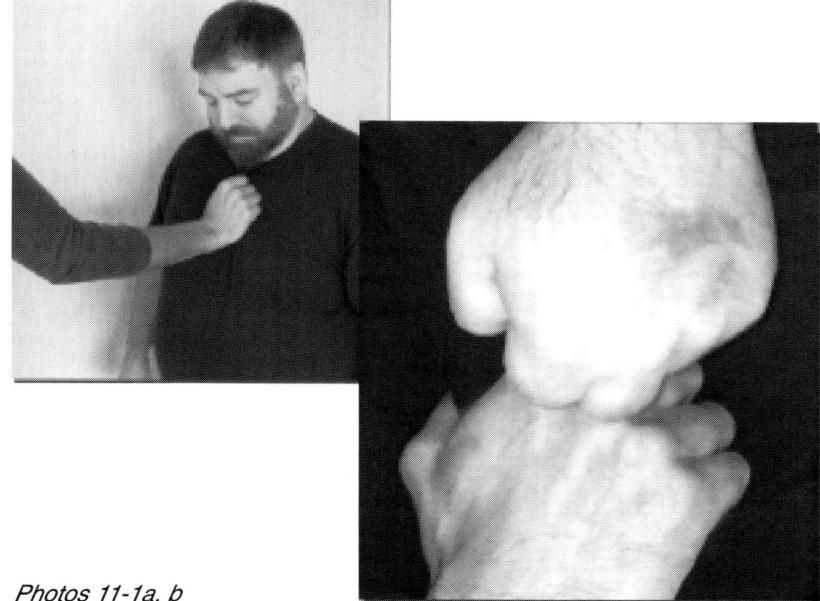

Photos 11-1a, b

I could also peel fingers off my clothes. Of the two, I'd choose the latter, because a knuckle rub would cause him to let go, but I wouldn't have control. If I were to grab my opponent's fingers, you could bet your little pinky finger, or his, that I wouldn't let go; I'd be causing all sorts of pain tweaking those fingers.

Let's move into more sophisticated responses. You could grab the back of the hand and move right into the Basic Lock (photo 11-2).

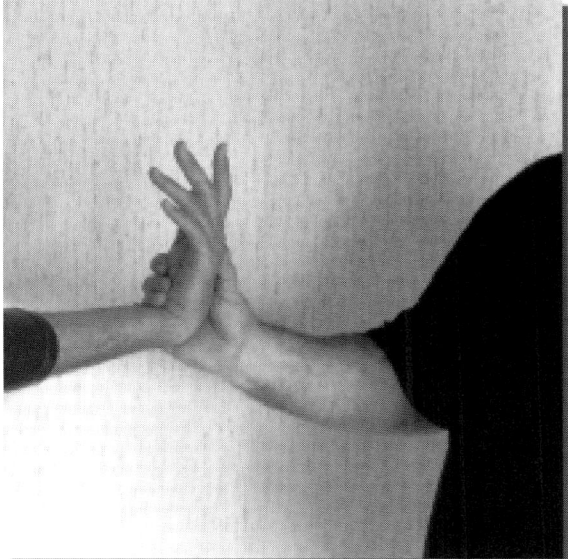

Photo 11-2

In order to effect the Basic Lock, you are going to have to peel off some fingers from the grab to your clothing.

As you already know, one variation on the Basic Lock is to grab by thumb. You still go in to the same lock, but instead of positioning your own thumb on the back of your opponent's hand, grip your opponent's thumb.

If you think about it, this makes a lot of sense. After all, since you have to peel some fingers anyway, you might as well strip the digit off right into the lock.

See Photos 11-3a through 11-3c on the next page....

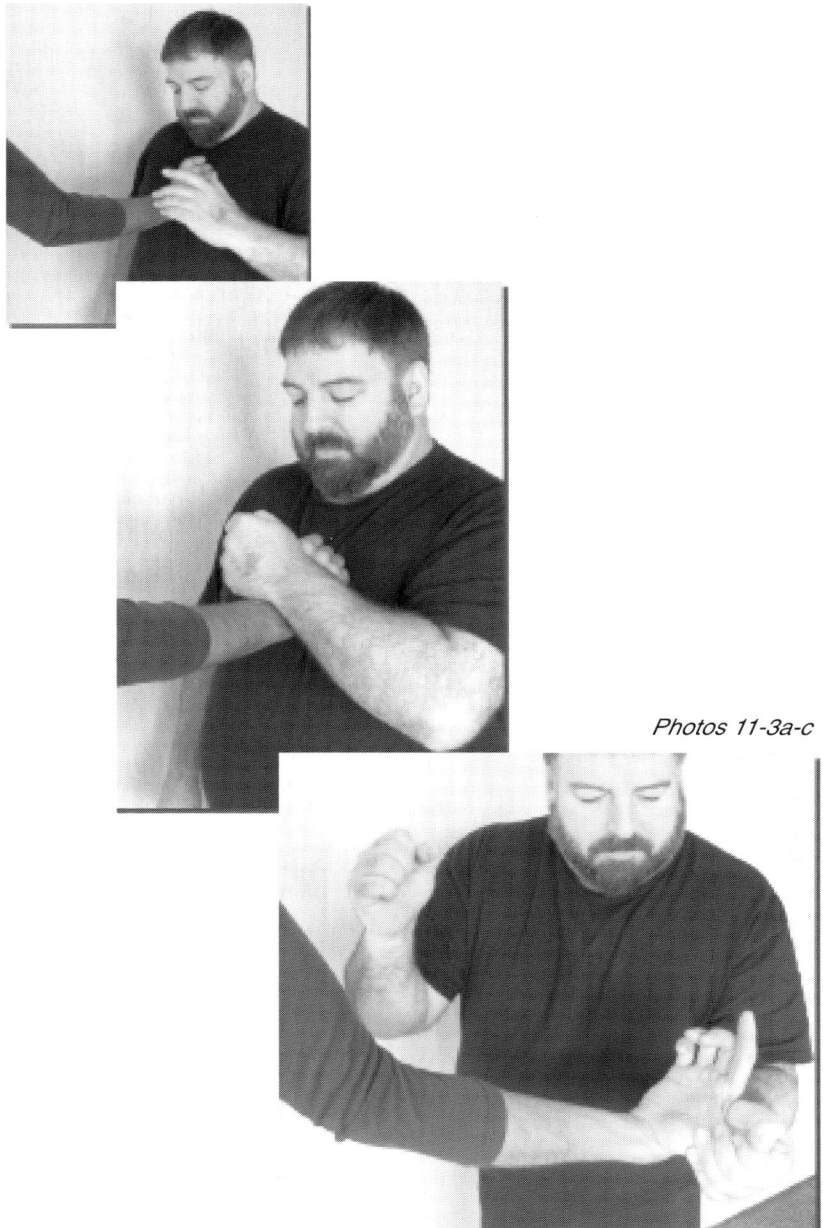

Photos 11-3a-c

So, what happens if you start the lock with your other hand?

If you start with your other hand, then the twist of the hand won't put your partner into the Basic Lock. The torque is going in the opposite direction. This is perfectly OK. It just means that you'll snap on a different wrist lock. So, if you reach with your other hand, then grab thumb-to-thumb, with your fingers peeling on the edge of your partner's hand nearest to the little finger (photo 11-4a-c).

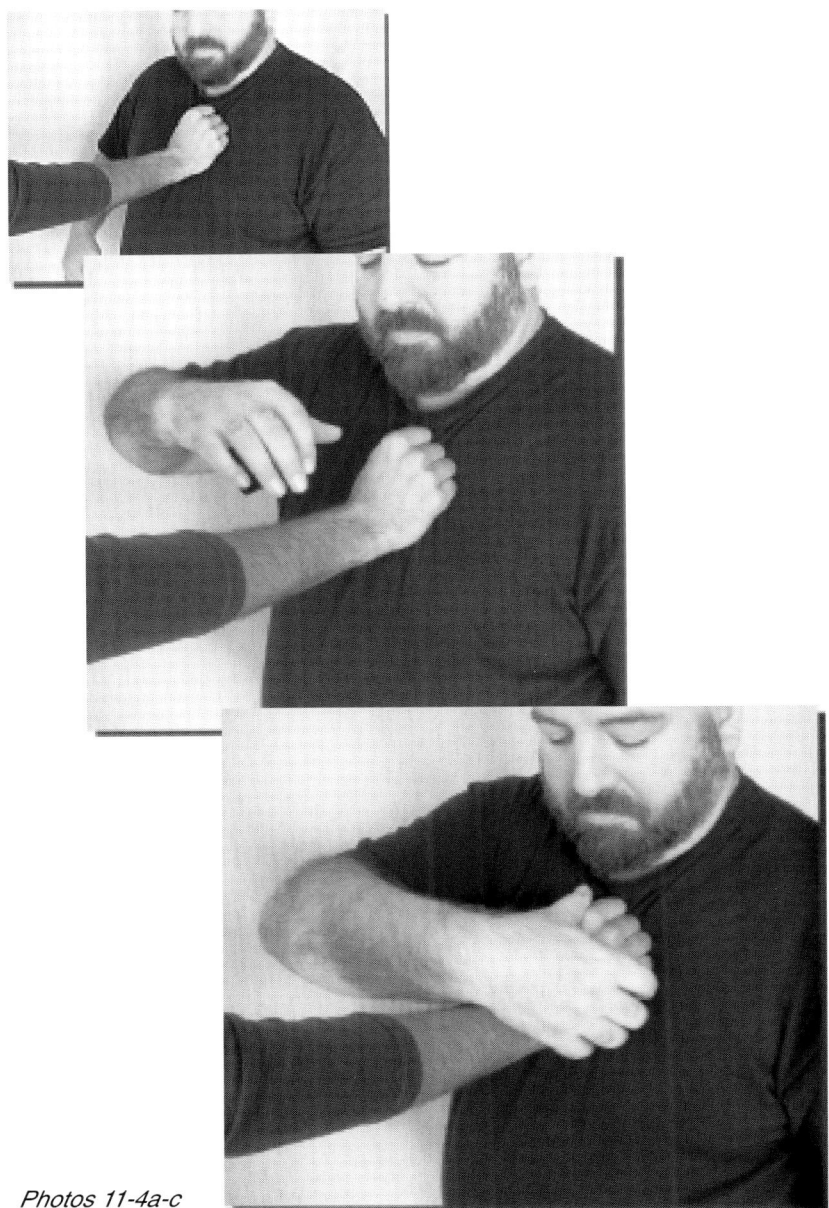

Photos 11-4a-c

Lift your opponent's hand off your clothes and twist and bend the arm, as you twist the hand into a thumb-down position.

This will take you right into the Double Ninety-Degree Lock (photos 11-4d-f).

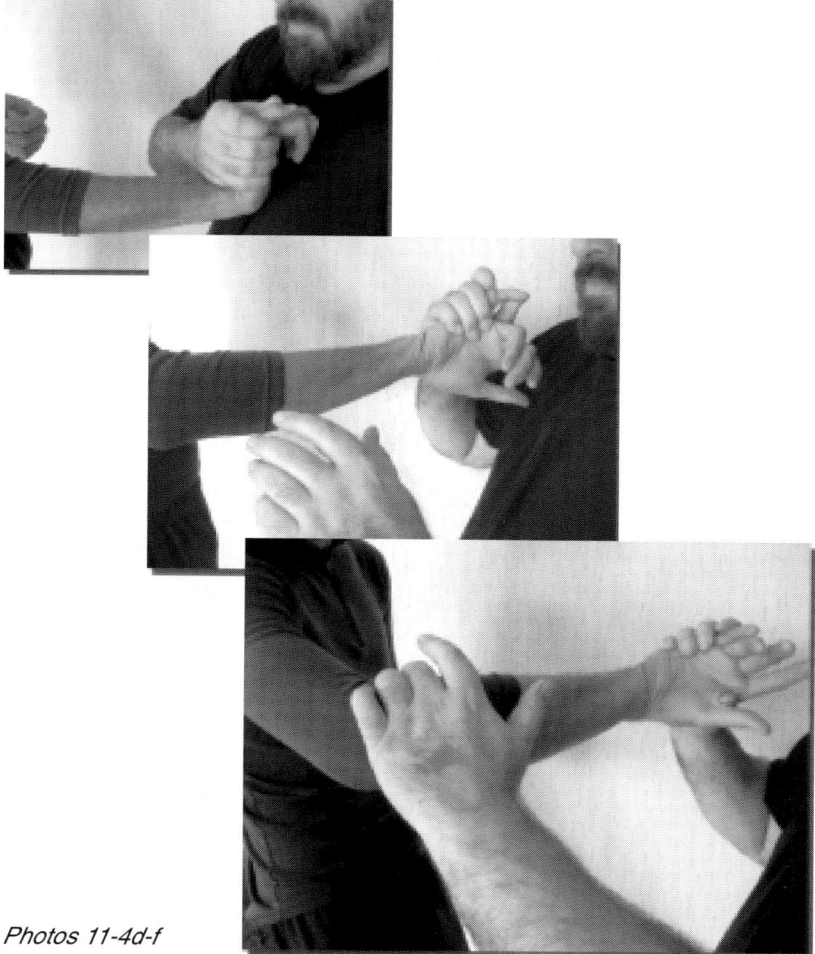

Photos 11-4d-f

While you are inventing your own responses, locks, applications, and variations, remember to add in some hits and kicks. You can always choose a more passive route in a real confrontation, but it's nice to know that the hits are there, if you need them.

Even a hit at the end of a good wrist lock can be useful and especially important in dealing with multiple attackers. You hit, then control, and hit some more ... as you move on to the next assailant.

You can also use a locked (and beaten) attacker as a human shield in a multiple attacker situation.

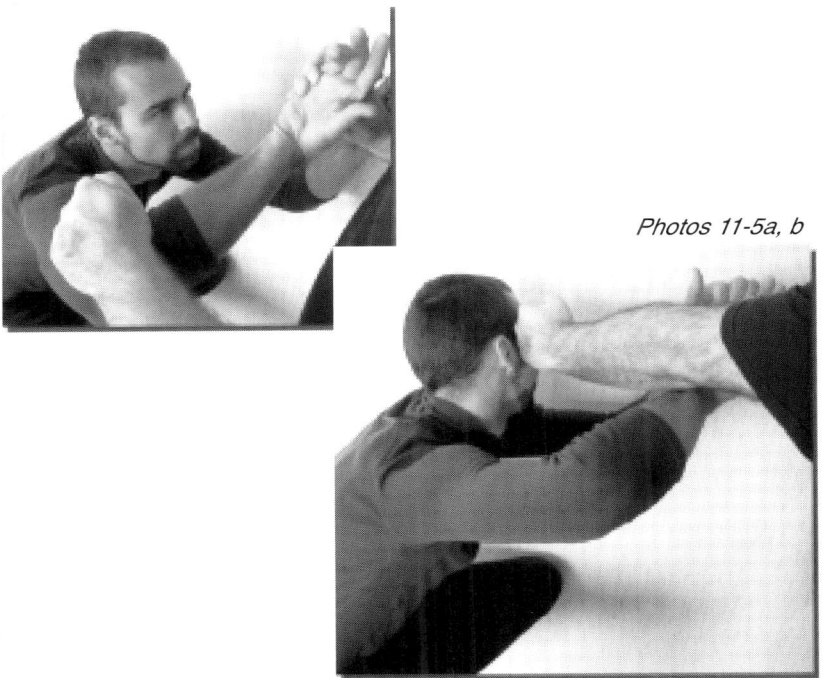

Photos 11-5a, b

We could continue in this manner and "invent" many other responses where the first movement is to deal with your opponent's grab hand.

We could, but then I'd be doing the work for you. You're the one who needs to go through this process.

Let's move on. We'll start from the initial grab, but instead of exploring more locks with the same hand, let's change ... hands.

Your opponent grabs you; start to perform the Basic Lock, but instead of continuing the pressure with your hand as it starts to touch your opponent's, use your other hand to effect the

Basic Lock – in a mirror of what your other hand was just doing. This is beautiful. Your opponent thinks and feels that you are about to put a lock on the grabbing hand, (the Basic Lock), but in reality, you're putting the very same lock on his (or her) other hand (photos 11-6a-e). If you're subtle, you will absolutely shock your opponent.

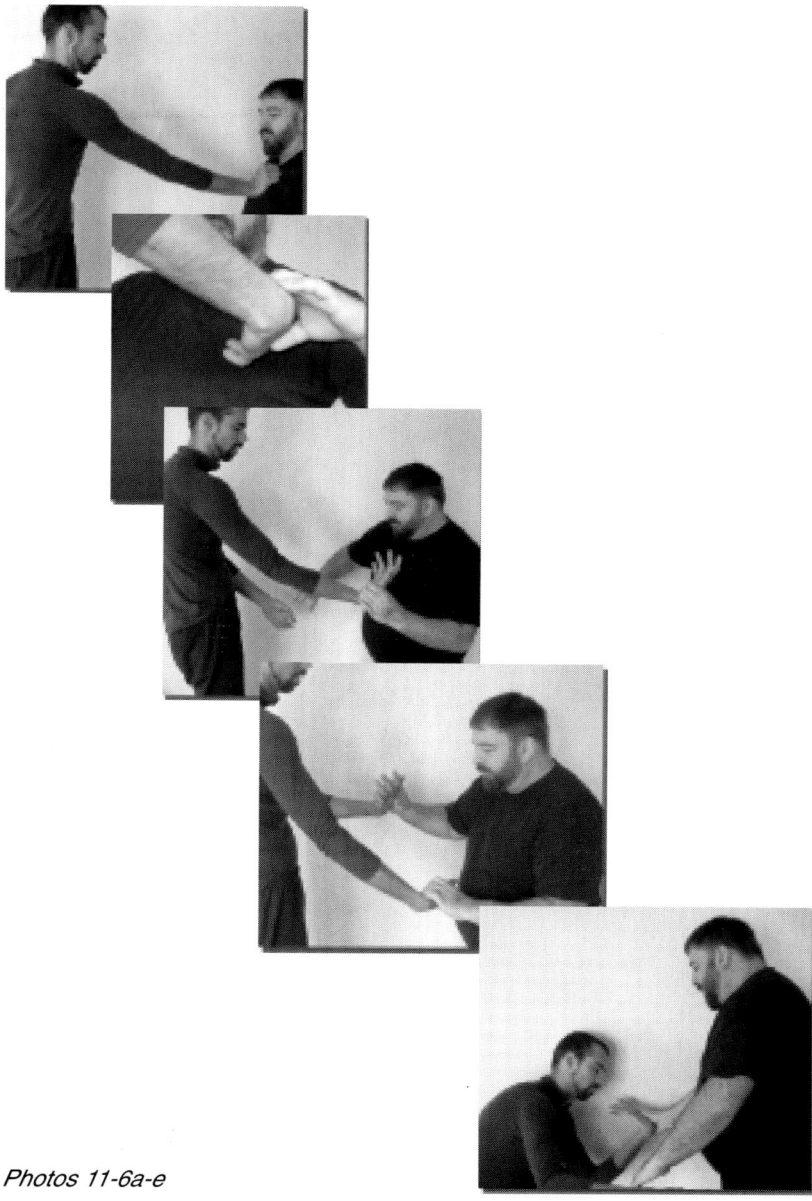

Photos 11-6a-e

Can you think of other locks to put on the free hand, like stepping through the space between the grabbed arm and body as in photos 11-7a-d?

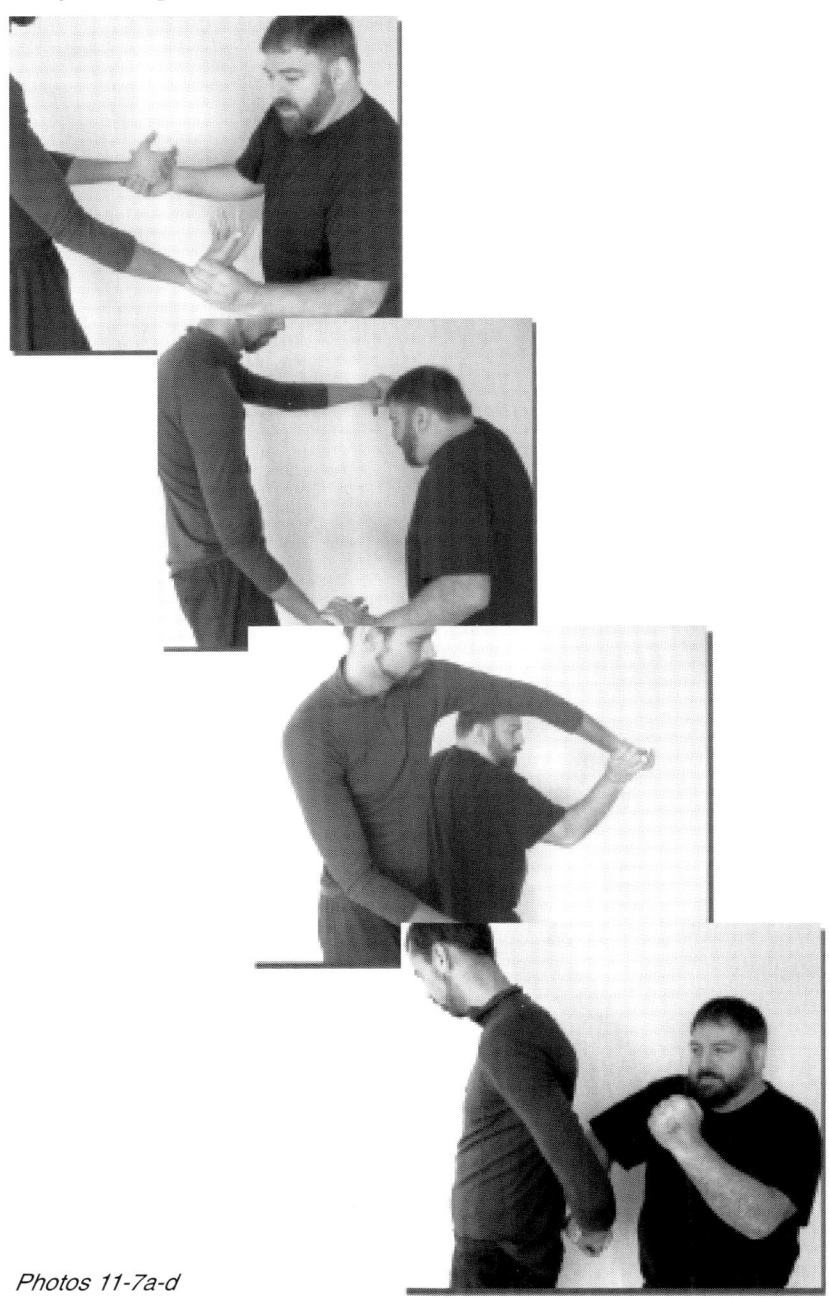

Photos 11-7a-d

Rather than just my giving you everything, which would not help your creative process one iota, it's time for you to take more control of the experimentation process.

Our first principle was to lock the hand that presents the immediate threat to you, even if the threat is in the form of a restraint.

The next principle was to go after the opponent's free hand, (definitely a finesse move).

Another principle is to temporarily forget the hand grabbing you, and to lock some other part of the body, like his arm. Did I forget to mention that sometimes I like to practice stepping through WITHOUT removing the grabbing hand first? Try this with other grabs and locks.

Now, It Is Your Turn

Your first task is to get from the grab to an arm lock, where pressure is exerted by rotating the pinky edge of the hand back toward the opponent's arm.

How might you accomplish this?

Somehow, get your opponent's arm rotated, so it's pinky-side up. Good luck!

After you play around with it, take a look at my solution on the opposite page (photos 11-8a-d).

Can you get to the arm bar? Your next task is to get from the first grab to an arm bar *in one move.*

You could get to the traditional position (photo 11-8d), but you could perform an even quicker one.

How would you put an arm bar-like pressure on your opponent without making him (or her) let go of his grasp of you, and without your having to pivot your body?

(I have faith that by now you can easily solve this puzzle.)

Experiment with your own solutions, and then take a look at the solution for the first task, on the following page.

Be sure to experiment, first. It's important.

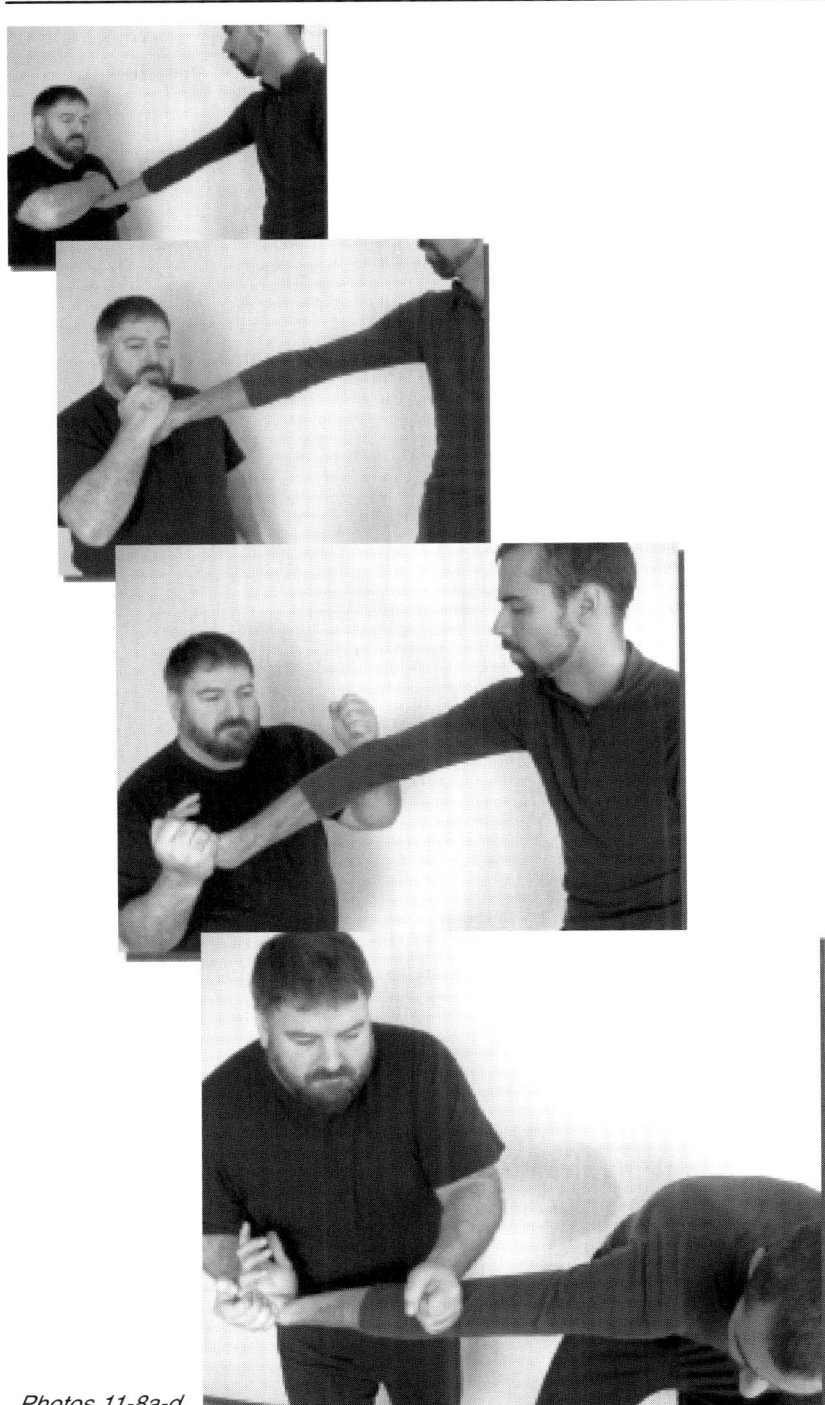

Photos 11-8a-d

How was your practice with the arm bar? Would you like a couple of more hints to help you develop real arm-bar skill?

First, if you get resistance while you are effecting your arm bar, try hitting. The instant you feel your opponent try to lift, punch – and then go right back into the arm bar (photos 11-9a, b). No pause.

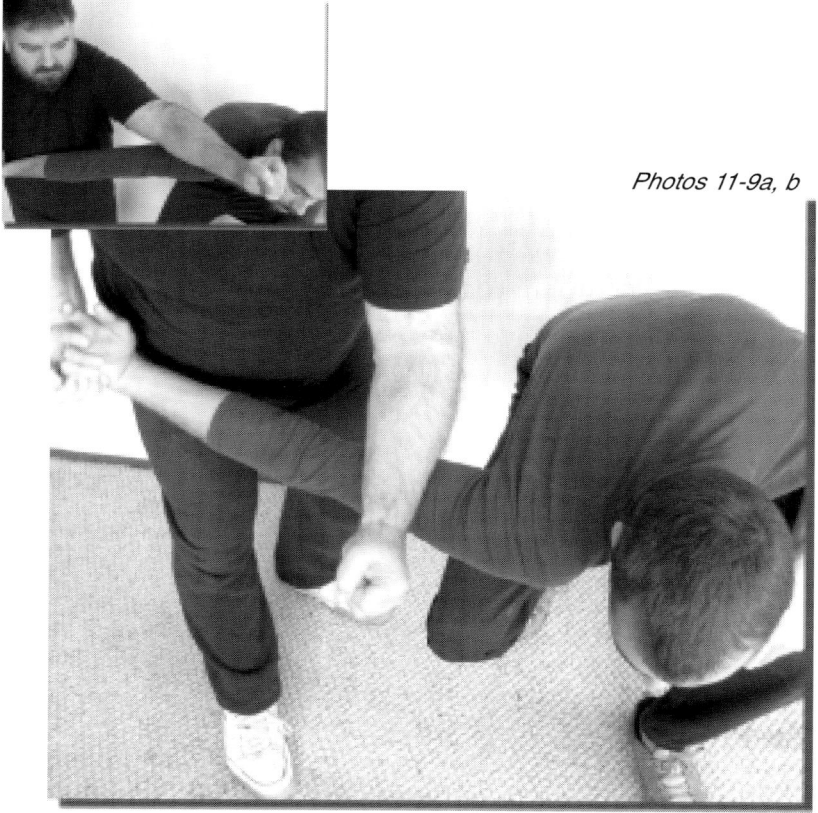

Photos 11-9a, b

Your second hint is that you can usually get into a move by executing a different lock first.

For example, could you go from the grab into a *Double-Ninety* (see pages 119-121), and then get from the *Double-Ninety* to your arm bar?

You'll have to bend his arm in toward your body, but again, you don't have to remove his hand from your shirt first.

Of course, what I really want is for you to get there in one move, as efficiently as possible; that's why I said that you don't even have to get your opponent to let go.

If your arm bar is accurate, the nature of the lock will force a release of your clothing.

Efficiency and Locking In Real Situations

See all that we were able to accomplish from one little grab. And there was so much more we could have done in response to the same grab.

Imagine the possibilities from all the various ways to grab the body. It's mind-boggling.

Once you are very comfortable with grab experimentation, you should eventually start learning to experiment with strikes.

Remember, there is an extra step involved with a strike. In a grab, your opponent grabs, and you can respond with a wrist lock. With a punch, for example, you have to stop or deflect the punch before you perform a lock. It's very, very difficult to convert your opponent's swift jab straight into a wrist lock.

Try catching a very fast punch; it's not a very comfortable feeling.

Strong blocks to slow opponents' strikes aren't always the best response either. We don't even have to go into the old two-step/one-step argument between the classical styles and the Jeet Kune Do descendants and off-shoots.

Here, the reason you may not want a heavy block is because it doesn't necessarily offer you enough control over the limb. It might knock your opponent's arm away, but it could also cause your opponent to pull the arm away. In both cases, you lose contact. Not good for locking.

With a solid block, you might even injure your attacker's arm, but it could still pull away. You want some type of deflection leaving you in a good position for a lock. I prefer to maintain contact, as I apply the lock.

Some gung fu styles, like Wing Chun, teach passive deflecting blocks (the *bong sao*, for example).

In Bruce Lee's style, Jeet Kune Do, many methods of slowing down an attack may be too brutal for what you're looking for.

It all depends on your ultimate goals for real self defense.

Maybe you should look into trapping. There's a whole world of trapping out there to explore. Give it a try. Write to me for advice on choosing martial-arts schools; I have some definite opinions.

Your ultimate goal may be to apply this whole ball of wax to real-life situations.

This ability could definitely be a major component in achieving expert status.

Start experimenting.

Learn to take everything. These practice sessions are your laboratory. Conduct lots of experiments, and get very proficient, before going out into the real world.

12

When to and When Not to Use Wrist Locks

In the martial arts, one tends to use the most practiced material in a confrontation. Also, recency of practiced material tends to put these moves on the "front burner."

If you're practicing these locks the way you should be, you're going to start relying on them more and more.

That's great, but ... you can't always rely on wrist locks to take everything. I wish that it were the secret to invincibility; while they are great tools, and they can save your life and the lives of others, they are only one facet of a complete system.

I'll say it over and over again; while I am a confirmed wrist-lock addict, I would not hesitate to send my fist through someone's face if it were the more efficient way, for example, to protect a loved one.

I will do everything I can to get out of a fight, but if I have to fight — in other words, I'm forced into it for a serious enough reason (not because someone "flips me off"), I will do whatever it takes, including, but not limited to, wrist locks.

Yes, I know the law in my home state.

You should too.

Then you make your decisions, and I'll make mine.

I don't take legal responsibility for your actions – I am not a lawyer, on the police force, versed in the laws of your area, a diety, or anyone else who can take responsibility for your actions or give you legal council.

I *am* someone who cares ... enough to tell you that real defense situations go into litigation all the time. Be careful. Avoid conflict. Get professional advice.

With all that in mind, here are some specific tips on when not to use wrist locks.

As you find situations of your own, you'll want to make your own list. Review your list from time to time, and you should have no problem remembering the danger signs.

When Not to Use a Lock:

- We've already mentioned this one in the last chapter; so it's a good place to start. **Don't take a punch straight into a wrist lock.**

  A fast jab comes in and leaves too fast for you to be able to rely on going into a lock. It's too risky.

  You need to slow down fast techniques to get them under control before you attempt to go into a lock.

- **In a serious confrontation don't trade locks with someone better than you.** Don't play the other person's game. If your opponent is better than you are at wrist locks, don't stay in that mode.

  Hit; kick; do something else.

  If he is better than you at hits and kicks, don't fight. If you fight someone better than you at ALL aspects of fighting, you will lose. (No, I don't have a degree as a rocket scientist, and I was still able to figure this one out.)

• Along those same lines, **don't try to out-muscle a muscle-bound attacker.**

Someone flexing huge muscles is not a candidate for your wrist locks, until you know how to generalize to the "resister energy." It's a Catch–22.

How do you learn to counter a resister, until you go against a resister? And should you go against a resister, until you already know how to counter one? Now, what?

There actually is a good solution.

Get into a class with, or befriend, a lot of muscle-bound martial artists. Really.

If you work out with these guys, you'll get used to, and comfortable with, that "energy." When you actually have to go against a *macho dude* (does anybody still use that expression?), it'll be a piece of cake.

Your big friends can help you work through this type of energy. Boy, will you get good — fast.

• **Don't use a lock on someone drunk.** Inebriation deadens pain. He (or she) just won't feel it.

If it's a lock that relies on a pain factor, you'll be going into the lock with a "negative score." A restraining hold, where there is no place for him to go, works better than one that controls with pain.

• **Don't wrist lock in the range of other weapons** including your opponent's fists and feet. Don't commit the common wrist-lock blunder of not considering all dangers around you.

The only time that it's OK to be in range of your opponent's weapons is when you have control with the pressure of a lock.

For example, you should have enough pressure with an arm bar, that your opponent's free arm can't reach you.

If he reaches up, you just apply a little more pressure to stop his motion. You should be able to control any attack made by your opponent's free weapons.

If the lock that you have on your opponent isn't effective enough to control all the other weapons, what good is it?

• **Don't wrist lock innocent bystanders.** Take my word for it, you are not the life of the party when you demonstrate your nifty locks on everyone unrequested.

Don't be a pest.

Save your discussions and practice sessions for other martial artists. Just because you got "religion," don't think that everybody else wants to discuss wrist locks with you.

• **Don't wrist lock a lawyer.** Generalize that to don't wrist lock anyone who might sue you.

Save it for self-defense, and be able to prove that's what it was *in a court of law.*

Have I mentioned recently that you should know the law?

It really is important that you take responsibility for your actions. I think that wrist-lock expertise should include knowledge of how wrist locking (and other forms of self-defense) is/(are) treated by the law. Don't you agree?

What are you going to do to find out about the laws in your area?

• **Don't rely only on your wrist lock.** Always have contingencies. You need several *outs* at all times.

If a lock isn't working, where are you going?

Are you going to continue trying to force it? Will you loosen him up with a swift kick to the shins, and then try the lock again? Will you rely on a pattern and *morph* into a different lock?

Let's end this chapter on a good note. Here are a few tips on things that you can and should do.

What You Should Do:

- **Do beat the snot out of your opponent first.** Wrist locks are much easier to apply if you've "loosened" up your opponent first.

This of course doesn't work if you're in a passive mode, but if you really have to defend yourself, use the wrist lock as the controller after you've disabled him to some extent.

It's safer.

- **Do try for the lock when your opponent's muscles are relaxed.** It's easier to effect a lock when you can get him as close as possible to the point of no return without his knowing.

You smoothly get him as far as you can, and then you snap the control on almost before he starts to resist.

Smooth subtlety is the mark of a true expert.

- **Do try locks when your opponent is distracted.** Use any form of misdirection that takes your opponent's attention off the limb to be locked.

You need to use the environment to your advantage, and that includes anything that distracts the opponent.

- **Do know what his "other" hand is doing.**

That includes feet. As you perform your lock, check the weight of your opponent's body. Which foot is it on? Can he kick you with his front foot, or is his weight on that foot, making it impossible for him to kick?

- **Do wrist locks when you need to impress other martial artists** or want to give an impressive demonstration to a lay audience.

- **Do a wrist-lock counter or reversal, when you feel a sloppy lock** being executed on your wrist, and you see that you are out of range of a punch or kick.

- And finally. **Be prepared. Practice against all types of attacks and attackers.** Different attacks necessitate different locks. Things may not go as you originally planned.

Do know a myriad of "outs."

13
Learning by Teaching

You should learn to teach, because by teaching you learn more throroughly. (In the last decade, several people have quoted the above phrase from this chapter. Maybe the chapter deserves a more than just a casual glance, whether or not you currently teach.)

I want you to teach. Not only because I claim over a decade of teaching at high school level or above, among my several professions, but because you really will learn so much by teaching.

You don't have to open a martial-arts school to teach. Some of the very best teachers I know teach out of their garages.

You don't even have to have a full class to profit from teaching. Showing a few friends at the same time will still give you the opportunity to experience the reactions (*energies*) of different opponents.

Teaching even one other person still offers a lot.

You don't get to feel the force of different types of opponents, but you still have someone asks you questions, someone with whom you can brainstorm, someone to help you to practice and perfect specific techniques, and more.

It's impossible for me to turn you into a professional teacher in the space of one chapter.

> If you are interested in becoming a better martial-arts teacher, take a look at my ebook **Secrets of Teaching Martial Arts More Effectively**. I also offer other ebooks on improving your martial-arts teaching skill.

Teaching martial arts for pay doesn't require a degree *in my state,* but I do advise that you get a black belt, at the very minimum.

Even a hard-earned black-belt degree, (not the advance by ~~dollars~~, I mean *numbers* crap — or worse yet, a mail-order degree**,) doesn't guarantee that you'll be a good teacher or have the business sense to run a martial-arts school.

You do learn to teach by teaching, but you must have or learn a certain amount of basic classroom sense, not to mention some business sense.

If you're really interested in learning to teach martial arts, write me. I can help.

> Note: Don't get me wrong. I think one can learn an awful lot from mail-order materials.
>
> Be careful; there are a lot of rip-offs and scams out there. There are also some great books and video tapes that are not available in stores. If you're opening a school, you really do need planned lessons, other than just those found through the mail.
>
> For a lot of martial arts, you need an expert there to correct and guide you. You also get to feel the move; this is a very necessary component to your gaining expertise. It's easier to feel the right *energy* from a teacher, than to learn it by fumbling around blindly with a practice partner.
>
> Both methods of learning have value; you need to experience both, so you can become a better teacher.
>
> Even if you prefer to study alone, I hope you see the necessity to also get trained by a live teacher.

This chapter contains tips specific for your improvement as a wrist-lock expert. Most of the tips are good and solid advice on teaching martial arts. While some of the tips will benefit your students the most, I have kept your goals in the back of my mind.

As your students improve, you improve.

Use the tips that apply to your situation. Discard what isn't useful to you. Start keeping your own notebook. Fill it with tips you learn along the way.

Keep lesson plans, thoughts on various moves, quotes to share with your students, and any other aspects of teaching that you want to track or be able to put your hands on easily.

Here are your first tips to get you started:

Tip #1

This advice comes in the form of a plea.

Treat your students with respect! Don't abuse those bodies. You are given a certain responsibility when you teach.

You can roughhouse and bruise only to the extent that everyone is benefiting from the experience. The occasional bruise is a natural by-product of good, hard martial-arts training; that doesn't include brutalizing students to massage one's ego.

Macho instructors who pick on their helpless students don't impress me one bit.

You'll get a lot more wear and tear out of your students if you check their fluid levels and change their oil regularly.

Tip #2

Break your patterns and even single locks into smaller components. It's easier to teach smaller segments of a move or routine.

It also helps you to analyze every little detail in order to further perfect your technique.

Start by breaking down the technique before you ever get to class. Plan in what order to present each component part. Have the students practice one part beyond the point of boredom.

You want them to perfect the individual movement as much as possible, before moving on to the next move.

Impress your students by teaching them the final counter in your routine as one of the first separate techniques. Then when you put the sequence together for the students, which by the way, will be very easy for them to learn since they practiced the individual components, you leave off the last counter.

When your students get to the "end" of the routine, you tell them that there is a specific counter.

Imagine their surprise when it ends up being the first technique that they learned that day.

On the practical side, by teaching them the last movement first, there is a less of a chance that they'll forget the last move of the routine. (Remember how you used to forget the last line of the speech or poem?)

They have already practiced the move *ad nauseam,* and they get to use it as the *coup de gras.*

Any sequence that includes some sort of counter or reversal can be broken down.

Tip #3

Have patience.

Help each student to find what he or she is good at; what each can really excel at.

It's your job to bring out the best in your students. If one of your students is lousy at arm bars, maybe he or she could really learn the Basic Lock.

There is something for everyone.

Helping each student find his or her own niche can be very beneficial to you. Maybe you can't get a particular student up to your level on everything that you do, but maybe you *can* get this student up to your level, or beyond, performing a particular lock.

Whenever this student successsfully puts that lock on you, it forces you to learn to counter a lock beyond previous skill. You will improve as well.

Note: People are often impressed at my wife's level of skill in the martial arts. Especially given her stature; she's 5' 2" and weighs less than 115 lbs.

Given her kind nature, she's naturally a compassionate teacher outside of the self - defense class.

On lookers can't believe that she can apply wrist locks with such force. When asked how she learned such "energy," she usually responds by pointing toward me with a comment like, "You see that big, hairy guy? Not only is he my husband, but he's my teacher and practice partner."

With a practice partner who outweighed her by more than 150 pounds, she improved very quickly. I needed her to really perfect some of these locks, so I could start to benefit as soon as possible.

Kate had to learn to exert enough force with her compact body, that my big frame would be challenged.

Tip #4

Overcome weaknesses. If Tip #3 was to teach your student to emphasize and build on what they're good at, Tip #4 focuses on the opposite.

Don't give up on their weaknesses.

Teach your students the discipline to do , with perfection, what they aren't now capable of. There is a special satisfaction when you achieve what you previously thought was impossible.

Follow your own advice and strengthen the weaker aspects of your techniques.

If you can't think of what to work on, I have a great idea. Read on....

Force ambidexterity in your students.

Most students are dominant with their wrist lock technique on only one side of the body.

You never know when your dominant hand will be rendered useless in a fight. All it takes is one well-placed strike to the back of your dominant hand with or without a weapon.

Wouldn't it be nice to be able to use your other hand with equal facility?

Beyond being super practical, learning to use both hands equally is a wonderful exercise in overcoming difficult obstacles. Again, you'll notice that some of the photos in this book are for right-handed fighters and others are for lefties. Learn to do all your techniques both ways. Even patterns.

I have made ambidexterity a requisite for promotion in the martial arts system that I teach.

If you really want to be an expert, learn every technique equally well with both sides of your body. It will also make you a better teacher. I don't care if I'm teaching left-handed students or right-handed ones, or both at the same time.

I can teach them on either side, and I can switch back and forth effortlessly. You should learn to as well.

Tip #5

Work on flexibility. Both you and your students could probably use it.

Stretch wrists especially, and legs, arms, back, and torso while you're at it.

Put the palms of your hands flat on a sturdy table lean forward on them (photo 13-1). Rotate your palms and continue stretching your wrists.

Photo 13-1

A good way to practice increasing flexibility is for your partner slowly to apply more pressure to a lock on your wrist. Hold the pressure as long as you can, but be careful. You don't want to strain anything. Relax.

Learn to take the hold further each time.

You are, in effect, increasing the distance to your specific *point of no return.*

Can you see the benefit of this?

You get more time to react. It becomes increasingly difficult to put a hold on you. You're less prone to injury.

There are plenty of books on flexibility. If you want a video on the subject, just look in the ads in any martial-arts magazine.

If you've learned flexibility exercises for your legs, apply the same principles to your wrists. Always be cautious when experimenting, but do experiment. This is the way you'll master the art of stretching.

> Note: Certain disciplines believe that remaining flexible will help maintain youth.

Tip # 6

Have your students pair off to work. Give them a move and have them brainstorm how to counter the move, or maybe what the next move in the series might be.

After the brainstorming session, bring everybody back together to share knowledge. No ideas are bad ideas.

During the brainstorm, try to change the impracticable ones to make them more workable. Give everyone a chance to try each good idea. You can learn a lot and bolster confidence during these work sessions.

Tip #7

Bring in guest experts. You can't be an expert on everything.

For example, say you don't have good leg take-downs, and you need them in order to close the distance for a specific wrist-lock technique. Bring in an expert to teach one of your classes.

You could pay the guest lecturer, or you could offer to return the favor with a lecture in your area of expertise. Maybe you could offer some other form of barter.

If you have a big enough school, or if you link up with another school, you could sponsor a big-name martial artist. Find out the cost ahead of time; then have your students sign up in advance.

If there aren't enough people, don't hire the expert. Find a volunteer. This way you won't lose any money.

You can also use your own students as guest lecturers. If one of them attends a seminar or a series of seminars in a different discipline, have them come back to class and make a presentation to you and the other students.

Even though they won't be experts after just one seminar, you may learn something new and useful.

Do you pay students?

The students can present it for free, just because it's a sharing of knowledge, or maybe you could pay each presenter with a free private lesson. Maybe a letter of appreciation with a fancy school seal on nice paper.

These small rewards may increase the quality of your presentations.

If you take all mini-seminars seriously, so will everyone else.

By the way, when I say seriously, that doesn't mean you can't have fun and even tell an occasional joke.

It does mean that you really try to learn from the presentations. It also means that you treat the temporary teacher , whether it be one of your own students or a guest from another school, with the utmost respect.

A time for learning is not a time for criticizing (my teacher taught me well).

Discard inefficient moves later — after you've had time to explore all of the possibilities. Don't "poo poo" moves in front of the presenter.

A particular move may just not be your cup of tea; it could be perfect for someone else.

Let others judge for themselves.

Tip #8

I have mentioned the following before, but it's worth repeating.

If you get serious about teaching, then you should learn the "other stuff." Don't get me wrong, wrist locks are great, but they are not a complete martial-arts system.

You might want to learn to take punches and kicks.

You also might consider learning to use weapons, or how to punch and kick. (See the Resource Section in the back for suggestions on weapons fighting and learning better punches.)

So what is the "other stuff"?

You should work toward some sort of certification in a progressive martial art, if you don't have it already, and you feel that it's necessary. (Remember, your real goal should be to learn, not just to be "certified.")

I say a progressive art, because it would be more likely to teach you street-fighting techniques. Depending on your goal, I advise you to stay clear of the "tournament styles." (Tournament styles are OK; they just aren't *my* cup of tea. I need more realism in my art. I hope I'm not offending you, but a lot of years of experience have taught me that *The Ring* is not *The Street*.)

You need to learn how to defend yourself at a real distance, not in a "sparring context." Combine an already eclectic art with your wrist-lock expertise, and you'll be ready to teach the masses, *or at least four or five people in your garage.*

Tip #9

As a serious teacher, someone who wants to go beyond just improving his (or her) own wrist locks, you should teach values.

Indirectly teach morality and ethics; teach by example. Don't teach religion. Don't get mystical.

Just teach your students to be good people.

Often, indirect teaching "sticks." How would you teach without shoving morals down your students throats? Teach them to help their partners up, how to avoid fighting, how to lose their ego, how to exhibit control in not hurting their practice partners, how to respect a "tap out,"and so on.

Tip #10

Don't be a "know-it-all."

You have to have confidence in yourself to inspire confidence in your students.

Be confident in your teaching ability. Be confident in what you know works (until such time that it doesn't). Be confident in your ability to explore for answers.

Don't be too cocky.

Don't belittle others in an attempt to boost your own ego. Be the nice guy. You'll get more opportunities to learn that way.

Reluctant Tip #11

Don't get sued!

This is the day and age of lawsuits in the United States. People are lawsuit-happy. You'll get sued if someone even trips over a crack in your sidewalk; I'm not kidding.

Get insurance if you're going to teach.

Learn about insurance release forms. Have a parental consent form for your students under eighteen. Get some specific legal advice. Don't take chances.

Teaching is a very rewarding activity; don't let greedy turkeys spoil it for you. Play it safe so it can be everything that you want it to be.

Remember, you are going to learn by teaching. Make it a quality experience, and enjoy.

14
Going Beyond Others to Become a Real Expert

How good do you really want to be?

What are your goals concerning wrist locks? I'm a firm believer in goals. I think you should write them down.

You can play with wrist locks all you want, but until you start working toward a particular outcome, you'll just be another "hacker."

Do you want to be able to avoid all locks put on you?

How would you like to reverse or counter anything put on you by your opponent? Is your idea of expertise knowing every lock in existence? So tip #1 has to do with goals.

Tips for Going Beyond Others to Become a Real Expert

Tip #1: Write your goals down. Turn them into a plan. Break the goals down into achievable, measurable smaller goals.

How are you going to know when you've reached the goal?

What are your practice sessions going to be like?

Work out the details.

Make your goals specific: If you say, "I want to get better at wrist locks," you probably won't get very far, but if you write down "I want to get better at arm bars," you're getting better, because it's a specific technique, rather than an entire category.

If you make it more specific with something like, "I want to learn three counters for a standard arm bar," that's even better. Remember, the more specific the better.

You could break those arm-bar counters down, add a practice schedule (the time element), and even touch on generalizing to really tighten up the goal.

I want to learn the wrist reversal to the arm bar, the Aikido lift, and the forearm-rotation reversal.

I practice these reversals every day for a minimum of ten minutes. I have reached my goal when I can do each reversal five times successfully on at least three different opponents.

I continue to practice these three counters for fifteen minutes a week to maintain my level of skill.

Tip #2: Go to different styles that incorporate wrist locks. Learn all that they have to offer: Really get to know each lock. Learn all of the situations where a particular style would incorporate the lock.

Do the practitioners use it as a reversal only?

Do they only try it from a left-hand-to-left-hand-grab?

Once you know exactly where that particular lock would be incorporated, then it's time to go beyond that style. Find more ways to incorporate the move. Could you get to the position from a punch-check combination? (Remember, avoid blocking, whenever possible, to be true to the philosophy of Bruce Lee.)

Could you use this lock for a weapon take-away?

If there is a certain sequence for getting into a particular lock, could you break in on the middle of the sequence?

For example, do you remember the Basic Lock two-handed sequence described Chapter 4?

It starts with a two-hand grab (photo 14-1a). You rotate the wrist upward and grab one of your opponent's (photo 14-1b).

You then rotate your grabbed hand back toward your body, releasing it from your opponent's grip (photo 14-1c).

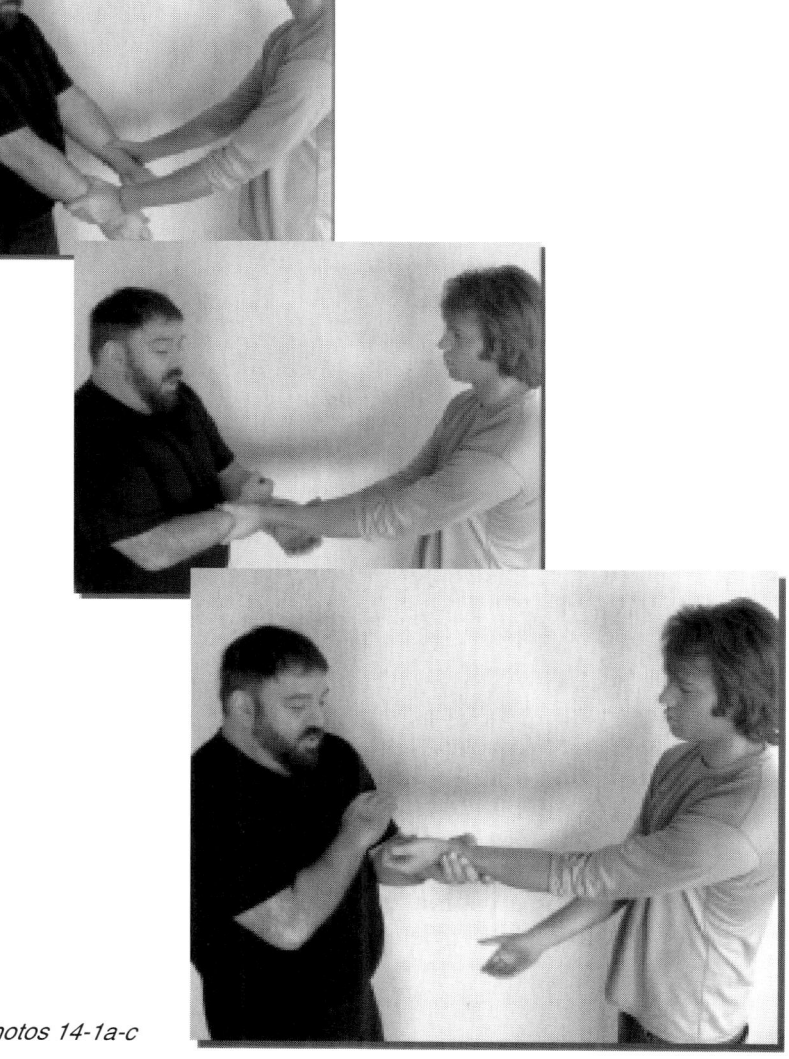

Photos 14-1a-c

After pulling your hand out of the grip, you're ready to execute a wrist lock (photos 14-1d-f).

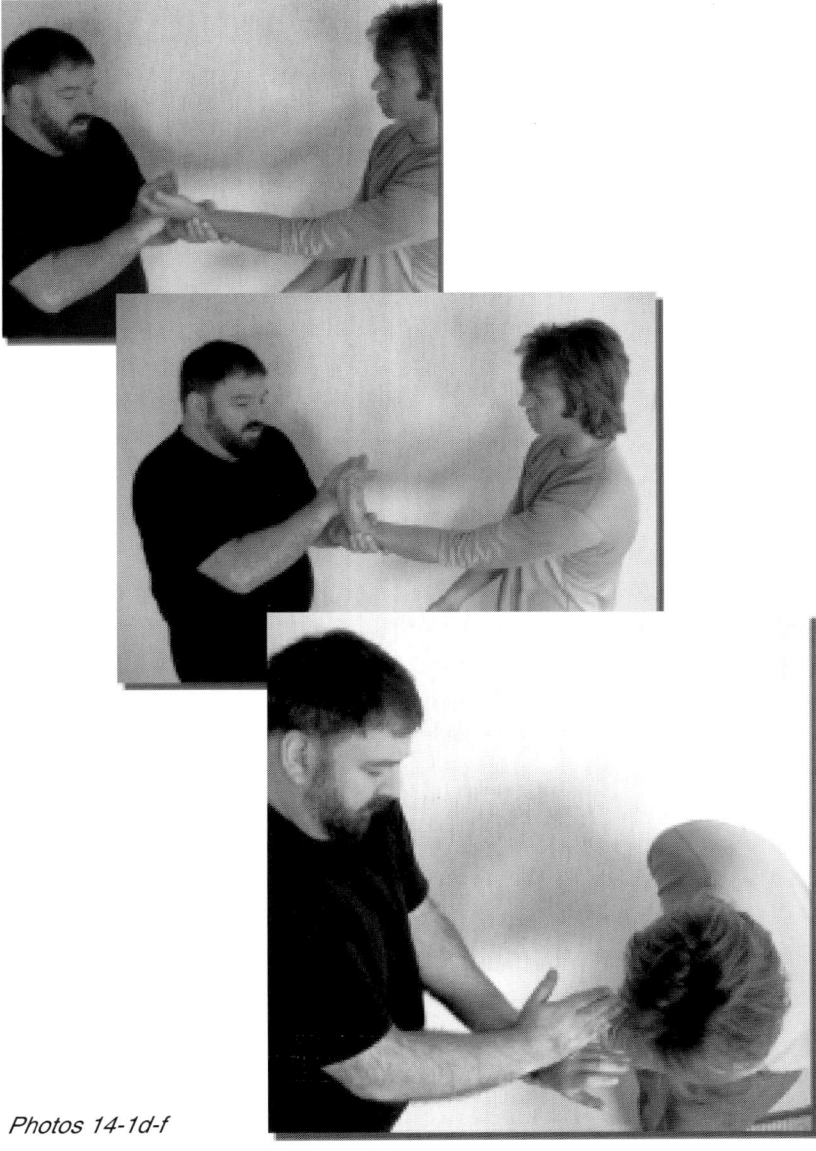

Photos 14-1d-f

This is the sequence that I first learned, and the sequence that I practiced repeatedly — first the grab, then the rotation, next the release, and finally the joint pressure.

One day someone put the lock on me. There wasn't any grab, or rotation, just "the lock."

Once I had learned that you could jump in and start at the point of applying pressure, it opened up many possibilities.

I used that particular lock everywhere.

I even used it in places where other locks or counters would have been more efficient. Forcing the lock from all positions was, in retrospect, a great exercise for learning more than what a particular style had to offer, but not a lot of it translated into the practical world.

Still, you should think about trying it yourself. It's a great mental exercise. It forces creativity. It's a kinesthetic brainstorming process that opens up a myriad of new possibilities.

Just remember to eventually discard the inefficient movements and keep the ones that lend precision to your system of martial arts.

You might need an outside source to help you evaluate these new applications to your locks. A third party may be detached enough to detect and help you eliminate some of the flaws to the new applications.

This outside source may help you by seeing openings in your defense. After all, you don't have eyes in the back of your head.

Tip #3: Generalize to different opponents. (See chapter 7.)

You need to get the feel of different opponents — especially those who are stronger than you are. Work out with hundreds of people, if you can.

Learn what works against whom. Learn what doesn't. Experiment.

Change angles and the amount of pressure you're applying.

Think of the confidence gained when you learn moves well enough to apply them on almost anyone, and the few that you can't, you'll already have discovered the counters in your practice sessions.

Tip #4: This tip is similar to Tip #2, however your goal is more specific. Analyze movements from one style, and blend them into counters from styles unfamiliar to your opponent.

Let's say that someone is putting a wide, slower lock from Aikido on you.

You could respond with a counter straight from Aikido. Then your opponent would counter your counter and so on. What if, instead of that first Aikido counter, you were to respond with a Small-Circle Ju Jitsu counter?

Your response would be with a quicker, shorter motion; you'd probably take your opponent by surprise.

Maybe your opponent was familiar with that last counter, or a similar motion in Aikido. So, your opponent responds. Fine! Who'd ever expect you to counter with a Chin-Na technique?

If, during a demonstration you ever have to explain how many styles you just incorporated in a matter of seconds, you really will be thought of as an expert.

Tip #5: Be more precise than your opponent on the *point of no return* and fool him (see page 30).

It goes both ways.

Not only do you want to be able to know how far your opponent can go with a movement before you won't be able to effectively reverse it, or even escape, but you want to be able to determine how far you have to go before you have enough pressure to hold your opponent.

Once you really learn these points (and remember, the points vary according to lock, opponent, body positions, etc.), you could try to fool your opponent.

Bonus Extra Tip

How would your opponent feel if he (or she) thought the lock to be successful, only to discover that you still had an extra six inches of movement to reverse the hold?

To fool your opponent you have to really make your enemy think that the hold has been executed correctly.

Torque your body at the appropriate time.

Wince when necessary.

Respond exactly as you would if you had really reached the point of no return. You may have to have a friend actually put the move on you over and over, so you can learn the proper response.

Analyze every minuscule reaction to the technique. Become a great actor. Fake the *point of no return*.

Tip #6: Have an arsenal of what to do when the lock isn't working.

If someone resists your lock, do you know where to go to instantly change it to another lock that works? If you don't, you should start with the patterns in Chapter 6.

Practice what to do when someone forcefully resists. Know where you're going next.

Don't always look for another lock in response. Sometimes the best response to someone resisting one of your locks is just to hit or kick your opponent.

It can be as simple as that.

You start to throw a lock on someone; he resists; you hit him. No fireworks. No fanfare. Just a simple kick or hit.

—But—

Why stop there!

I use the hit to loosen them up; then I either reapply the same lock more forcefully, or I flow into a completely different lock.

It's funny how one forceful elbow-jab between the shoulder blades will make my opponent pliable enough to throw on a bent-arm lock (photos 14-2a, b).

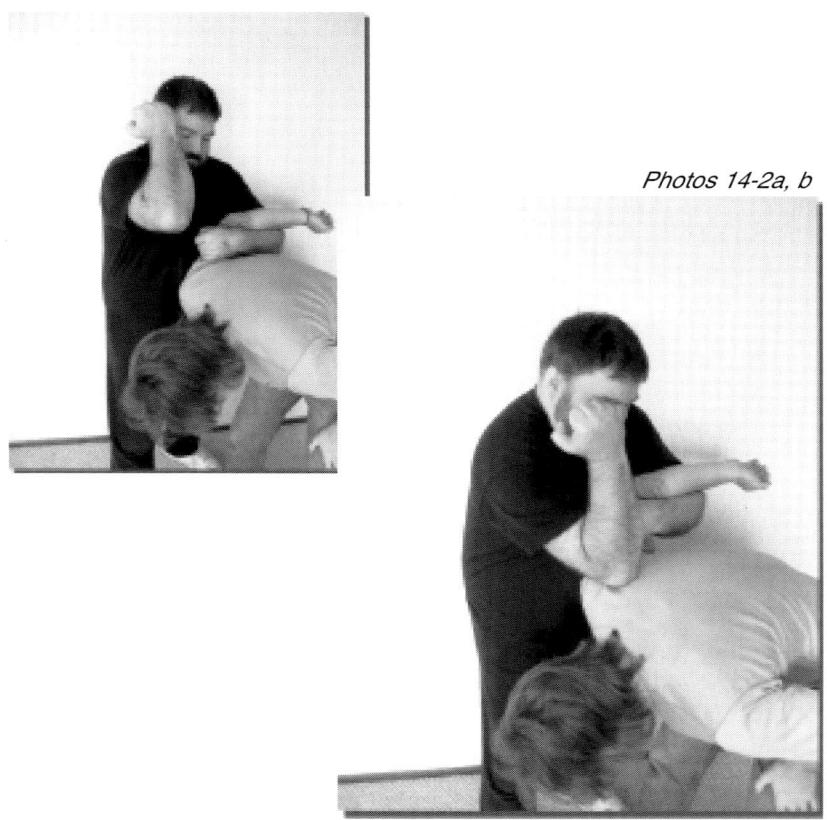

Photos 14-2a, b

Tip #7: Become an encyclopedia of wrist locks.

Learn everything by name (refer to Chapter 2). Become the knowledgeable expert. Know the different names for the same move.

What's the Chinese name?

How about the Japanese name for the same motion?

Different disciplines call the same techniques by different names. Is it a "back fist" or a "back knuckle"? Or even a type of a "Rabbit Punch"? Are you performing "Osoto Gari," or are you performing an "outside hip-throw"?

Know the names of everything. Be able to remember more locks than anyone else.

And for heaven's sake, be able to apply all of them successfully.

You'll feel proud when everyone starts coming to you with questions like "Do you remember the lock where you grab them like this and and drop them to the side?"

Tip #8: Don't always sit on the sidelines.

I know that to learn, you have to be receptive.

You have to quiet yourself for a minute and let someone else do the explaining. Step back and really examine the technique—analyze everything.

Sometimes the strong silent types miss out on a lot. Sometimes, experiential learning is by far the best. You have to feel it to learn it. But, sometimes you just have to jump right in.

If you go to a seminar, PARTICIPATE (if you can).

Tip #9: Make up your own set of tips. As you set goals and pursue them, you'll find great advice along the way.

Why not make your own book of tips, just for you? Collect tips from your martial-arts teacher(s), books on wrist-locking styles, seminars, DVDs, and so on.

Along with things to do, you should have a list of definite "no-nos."Don't focus on them too much; you don't want to emphasize the bad to the point that you now occasionally respond with those incorrect moves.

Whenever you study the bad, be sure to have a positive replacement technique to take its place.

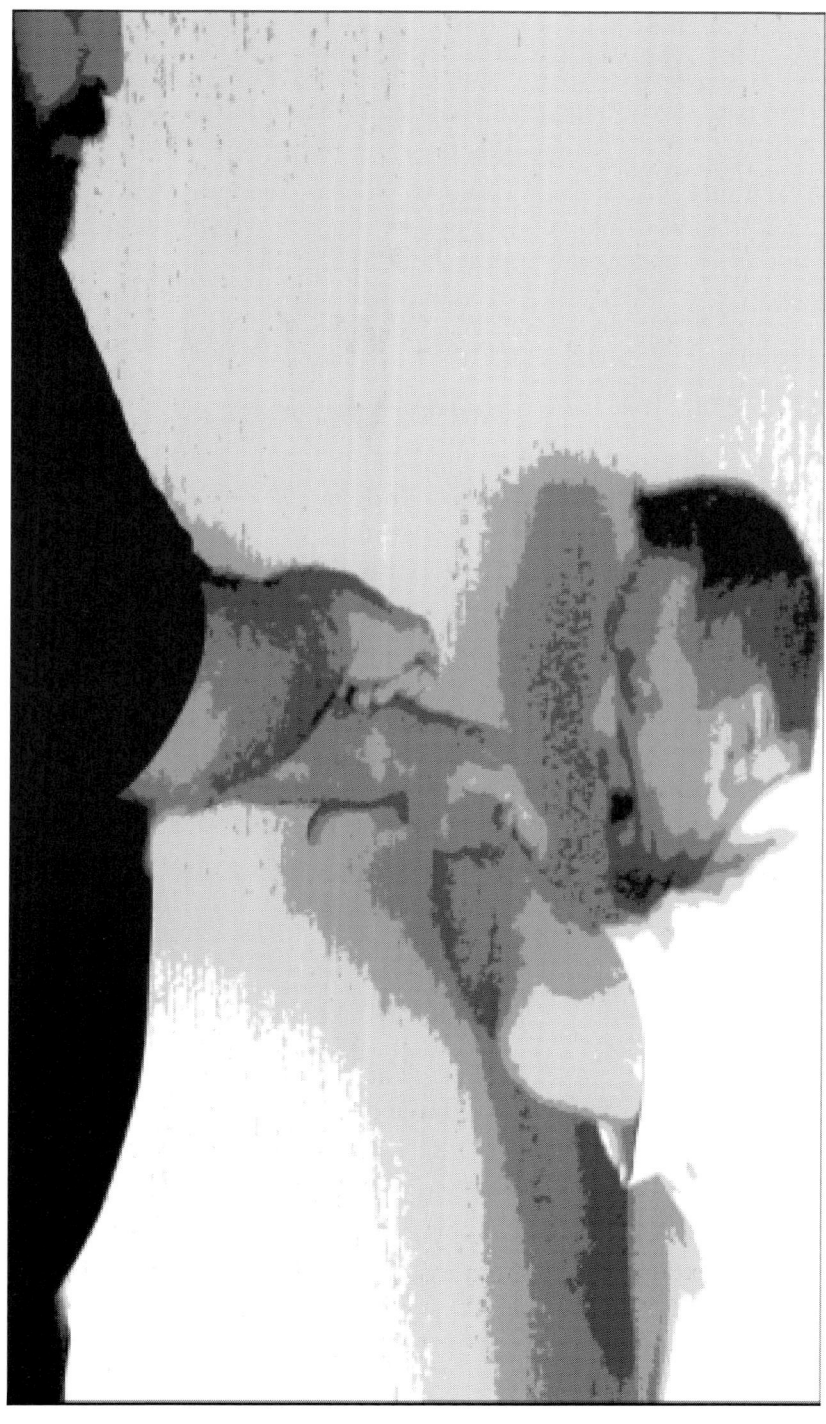

15
You'll Know You're an Expert When ...

As I stated in the introduction and the chapter on practicing, different people have differing definitions of "expert." I am sure you have an interpretation of the ideal, as well.

What are your goals concerning wrist locks?

You will have to come up with your own interpretation of expert. To be frank, to a certain extent your definition of *expert* won't mean anything, unless others accord you expert status. While it is true that you shouldn't change your life to fit the molds of others, you may feel more of an expert, if your mastery has been accepted, or at least recognized, by others.

I have some opinions about what expert status really is. (So, what else is new?)

Read and decide for yourself .

You don't have to be true to me, only to yourself. Who knows? I may have forgotten something in my definition that is of paramount importance to you. That's fine. You are creating your own definition, just as I have created mine. Here are some ideas to consider....

You know a lot

In my mind, a wrist-lock expert can do many locks.

And this expert can do them instinctively, if not almost effort-lessly. It's always better to know a few verywell, than many sloppily executed locks.

In this case, to be a true expert, you should be competent, and have a big repertoire from which to choose.

Others in your community (school, city, leagues, style, etc.) think of you as an encyclopedia of locks. If they are having trouble remembering a specific lock, they would likely come to you.

You seem to have an almost eidetic memory for this stuff.

If you're more conscientious than I, you'll take the time to memorize all the names for all the moves, in all the languages, for all the styles.

Be able to cross-reference a move from memory.

The reason I haven't bothered memorizing everything, although I do have a lot of specific names stored in my "garbage" head, is that I like coming up with more-practical, and sometimes comical variations.

If you remember in Chapter One, some of these names developed as a result of my students, and some I developed. In either case, most all are practical names.

> OK, I took some liberties with names like *Uncle Fred*, or *The Weird Lock With No Name.* To tell the truth, a little humor does help to jog the memory.

Whether or not you memorize names for these moves, you should know so many moves, that you're afraid you'll forget some. This is one component of being an expert.

> By the way, you do have a *wrist lock notebook,* don't you?
>
> In my **Home Study Punch eCourse**, I insist that students keeep a punching notebook.

You've Taken from Other Styles

Another component in my book is not being limited to one style. You've researched the styles that have lots of locks including Aikido, Jujitsu, the Filipino arts, and Chin Na.

Don't forget to include the progressive arts, like Jeet Kune Do, and its relatives – they use whatever works, including wrist locks.

You should also spend some of your spare time researching the styles that aren't known for their wrist locks. You may discover some gem, and also you do want to know what the other styles are capable of.

Research so many styles, that you start to feel that there's nothing new under the sun.

Now, you're starting to feel like an expert, right?

You can Counter Anything and Everything

Nothing gives you a problem. You can counter whatever comes your way.

You know so many moves, and so many counters and reversals to these moves, that nothing amazes you.

You smoothly flow into any number of counters; (you've researched Aikido to work on your smoothness).

And if, by chance, someone does pull a new one on you, it won't matter. You'll "fake it" with something impromptu – this impromptu move will work perfectly, because it's based on prior knowledge.

I can't even begin to tell you how much being able to counter anything adds to your confidence. Instead of a pit in your stomach, when someone tries to lock you, a smile breaks out on your face. You know your locks. This is your game.

You Prevent Others from Successfully Locking You

...although to learn a new lock, you have to allow it to be put on you to learn the counter. We've already discussed reversals.

That's one way (or actually hundreds of ways) to prevent yourself from being locked. Make sure you're versed in the point of no return. That knowledge is crucial to avoid being locked.

Don't let yourself even get close to that point.

Counter early.

Can you shift your weight, change your position, or tense your muscles to avoid having a lock or throw put on you?

One key to preventing being locked or thrown is to counter them before they happen. Now, that's countering early. Even if you counter early, still try to counter smoothly.

You Have Truly Learned to Generalize

You have practiced with so many different people , that you can easily adjust to different "types" of opponents.

You easily adapt to differences of strength and speed in your opponents.

You have worked out with so many people, that you recognize similiarities of style. One muscle-builder is just like another to you. The super-flexibles will stick out like a sore, *double-jointed* thumb. You won't be nervous, because it will all feel familiar.

You Invent Your Own

You teach yourself new moves. You establish your own routines. You can take an opponent where he has never been, because you're using your own sequences and combinations. An unfamiliar route will confuse your opponent.

Since your own combinations include a number of "outs" to any given move, if something isn't working, you instantly adjust to something more suitable.

You constantly experiment and play with new moves.

Your experimenting will give you more of an unorthodox style. Have I convinced you yet that this maverick style has its advantages?

Even the good technicians won't be quite able to get a handle on what you're doing. The frustrating thing to your opponents is that, even with this unorthodox style, you're so damn smooth.

You are practiced.

You can switch from orthodox to unorthodox, and back, at will.

You Have Mastered All of the Subtleties

You have studied all joints and protuberances. You know all the angles. You can finesse a move that others might mess up.

Rather than just blatantly resisting everything, you seem to give in to your opponent's force.

Always resisting is amateurish. You allow your opponent to twist you into familiar positions, which, unbeknownst to him, *are* desirable to you.

There is a certain smoothness that one can only acquire through thousands of repetitions, with constant, minute adjustments. Over time, you become a "pro."

It shows.

By exhibiting the subtlety of your art, you make it look easy.

Basically, You're Invincible When it Comes to Locks

No one can put you down. The opponents are battling you on your turf.

If wrist locking is the game, you're an expert. The closer you come to this ideal ...

When you meet your equal, it will be in a pedagogical atmosphere, if you are fortunate.

You'll be able to amicably discuss techniques. You might even make a friend.

And if you just happen to mention this book, and he (or she) has never heard of it before.... (Thanks for the plug, or could it be that this book will never be mentioned, because it is your *secret weapon*?)

Remember, the above is just my point of view. Half the fun of becoming an expert is the task of defining what you yourself want to become. And yes, your definition may change as you progress.

That's OK.

Your eyes are being opened; you're seeing new possibilities. Go for the gold.

Make sure you go beyond this book.

This is just the beginning. I'm excited for you.

If you don't know where to go from here, check the Resources section of this book. Explore what interests you.

If you still don't know where to go, write me. Give me an idea of your goals (in the martial arts would be nice, too), and I'll make a few suggestions.

I want you to feel confident and excited as you progress to expert status.

If that means providing more books and ebooks on wrist locks, then I'll oblige. If you need other practical martial-arts information, I'll do my best.

Sometimes having another perspective on a wrist lock problem can mean the difference between frustration and an easy solultion. Write, if you need help.

May you continuously progress, never stagnate, and occasionally pause to enjoy the journey.

Sincerely,

Keith

Bonus One: Fancy 90 With A Throw

Putting together this revised and updated edition of *Wrist Locks* got me so enthusiastic that I have started working on a second wrist-locks book.

I thought you might like a preview of what's to come.

Not only will you see more locks featuring my wife, my martial-arts students, and me, but in the next volume, I'd like to include a few wrist-lock nuggets from my teacher, Steve Golden.

For example, here are a couple of next steps for your Double Ninety-Degree Wrist Lock:

Have a practice partner reach for you (photo B1-1a).

Photo B1-1a

As your partner reaches, you grab the extending hand. Grab the hand, thumb to thumb (photo B1-1b).

Photos B1-1b

Twist your partner's hand to a thumb-down position and continue on into the *Double 90* (photo B1-1c, d). Are you with me, so far?

Photos B1-1c, d

This Is Where It Gets Interesting

Do you have pressure on the locked wrist? OK, it's time to reposition your grip. Remove the hand pushing down on your partner's elbow, and reach up on the inside, from underneath, as in Photo B1-2a.

Photo B1-2a

Continue on and lock your wrist on top of your partner's (photo B1-2b). Maintain a bend in both the elbow and on the wrist. Also, keep the free hand from reaching out to you with your locking pressure.

Photo B1-2b

And if you are Steve Golden, the chances are you'll find a finger tweak, to add even more pain (photo B1-2c).

Photo B1-2c

Your *Double 90* modification – should we call it a *Forward* Chicken Wing? – doesn't have to end with the finger tweak. Steve has the perfect pressure applied, to continue into a throw.

Photo B1-2d

Bonus Two: A Triple Finesse

Do you remember Lock #11 from Chapter Four? This second bonus may look like Live Long and Prosper, but this finger lock has more finesse.

You'll see:

Finesse #1

In several places in this book, I emphasized distracting by faking a lock on the other hand. It was a great distraction.

Well, Steve Golden gets the same effect with a shove.

Steve shoves his opponent, as he grabs the hand about to be locked (photo B2-1a, b). This shove is the first finesse.

Photo B2-1a, b

Finesse #2

With Live Long and Prosper, you grab the forefinger and second finger with one hand, and you grab the third finger and little finger with the other.

In this bonus lock, Steve grabs the second and the third fingers. That's right, he forgets about the thumb, forefinger, and pinky (photo B2-1c).

This proves that if you understand the controlling pressure, you can vary how you grab the fingers or even the wrist.

Work it out and practice it formally.

Photo B2-1c

Finesse #3

Earlier in the book, I suggested that you plough your attacker's elbow straight into the ground – advice gleaned from Steve.

Here, instead of shattering the elbow which might not work on the soft grass, Steve lays his opponent flat on the ground, face down (photo B2-1d).

Can you figure out this last finesse? How would you adjust the pressure to control someone slowly to a downed position?

Hint: Take a step or two backwards, as you apply pressure.

Of course, once you have mastered these three finesses, feel free to apply them to your other locks.

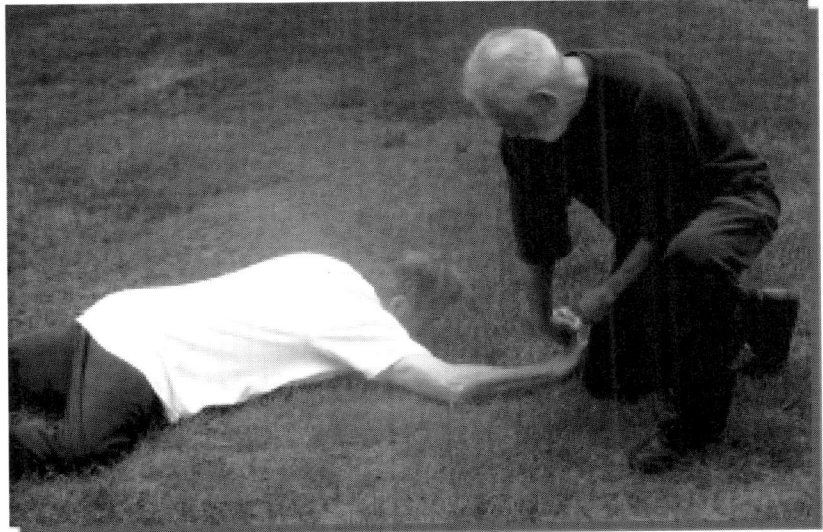

Photo B2-1d

More contributions from Steve Golden ...

Did you know that there is a second wrist locks book in the works?

In it, we'll continue the exploration of wrist locks, finger locks, joint locks, and arm bars. You can also expect more contributions from Steve Golden.

You'll see some interesting variations on locks discussed in this book. ➡

Can you imagine a practical application where you effect this lock? ➡️

And then you smoothly flow into this lock and hold. ⬇️

You'll take familiar locks to new heights ... (or lows )!

Resources

I have enjoyed sharng some of what I know about wrist locks with you. It has been a pleasure.

Some of you would like to read more of my words about martial-arts and self defense. I have been on the Internet for a long time, so it's very easy to find articles, reports, ebooklets, ebooks, and books that I wrote.

Start your search at **www.KerwinBenson.com**

Since the first edition of *Wrist Locks*, I have written over a dozen books and ebooks on martial arts and self defense. The following recommendatons are a few of my favorites.

All of my books and ebooks come with a money-back guarantee, because I want my writing to be a good fit with your martial-arts needs and wants.

Take a look at the following:

Do You Want to Punch Harder, Faster, and More Efficiently?

Learn quickly and efficiently with the **Home Study Punch eCourse**.

The 5 Volumes include **Punch Fundamentals**, **Develop Explosively Powerful Punches**, **Super Speed Punches**, **Defensive Punching,** and **Punch Strategies**.

This 65-Lesson eCourse is available for immediate download.

A Quick Knife-Fighting Lesson for Self Defense

Let's take a moment, right now, to talk about knife-fighting self defense. I firmly believe that in a real knife fight, you need two skills. They are of paramount importance.

In a real (life threatening) knife fight, you have to:

- Make sure that every response or action you take directly slashes or stabs your enemy.

- React automatically, without thought.

Think about it. If you exchange knife strikes with someone who is direct – every move an attack – then the first time you block or perform some other inefficient move, it's over.

And while it's OK to carefully consider the situation, if you find the need to defend yourself, once the real fighting begins, you only have a little time to react. That's just the way it is.

I have several ebooks on knife fighting, and several different epackages available. Whether you choose a beginning knife-fighting epackage or a more advanced set of ebooks, make sure that the epackage includes **10 Days to Better Knife Fighting**.

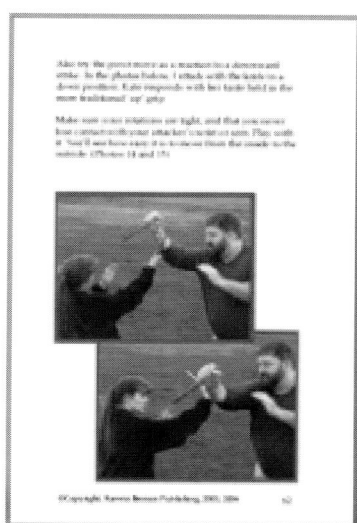

10 Days to Better Knife Fighting teaches you to make every response an offensive move -- a cut or stab of your own. And through a series of exercises, it will teach you to make those responses automatic.

Develop speedier knife reactions now. Ebooks available at:

www.KerwinBenson.com

Finally! A Parable About Staying Safe in Dangerous Times

(Makes a great Gift for Loved Ones and Non-Martial Arts Friends)

This is a story about a mother and daughter who want to find safety and comfort in dangerous times, in their city, and any place they visit.

The mother, Danielle, is insistent that they don't take martial-arts classes.

But, they end up taking lessons from Sam ... a martial arts expert. Instead of martial arts , they learn lessons in *Tiptoeing to Tranquility*.

As Danielle, and her daughter, Jessie, journey through entertaining exercises in finding security in their city, you will pick up valuable tips to apply to your own life.

Imagine leading a more tranquil life, free from fear.

Tiptoeing to Tranquility: The Parable for Finding Safety and Comfort in Dangerous Times is the story that will show you how. Available in soft cover.

> If you have any difficulties finding books, ebooks, or articles by me, email me:
> keith@keithpascal.com
> I will always help, when I can.

These aren't all of my books and ebooks, just some of my personal favorites. I have others, like *Knockdown Punches*, *58 Martial-Arts Motivation Questions Answered*, and so on.

As I mentioned before, you are welcome to email me. I'll do my best to direct you to the appropriate article, report, ebook, or book. Some of my recommendations might be free; others are for paid information. In both cases, I am doing my best to answer your need.

Wrist Locks Recommendations

As you read this book, I am already working on my next wrist-locks project. Yes, wrist locks and joint locks are a passion of mine. They have been for years.

Make sure to stay in touch. I'd be happy to update you on current wrist-locks how-to information.

Keith

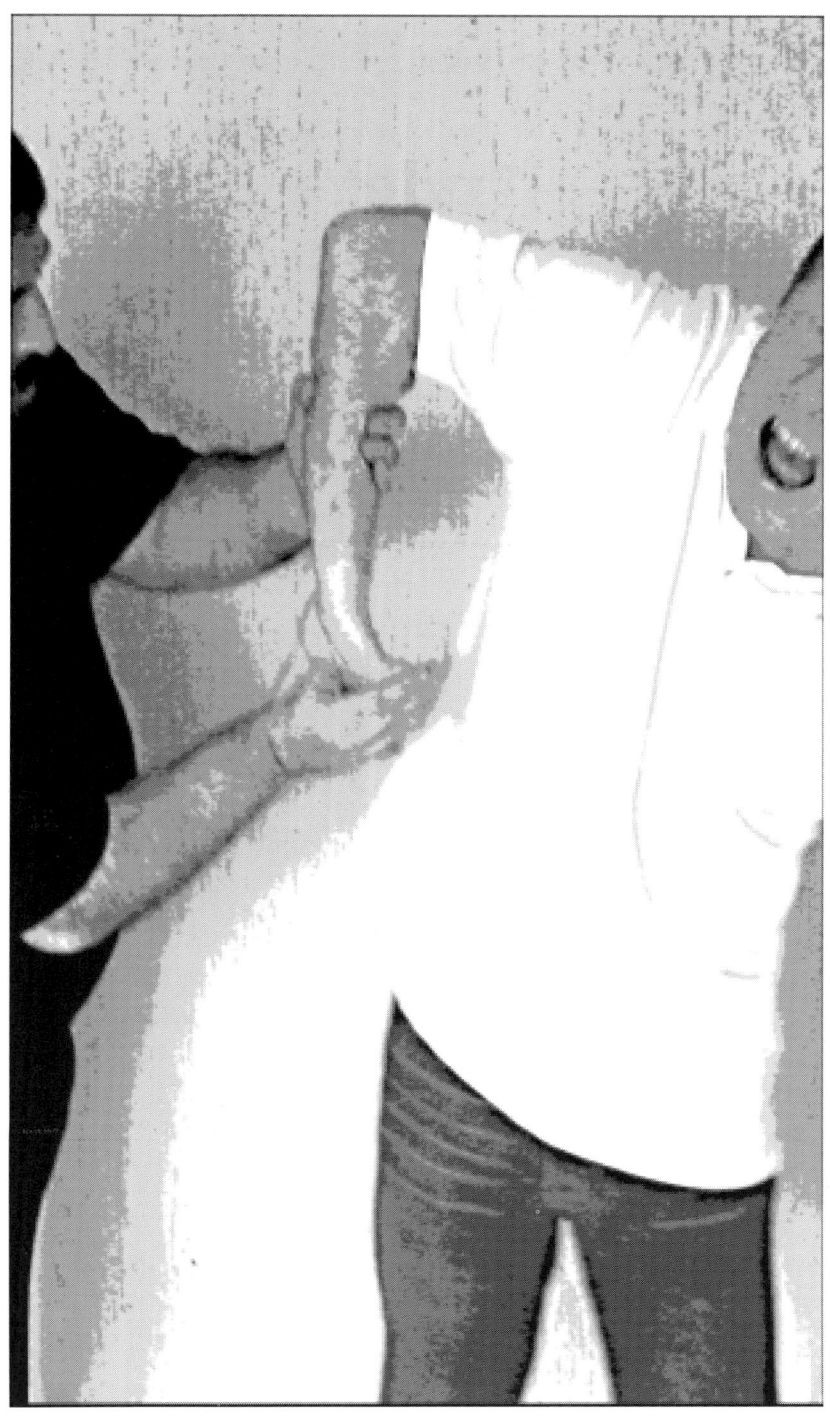

Index

A

B

J

K

L

M

T

U

V

W

Y

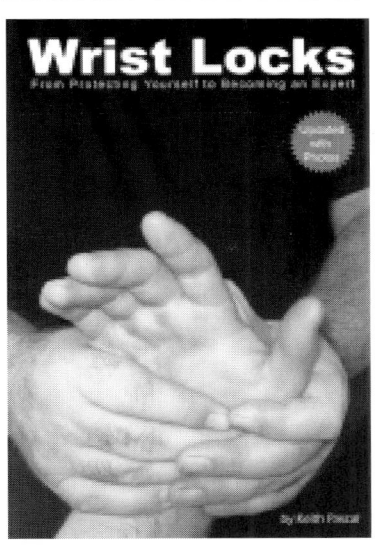

~Notes~

~Notes~

~Notes~